The Constitution of France

A Contextual Analysis

I0121621

Sophie Boyron

·H A R T·
PUBLISHING
OXFORD AND PORTLAND, OREGON
2013

HART PUBLISHING

Bloomsbury Publishing Plc

Kemp House, Chawley Park, Cumnor Hill, Oxford, OX2 9PH, UK

HART PUBLISHING, the Hart/Stag logo, BLOOMSBURY and the Diana logo are
trademarks of Bloomsbury Publishing Plc

First published in Great Britain 2013

A catalogue record for this book is available from the British Library.

ISBN: 978-1-84113-735-3

Typeset by Hope Services Ltd, Abingdon

To find out more about our authors and books visit www.hartpublishing.co.uk. Here you will find
extracts, author information, details of forthcoming events and the option to sign up for our
newsletters.

THE CONSTITUTION OF FRANCE

The centrepiece of this work is the French constitution of 1958, portrayed by the author as an innovative hybrid construct whose arrival brought the constitutional stability that had eluded France for centuries. But the creation of the 1958 constitution was not an isolated act; it represents part of an evolutionary process which continues to this day. Even though it is codified, the constitution of the Fifth Republic has evolved so markedly that some commentators have dubbed the present institutional balance the 'sixth Republic'. It is this dynamic of the constitution which this book seeks to explain. At the same time the book shows how the French constitution has not developed in isolation, but reflects to some extent the global movement of ideas, ideas which sometimes challenge the very foundations of the 1958 constitution.

France – pictorial narrative

The heart of the composition depicts Marianne, France's national emblem of Liberty and Reason. Marianne's posture, with right hand clutching the French flag, is inspired by Eugène Delacroix's 'La Liberté guidant le peuple' – but her head is juxtaposed with the French Coat of Arms and the monogram 'RF' for République Française. Marianne's left breast is roped onto the famous Republican motto: 'Liberty, Equality, Fraternity', shortened to 'LEF'. On Marianne's left, scales of justice are fused with a guillotine – symbolising the reign of terror – partially obscured by billowing smoke from the storming of the Bastille in 1789. Below the initials of the Republican motto, stands the entrance to the Cour du Mai of the Palais de Justice. France's first chamber (the Assemblée Nationale) with its facade etched with '1958', referring to the year of the adoption of the current Constitution of France and the 5th Republic associated with President Charles de Gaulle. His statue – striding over the Parliament holding Roman swords – echoes Jacques-Louis David's Oath of the Horatii (David was an active supporter of the French Revolution). The Eiffel Tower, still in the process of construction, is intended to project de Gaulle as modern man and the modernity of France. There is an assembly of citizens in conversation, representing the ownership of the 1958 Constitution by the people.

Constitutional Systems of the World
General Editors: Peter Leyland and Andrew Harding
Associate Editors: Benjamin L Berger and Grégoire Webber

In the era of globalisation, issues of constitutional law and good governance are being seen increasingly as vital issues in all types of society. Since the end of the Cold War, there have been dramatic developments in democratic and legal reform, and post-conflict societies are also in the throes of reconstructing their governance systems. Even societies already firmly based on constitutional governance and the rule of law have undergone constitutional change and experimentation with new forms of governance; and their constitutional systems are increasingly subjected to comparative analysis and transplantation. Constitutional texts for practically every country in the world are now easily available on the internet. However, texts which enable one to understand the true context, purposes, interpretation and incidents of a constitutional system are much harder to locate, and are often extremely detailed and descriptive. This series seeks to provide scholars and students with accessible introductions to the constitutional systems of the world, supplying both a road map for the novice and, at the same time, a deeper understanding of the key historical, political and legal events which have shaped the constitutional landscape of each country. Each book in this series deals with a single country, or a group of countries with a common constitutional history, and each author is an expert in their field.

Published volumes

The Constitution of the United Kingdom
The Constitution of the United States
The Constitution of Vietnam
The Constitution of South Africa
The Constitution of Japan
The Constitution of Germany
The Constitution of Finland
The Constitution of Australia
The Constitution of the Republic of Austria
The Constitution of the Russian Federation
The Constitutional System of Thailand
The Constitution of Malaysia
The Constitution of China
The Constitution of Indonesia

Link to series website

http://www.hartpub.co.uk/series/csw

To Stewart

Contents

Table of Cases

European Court of Justice

European Court of Human Rights

Conseil constitutionnel

Conseil d'Etat

Cour de cassation

German constitutional court

Table of Legislation and other Instruments

United Nations

European Union

Directives

France

United States of America

International

1

French Constitutional History

A Difficult Coming of Age

⎯⎯◆⎯⎯

The Constitutional 'Big-Bang': The Revolution of 1789 – The Difficult Implementation of Constitutionalism – Understanding French Constitutional History – Conclusion: The Merger of Constitutional Traditions?

HISTORY IS KNOWN to help with the understanding of uncodified constitutions but it should not be underestimated as a grid of explanation for codified ones. In fact, constitutional history is paramount when it comes to the development of ideas, concepts and institutions in French constitutional law. Even though the present constitution was adopted relatively recently, many of its choices and provisions can be traced back to a determining event in the constitutional past. Indeed, the 1958 constitution is the direct result of a long evolution. Relevant aspects of this history must therefore be brought to the attention of the reader.

French history is often divided into two periods: pre and post Revolution. This representation seems to be particularly prevalent when it comes to constitutional history. It emphasises the ideological, societal, cultural and legal break that took place in 1789 when a revolution overthrew absolute monarchy. The events of 1789 are used to mark the beginning of 'modern' constitutional history in France: the new political elite wanted a fresh start and with revolutionary zeal, the old legal system – institutions, legislation, rules and all – was soon abolished in its quasi-entirety. Consequently, the presentation of constitutional history will begin with the events of 1789.

Although this chronological survey will be used mainly to highlight the difficult acclimatisation of classical constitutionalism in France, attempts will also be made to organise the historical data and explain this apparently chaotic constitutional evolution. This will help in understanding the provisions and practices of the present constitution.

THE CONSTITUTIONAL 'BIG-BANG': THE REVOLUTION OF 1789

The Revolution of 1789 is often portrayed in France as a real watershed in both political and legal terms. Modern constitutional history is often deemed to have begun with this quasi-mythical event. Not only did the revolutionaries establish a completely new constitutional settlement with a new organisation of society to boot, but they founded the legitimacy of this new system on a clean break from the past. One may wonder whether this representation of history was not the first of many symbolic representations which are so powerful in French constitutional law. In fact, legal historians warn us against accepting unquestioningly this divide: many post-revolutionary institutions have traceable roots to pre-revolutionary ones.[1] As far as constitutional change is concerned, the Revolution of 1789 creates a clear discontinuity which hides unnoticed in its midst a thread of continuity.

Before the new constitutional settlement is examined, it is necessary to investigate the reasons which led to the Revolution of 1789. To grasp the magnitude of the change established by the revolutionary settlement, one must understand the pre-existing monarchical order and its problems.

The Reasons for the Revolution of 1789

To survey in a few paragraphs the reasons and circumstances leading to the Revolution of 1789 may seem at best foolish and at worst doomed to failure. Like many events of this magnitude, the Revolution was not the result of one easily identifiable factor, but the complex combination of many. Ideological, philosophical, economic, monetary, social, political, constitutional and administrative factors (to quote the most important) all conspired to create an extremely unstable (one might say explosive) situation in France prior to spring 1789.

---

[1] See J-L Mestre, *Introduction historique au droit administratif français* (Paris, Presses universitaires de France, 1985).

Administrative and Judicial Organisation

By the end of the eighteenth century, the administrative and judicial organisation of the French territory was obsolete and inefficient.[2] France was divided into *provinces* and each *province* had a top court – called *Parlement* – which applied the law and developed rules and principles independently from those of other *provinces*. In addition, a multiplicity of lower courts, which had been reformed in successive waves, competed against each other. Furthermore, the northern *provinces* and *Parlements* resorted to customs and unwritten rules while those in the south favoured written provisions and the Roman law. Consequently, there was no uniform application of the law throughout the kingdom. To add to this complexity, all ecclesiastical matters were adjudicated upon by a separate judicial system. The country harboured competing legal systems and a great many efforts were spent 'clarifying' the jurisdictional divide between the various courts. Finally, cases often went on for a considerable time, sometimes spanning many generations and in some cases, even ruining the parties in the process.[3]

The administrative organisation of the country was similarly shambolic. In the sixteenth century, a body of controllers – the *intendants* – was created to tour and control the *provinces* with regard to taxation, the army and justice. Although these were meant to be temporary positions, by the eighteenth century, the *intendants* were a permanent fixture and had become the king's representatives in each *province*. This acknowledged the failure of the administrative mechanisms already in place: the *intendants* battled constantly with the *Parlements* and kept an eye on the *fermiers-généraux*, responsible for levying taxes. The monarchy was losing its administrative grip over the country.

Constitutional Challenges

French kings traditionally ruled as absolute monarch and did not recognise many (if any) limitations to their power and sovereignty. Unlike the British Crown, which had been forced to give up a number of its prerogatives and was working with the Parliament, the French Crown

---

[2] See J-P Royer, J-P Jean, B Durand, N Derasse and B Dubois, *Histoire de la justice en France*, 4th edn (Paris, Presses universitaires de France, 2010) 47.

[3] Judges were paid directly by the parties. This guaranteed independence from the Crown but meant that judges had little incentive to deliver a speedy judgment.

managed to eschew such political and constitutional restrictions. Although created in 1302, the Etats-Généraux, the Parliament of the time, had not been convened since 1614.

Paradoxically, there was a long-standing challenge to the authority of the king. In practice, the *Parlements* imposed serious limits on the will of the sovereign. This was possible because of the technique used to bring into force the king's proclamations. Proclamations did not have legal effect until registered by the *Parlements*. This registration ought to have been automatic but the *Parlements* used it to contest reforms that did not meet with their approval. When in the decades preceding the Revolution the monarchy attempted to put in place much-needed reforms, it was repeatedly thwarted by the *Parlements*.

Economy and Finance

The finances of the realm and the state of the economy are often presented as the catalysts for the Revolution of 1789. The task of levying taxation was contracted to the *fermiers-généraux*: they agreed to pay the Treasury a predetermined sum each year and were entitled to keep any surplus. This system of taxation was antiquated, inefficient, institutionalised abuse and led paradoxically to high levels of tax evasion. By the end of the eighteenth century, the French monarchy was slowly starved of tax revenue while it was spending heavily on supporting the War of Independence in America. As the finances of the kingdom reached dangerous levels in the 1780s, an overhaul of the tax system became necessary. The monarchy was close to bankruptcy.

In addition, the French economy was affected by a deep economic crisis. The 1786 free trade agreement with the United Kingdom impacted French industry badly. Unable to compete with cheaper imports (particularly textiles), many industries struggled and unemployment rose rapidly.[4] This led to major riots in Paris in August 1787 and again in May 1788. Also, a very poor harvest in 1788 led to a massive increase in the price of flour and bread – the staples of the time.

---

[4] In the Champagne and the Rhône regions, 50% of the population was out of work.

Organisation of Society

The class system in eighteenth-century France goes back for the most part to the Middle Ages. Society was formally divided into three classes: Nobility, Clergy and Third State. The Third State was a disparate group including artisans, the peasantry and bourgeoisie. The finances of the Nobility were precarious and many aristocrats came to rely on paid positions at court. While political power was mainly in the hands of the Nobility and High Clergy, economic power was slowly transferred to the bourgeoisie. This divide would be difficult for any society to countenance in the long term. Furthermore, the finances of the monarchy were such that successive monarchs sold positions and titles to the bourgeoisie. For instance, the bourgeoisie acquired judicial positions in this way and joined the ranks of the Nobility. However, this gave the bourgeoisie little access to real political power (but explains the systematic opposition of the *Parlements*). Overall, the class structure was rigid. The 1789 Revolution allowed its transformation and led to a sudden change of elite with the bourgeoisie replacing the Nobility at the helm of the State.

Philosophical Movements

The situation in France, as described above, was all round difficult and chaotic. It is not surprising, therefore, that philosophical movements were born in reaction. The second half of the eighteenth century has been baptised the period of the Enlightenment by reference to the ideology which aimed to shed a new light on all aspects of society and combat the deep errors ingrained in the monarchical regime: it attacked the organisation of society (mainly its class system), it contested the political value and efficiency of absolute monarchy, rejected the economic choices of a badly reformed feudal system, and denied the right of any religion to organise society and political power. The movement of the Enlightenment wanted to establish rationality as a founding principle for a new organisation of society. From this follows a right of all men to formal equality. Furthermore, it reduced religion to a branch of philosophy. While the monarchy found in religion the source of its political and moral legitimacy, democracy would provide the legitimacy for this new society.

The review of the various factors that culminated in the 1789 Revolution leaves an impression of inevitability and doom. While it is impossible to decide which factors were truly crucial, their combination was decisive.

The First Constitutional Settlement and Its Failure

As mentioned above, by 1789 Louis XVI needed to pursue essential fiscal reforms. On 5 May 1789 the king finally convened the Etats-Généraux. Members of each class were elected by their peers in Paris and in each *province*. Many representatives of the Third State brought demands with them: people wanted formal equality, the adoption of a codified constitution, the reform of the administration, but nonetheless the continuation of the monarchy. This reflected the belief of many revolutionaries: a constitutional monarchy was seen as an appropriate solution. Although with 578 members, the Third State[5] outnumbered the Nobility (270 members) and Clergy (291 members) combined, the votes were counted per class; the Third State was systematically outvoted. Immediately, representatives of the Third State began to formulate two demands: that the votes be counted per person and that all three groups sit together. The continued refusal of the Nobility and Clergy[6] to accede to either demand led the Third State on 17 June to rename itself the 'National Assembly', thereby clearly proclaiming the sovereignty of the Nation. In the same sitting, the new Assembly authorised the temporary levy of the new taxes.

At first, the king refused to recognise the new Assembly and annulled its resolutions. However, by 27 June the king acquiesced in the merger of all three classes into the National Assembly. In the meantime, the National Assembly had taken an oath on 20 June to give the country a new constitution. On 9 July the National Assembly renamed itself the 'Constituent Assembly'. The storming of the Bastille on 14 July transformed this legal revolution into a popular uprising. The Constituent Assembly proceeded to draft a constitution establishing a constitutional monarchy and enshrining a declaration of the rights of man and citizen. Furthermore, on 4 August 1789 many aristocratic privileges were abolished and the guilds dismantled.

---

[5]   It was composed mainly of lawyers.

[6]   While all members of the Clergy had joined the 'National Assembly' by 19 June, no member of the Nobility followed suit.

The first constitution was adopted on 3 September 1791; it incorporated the declaration of the rights of man adopted on 26 August 1789. The constitution possessed some interesting characteristics: sovereignty was placed in the French people, and both Parliament and the king were only representatives of the people. A strict separation of powers existed between the Legislative Assembly and the Executive. The Assembly passed legislation and authorised all public spending. The king headed the administration of the kingdom. He could not dissolve the Assembly and the ministers appointed by the king were not responsible to it. Nevertheless, the king had a temporary legislative veto. This first constitution may have placed sovereignty formally in the people but the people did not exercise it much. A system of indirect suffrage was adopted for the elections to the Assembly and the right to vote was recognised only for citizens paying a significant amount of tax. Also, all domestic servants were barred from voting.[7]

From the beginning, the constitution was implemented and applied in an atmosphere of suspicion and distrust: the attempt by the king and his family to flee the country in June 1791 was perceived as bordering on treason. On 10 August 1792, the king vetoed two key pieces of legislation. In response, the crowd invaded the royal residence and Louis XVI was taken prisoner. Another Constituent Assembly was called to draft a new constitution. With the execution of the king on 21 January 1793 began a long period of constitutional instability.

THE DIFFICULT IMPLEMENTATION OF CONSTITUTIONALISM

French constitutional law rests on a striking paradox: while the change of constitutional paradigm happened very quickly in 1789, it took a further 200 years for democracy to be fully embedded in constitutional and political practice. In contrast with the United States, where the 1776 constitution generated political stability, France endured a long period of political and constitutional instability punctuated by revolutions, coups and civil war.

French constitutional law has been tainted by these difficult beginnings. Constitutional lawyers and politicians have struggled to establish

---

[7] They may not be independent enough to express an opinion other than the one held by their master. It is estimated that only one man in six was entitled to vote.

a system that engenders political stability. Every so often, a new constitution was drafted in an attempt to create this elusive stable and democratic regime; and more often than not, the experience ended in a coup or revolution. To rid France of this constitutional malaise, drafter after drafter tried new constitutional recipes, invented new mechanisms, fashioned new institutions. In many ways, this is the creed of classic constitutionalism 'à la française': in a triumph of optimism over experience, constitutional lawyers and politicians adopted constitution after constitution, in the hope that one day they would discover the right one. The philosophy of the Enlightenment taught French revolutionaries to believe in the power of constitutional law to tame and shape the political system. Accordingly they believed that a well-written constitution would suffice to capture, frame and submit political behaviour and practices to the law. Soon, the failures of past constitutions were explained by the inadequacy of the specific constitutional instrument: the inability to devise the necessary mechanisms, to create the appropriate provisions or to design the right institutions. This led drafters to experiment constantly in search of the elusive perfect constitution. Consequently, new constitutions were often written in a reaction to the previous constitutional effort. At first, constitutional systems swung violently from parliamentary to presidential regimes, from constitutional monarchies to republics, from unicameral to bicameral parliaments, from indirect to direct suffrage.

Over the last 200 years, most types of constitutional system have been tried in France. A chronological presentation of this evolution aims to dispel any lingering belief that following the king's execution, the revolutionaries managed to establish a stable popular democracy.

The First Republic and the *Terreur*

By 1792, constitutional monarchy had failed and this system was abandoned. The constitution of 3 September 1791 was barely in force when Louis XVI was deposed, but it was set aside and a new Constituent Assembly – the Convention – was convened. From now on constitutional change would be envisaged only as a complete break.

However, the rejection of the first constitutional monarchy threw the political system off balance for some time. It radicalised political attitudes and discourse and destroyed any chance of achieving political stability. At first, democracy seemed to take root. The franchise was widened for the elections to the new Convention: all men of 21 years of age and in employment (with the continued exception of domestic servants) were given the right to vote.[8] Still, the system was indirect and the link between the people and its representatives weak. These elections suffered from a record level of abstentions.[9] Although the Convention started work on the new constitution, the drafting was slow. It required a considerable amount of parliamentary time which would have been better used tackling the mounting challenges that the country faced: a coalition of European powers had declared war against France and a strong counter-revolutionary movement was rising, particularly in the west of the country. In addition, the fierce struggle of political factions in the Convention led to a first draft being discarded. Finally, the constitution of the first Republic was approved by referendum and proclaimed on 24 June 1793. It contained interesting innovations with regard to the expression of popular sovereignty: it recognised (male) universal suffrage and introduced mechanisms of direct democracy. However, this constitution never came into force. Instead it was decreed on 10 October 1793 that the Committee of Public Safety[10] would become a revolutionary government for the duration of the war. This set the scene for the regime of the *Terreur:* soon the Committee headed by Robespierre established an unparalleled dictatorship, the excesses of which were justified by the need to protect the republic. The brutality of the regime reached new heights in spring 1794: the systemisation of summary trials led to hundreds of executions. On 27 July 1794, with the arrest of Robespierre, the regime led by the Committee of Public Safety came to an abrupt end. As it was felt that the constitution of 1793 was tainted by association and would not have had the support of the remaining political factions, the drafting of another constitution began.

[8] It is estimated that the electorate grew from 4 million to 7.5 million for a population of approximately 29 million.

[9] It is believed that only 700,000 electors, residing mostly in large cities, voted: see 'Elections' in J Tulard, J-F Fayard and A Fierro (eds), *Histoire et dictionnaire de la Révolution française: 1789–1799* (Paris, Robert Laffont, 1987).

[10] Originally, the Committee of Public Safety was one of the parliamentary committees of the Convention.

The Constitution of 22 August 1795 – The *Directoire*

Constitutional lessons were being learnt and the new constitution was drafted in reaction to the constitution of 1793. The committee set up to draft the new constitutional text hoped to avoid the terrible and recent excesses. To begin with, the drafters turned away from the idea of popular democracy, and rights proclaimed in former declarations were abandoned. Furthermore, the fear of dictatorship was palpable and innovations were introduced to guard against such an eventuality. For the first time, the Parliament was divided into two chambers, the Conseil des Cinq-Cents (the Council of the Five Hundreds) and the Conseil des Anciens (Council of the Elders). The legislative procedure reflected a naïve division of labour: to the Conseil des Cinq-Cents the right to draft legislative proposals and to the Conseil des Anciens the right to adopt or reject them. Also, the Executive became a collegiate structure of five 'directors'. Appointed by Parliament for five years but renewable every year, this college had little democratic legitimacy. With the presidency revolving every three months, the Executive's continuity (but also its efficiency) was compromised. Finally, the roles and powers of the legislature, Executive and judiciary reflected a strict separation of powers. The new constitution came into force in November 1795 but the new regime inherited particularly difficult circumstances – a deep economic crisis, the return to war in spring 1796 and a deeply divided society. Although a political compromise aiming to provide political stability had been reached prior to the entry into force of the constitution, the frequent elections weakened it constantly. Consequently, the *Directoire* was plagued with political instability, conflicts between factions and coups. These struggles were so intense that they affected the integrity of the political system, not to mention its ability to govern the country effectively. Unsurprisingly, the coup of 9 November 1799 led by General Bonaparte brought the regime of the *Directoire* to an end.

The Constitution of 13 December 1799 – From the *Consulat* to the First Empire

In 1799, Napoléon Bonaparte turned to ancient history for inspiration. Not surprisingly, Napoléon Bonaparte was particularly interested in the

Roman system of temporary dictatorship. He believed in a strong Executive legitimised by popular support. The *Consulat*, and later the Empire, established this caesarian tradition, which has reappeared at regular intervals in France. Indeed, the constitution of the *Consulat* was drafted so as to establish the supremacy of the Executive over the legislature. The legislative power was weakened by its division between three institutions: Tribunat, Legislative Assembly and Sénat (Senate). None was granted the right of initiative and while the *Tribunat* could only debate legislative proposals without amending them, the Legislative Assembly could only adopt or reject them without debate. The Sénat, which was not a legislative chamber, controlled the constitutionality of texts and chose the consuls, the members of both houses, the judges of the Cour de cassation[11] and the state auditors from national lists. Although the regime claimed to find its legitimacy in the people, the democratic character of the electoral system was a facade: electors were only required to draw up lists of candidates which the Sénat or the First Consul used to nominate various appointees.

Even though executive power was exercised by three consuls, the First Consul had considerably more powers that the other two; the collegiality of the Executive was mostly fictitious. Finally, the Executive was supported by the newly created Conseil d'Etat which drafted legislative proposals and resolved administrative disputes.

Soon this personal exercise of power led to a logical transformation: on 4 August 1802 the First Consul, Napoléon Bonaparte, was confirmed in office for life by plebiscite and on 18 May 1804 he was made Emperor with a hereditary line of succession. In France, Napoléon I intensified his programme of legal and institutional reforms. Over the border, he led the French army in numerous campaigns. The disastrous campaigns of Russia and Germany weakened the legitimacy of the regime. On 2 April 1814, following the capitulation of Paris, the Sénat proclaimed the forfeiture of the Emperor and his family. French politicians began to prepare the way for a return of the monarchy: the throne was offered to the late king's brother, then in exile. The defeat at Waterloo sealed the fate of the Empire: Napoléon I was exiled permanently to Saint Helena.

---

[11] The Cour de cassation was and still is the supreme court for the private law courts.

The Restoration – A Relative Stability

In April 1814, the Count of Artois, and future Louis XVIII, was offered the throne and a new constitution was drafted by the Sénat. He accepted the throne but rejected the draft constitution: not only did he disagree with the content of this document,[12] but he did not wish to be seen to have accepted political power on condition. Instead, he bestowed on the French people a constitutional charter drafted with his consent.

The stability and moderation of the British system seemed attractive after the violent upheavals of the last decade and it served as a model for the institutions of the restoration. Legislative power was vested in a parliament with two chambers: the House of Deputies and the House of Lords. The Lords held life or hereditary peerages and the deputies were elected with a restrictive electoral system: to vote, one had to pay 300 francs in taxes and be at least 30 years old.[13] The resulting electorate was so narrow that there were only 100,000 electors among a population of nine million adult males. Executive power was vested in the king who appointed and dismissed ministers. Neither the king nor the ministers were politically responsible before Parliament. However, in practice, ministerial responsibility started to emerge. To break stalemates or avoid conflicts between Executive and legislature, the king resorted to his power of dissolution of the lower house.[14] Slowly, the regime evolved into a parliamentary system. Furthermore, Louis XVIII was an astute politician and under his leadership, the restoration and its institutions were a success. However, the constitutional monarchy started to run into difficulty after his death. Charles X, his younger brother, ascended the throne in 1824. He hoped for a return to absolute monarchy and was supported by the ultra-royalist faction. In 1829, while the House of Deputies had a clear majority of liberal and moderate royalists, the king appointed an ultra-royalist to head the government. Soon, the king clashed with Parliament and the lower chamber was dissolved. Although a stronger majority of moderate royalists was returned to the house, the king banned freedom of the press, amended the electoral system and

---

[12] The draft constitution specified in article 2 that the French people called Louis-Stanislas-Xavier of France freely to the throne.

[13] Furthermore, to be a candidate, one had to pay 1,000 francs in taxes and be 40 years old. There were only 17,239 potential candidates in 1814.

[14] The House of Deputies was dissolved in 1815, 1816, 1823 and 1827.

dissolved the house again. This proved a step too far: in 1830 a revolution forced the king into exile.

Many believed that the king and not the constitutional monarchy was to blame for this recent failure. Consequently, the charter was amended in July 1830 and Louis-Philippe, Duke of Orléans[15] was offered the throne. In fact, the legitimacy and source of sovereignty of the new king was a serious issue from the beginning: on the one hand, Louis-Philippe did not have much monarchical legitimacy as he came to the throne on a revolutionary wave and on the other, he could never hope to incarnate popular sovereignty. This equivocal position was not helped by the amendments to the constitutional charter. The powers of the monarch were further reduced: he lost the right to suspend statutes when the security of the realm was at risk and he shared the right of legislative initiative with Parliament. The interpretation and application of the charter became more parliamentarian. However, the political majority necessary to ensure the stability of the new regime was elusive throughout the reign. Although the king and the regime were popular at first, the democratic credentials of the regime were eventually questioned. In 1847 failure to extend the franchise coupled with a deep economic crisis led to the organisation of the 'campaign of the banquets' by the opposition.[16] On 22 February 1848, the king prohibited a banquet in Paris and inadvertently triggered a revolution. He was forced into exile.

The Second Republic – The Constitution of 4 November 1848

The revolutionary movement that swept across Europe in 1848 led to yet another constitutional experiment. In a bid to depart from the emerging parliamentary system, the drafters of the 1848 constitution adopted a presidential regime and made a number of choices: to avoid unnecessary conflicts, the Parliament was to have one chamber only and all executive power was given to a single man, the President of the Republic. The President was meant to be subordinate to Parliament and simply implement its will. However, both Parliament and President were elected with direct universal suffrage. Finally, a strict separation of

[15] The family of Orléans represented the junior line in the order of succession but was next after Charles X and his heirs were set aside.
[16] The public were invited to banquets during which the opposition would debate controversial issues.

powers was established between the two. This constitutional mix may have been enough to destabilise any regime, but the result of the elections sealed its fate. While Louis-Napoléon Bonaparte, nephew of Napoléon I, was elected on 10 December 1848 as the first President of the Republic, the parliamentary elections returned a royalist majority on 13 May 1849. Three years of deep instability and strife between Executive and legislature followed. On 2 December 1851 Louis-Napoléon Bonaparte led a coup, took the title of Prince-President and began the drafting of a new constitution.

The Constitution of 14 January 1852 and the Second Empire

Although Louis-Napoléon Bonaparte did not proclaim himself Emperor immediately, the constitution of 14 January 1852 needed little alteration when on 2 December 1852 the second Empire was finally proclaimed. With the 1852 constitution, Louis-Napoléon Bonaparte internalised the advances made by constitutional theory and practice since the last Empire. Not only was the Prince-President the driving force behind the new political system but he was also the only representative of the people. While the Sénat, the higher chamber, played an important role of control of constitutionality, the Legislative Assembly had a rather limited legislative role: it could debate and vote the proposals put forward by the Executive but all its amendments had to be approved first by the Conseil d'Etat. Ministers could not belong to the Legislative Assembly and the Assembly had no control over them. Ministers held their office entirely at the pleasure of the Prince-President. Consequently, in the 1852 constitution the Parliament was clearly marginalised. When it came to parliamentary elections, the constitution resorted to universal suffrage. However, these elections were totally manipulated by the central government and very few candidates of the opposition were ever elected. Nevertheless, the second half of the Empire saw an era of political liberalisation and the return to a more parliamentary practice of the regime. With it came demands for more civil and political rights. Although in its last years, the imperial constitution was amended in an attempt to establish a parliamentary democracy, the resounding defeat in the Franco-Prussian War of 1870 sealed the fate of the second Empire and forced Napoléon III into exile.

The Third Republic and the Constitutional Statutes of 1875

The uncertain beginnings of the third Republic were a complete contrast to the experiences of previous regimes: at first, no attempt was made to draft a constitution. Even when the system was consigned to paper, the resulting constitutional documents were considerably more informal and less detailed than past attempts. Ironically, this may have been the reason why the third Republic provided the longest period of constitutional stability in French history since 1789. The five years between the fall of the second Empire and the adoption of the constitutional statutes of 1875 allowed politicians to choose between various options and the political system to settle into a routine. In 1871 the royalists obtained a clear majority in the newly elected National Assembly and supported a restoration. For this reason, the political institutions of the third Republic were inspired by the advances in parliamentary democracy made during the restoration period. However, the intransigent attitude of the heir to the throne made a restoration impossible. With the passage of time, the republican choice came to be seen as a safe and desirable option. In fact, this waiting game allowed two constitutional traditions to merge together: the parliamentary tradition of the constitutional monarchy and the republican tradition of the Revolution. This fusion was the foundation of the system of government finally enshrined in 1875.

The three constitutional statutes adopted over a period of seven months in 1875 put into place a parliamentary regime, many traits of which have left an indelible mark on French constitutionalism. The Executive was divided between the President of the Republic and the Government as it is today. The President of the Republic was elected by both chambers and consequently had little legitimacy. Although the position of head of government did not exist in the 1875 constitution, the President of the Council (of Ministers) filled this role from 1879. The Parliament consisted of two legislative chambers as it does today also: the House of the Deputies, elected by direct universal suffrage and the Sénat, elected mostly by indirect suffrage.[17] Although the two chambers rested on different legitimacies, they passed legislation and brought the Government to account in the same way. During much of the third Republic, governments were unable to find a stable majority in Parliament. This ministerial instability was exacerbated by the fact that governments

---

[17] There were 75 members for life in the Senate until August 1884.

were responsible before both chambers.[18] Consequently, successive governments found it difficult to implement coherent legislative programmes. The necessity to take adequate measures during World War I saw the emergence of the *décret-loi*.[19] According to this practice, the Parliament authorised the Government to legislate in discrete areas. Arguably, this was contrary to the constitution as the first article specified that legislative power was exercised by both houses. Furthermore, the return of governmental instability after World War I made the *décret-lois* necessary and from 1924, the use of this device became standard. Although constitutional reforms to redress these dysfunctions were envisaged, none ever succeeded. From May 1939, Parliament bestowed all necessary power on the Government to organise the defence of the country; and following the French defeat and armistice, the Parliament granted to the head of government, General Pétain, all powers to amend the constitution on 10 July 1940. This sealed the fate of democracy and led to the fascist regime of Vichy. Nevertheless, the third Republic had been instrumental in furthering the advances of democracy prior to that: legislation proclaiming freedom of assembly, freedom of association and many trade union rights was adopted in this period.

The Fourth Republic – The Constitution of 27 October 1946

At the end of World War II, the French people decided by referendum against a continuation of the third Republic. However, the adoption of a new constitution proved eventful. A first draft was rejected unequivocally by referendum on 19 April 1946.[20] When a new constitution finally came into force on 27 October 1946, it resembled the system of the third Republic: the Parliament had two legislative chambers – the National Assembly and the Council of the Republic – and the Executive was divided between a President of the Republic and a Prime Minister. Still, as Parliament was held responsible in large part for the problems of the previous regime, a few provisions were meant to curb this institu-

---

[18] The Sénat brought down seven governments during the third Republic.
[19] The *décret-loi* is a cross between an Act of Parliament (*loi*) and a statutory instrument (*décret*). It is similar in content to an Act of Parliament, but adopted the same way as secondary legislation.
[20] The French people were believed to have rejected the text because of the single chamber Parliament and the new declarations of rights.

tion. For instance, the powers of the second chamber were reduced: it could no longer dismiss the Government and its amendments could be circumvented by the National Assembly. Also, the constitution adopted a strict procedure for the National Assembly to dismiss the Government. In short, all was done to ensure that the new regime would not follow in the footsteps of its predecessor. Ironically, these changes may have reignited the previous difficulties. Between 1946 and 1958, there were a total of 21 governments. In fact, the conditions for dissolution of the National Assembly were so exacting that dissolution was no real threat.

Also, the choice of proportional representation for the elections to the National Assembly led to a relatively large number of smaller parties being represented and made it difficult for a stable parliamentary majority to emerge. The political context of the time compounded these problems. The pool from which coalition governments were chosen was artificially reduced: the left-wing alliance, responsible for the adoption of the 1946 constitution, was compromised by the advent of the cold war. By May 1947, it had become unthinkable to allow members of the communist party to join the ranks of the Government. The choice of coalition parties was restricted largely to the centre of the political spectrum.

The political context adumbrated above explains partly the inactivity of the Parliament of the fourth Republic. Although Parliament was often accused of interfering in all and everything, it was impotent when it came to important decisions. As soon as a government seemed poised to implement an important policy, it was often rewarded by a vote of no confidence. In the end, this inactivity would doom the regime.

During the fourth Republic, many French colonies became independent and for a large majority, the process was smooth. Unlike other colonies, Algeria was regarded administratively and territorially as part of France and a large French population lived there. The independence of Algeria divided public opinion and political parties alike. Soon, the Algerian crisis became a war of independence and the situation grew more difficult by the day. It is against this background that the fourth Republic met its end.

From the Fourth to the Fifth Republic

On 13 May 1958, a French crowd invaded the government buildings in Algiers and established a committee of national security. Neither police nor army intervened, thereby signalling their passive support for the rebellion. The army was in a particularly difficult position: while it was committed to stay in Algeria and protect the French population, the increasing number of dead and injured among young conscripts was turning many French families against the war. While French citizens in Algeria worried about being abandoned, the rest of the population had begun to shift in favour of independence.

The rebellion in Algiers was all the more problematical in that its timing coincided with the fall of yet another government in Paris. Although negotiations had taken place to appoint Pflimlin, the new Prime Minister was suspected of supporting independence and his appointment was immediately compromised. In view of this situation, the President of the Republic turned to the army and requested that it end the rebellion in Algiers, but to no avail. On 14 May, General Massu called for de Gaulle to return to politics.[21] This request was repeated the next day by General Salan. This time, de Gaulle gave a press conference and replied that he was ready once more to assume power. Things turned critical on 24 May as the rebellion spread to Corsica. By then, political power was divided between the constitutional power of the Government in Paris, the factual power of the committee of national security in Algiers, and the moral power of de Gaulle. On 27 May, de Gaulle demanded in another press conference that the army abandon its plans for a military coup the next day. On 28 May, Pflimlin resigned and the political crisis deepened. At this juncture, the President of the Republic, Coty, issued an ultimatum to the Parliament: he would resign if Parliament barred the return of de Gaulle to power. On 31 May de Gaulle, having demanded that a new constitution be drafted, chose the members of his Government. The Government was approved by the National Assembly on 1 June and a constitutional statute authorising the drafting of a new constitution was passed by Parliament on 3 June: it settled the drafting process and listed the principles to be included therein. This aimed to provide distance for the future constitutional settlement from past experiences (for example the events of July 1940) and protect its legitimacy. The new constitution was drafted over the summer and was endorsed by the French people in a referendum of 28 September. It came into force on 4 October 1958.

---

[21]   He left politics for the duration of the fourth Republic as he disagreed with the regime.

UNDERSTANDING FRENCH CONSTITUTIONAL HISTORY

With the speed of French constitutional change comes the realisation that the ideal of constitutionalism and democracy did not take root easily in France. The Revolution of 1789 was only the beginning of a long and tortuous road.

If at first the development of French constitutional history seems haphazard, it is possible to identify some distinctive trends and bring some order to this apparent chaos. Also behind this rich and complex history, it is possible to discover a certain conception of constitutionalism, a conception which has been partly responsible for the way constitutional history unfolded.

The Mechanisms of Constitutional Change

Although constitutional change in France appears random and chaotic, it can be explained and even ordained by reference to the systematic way it took place.

Chain Reactions: The Micro-Level

New constitutional instruments were often drafted in opposition to previous texts and regimes. At a micro-level, constitutional change would often consist in a series of chain reactions. Constitutional practices and experiences of one regime would inform the drafting and adoption of the next. This is exemplified by the innovations found in the constitution of 22 August 1795, drafted soon after the fall of Robespierre: for the first time Parliament comprised two chambers and the Executive was headed by three *directeurs*. This institutional structure was clearly adopted to prevent a dictatorship of either branch of government: while the legislative chambers would keep each other in check, the collegiate nature of the Executive would make it difficult for a dictator to rise to power. However, the drafters may not have realised at the time that this complex institutional structure multiplied potential conflicts. Interestingly, a few regimes and failures later, the constitution of the second Republic would return to a single-chamber Parliament and to a single-person Executive in a bid to avoid unnecessary conflicts.

Generally, new provisions were drafted and new institutions created in an attempt to quell undesirable practices and behaviours. The presentation of such an attempt spanning the last three constitutions throws an interesting light on this phenomenon. The third Republic suffered from chronic governmental instability and coalition governments struggled to legislate through Parliament. When the outbreak of World War I made it necessary for the business of government to be rapid and efficient, a new device (the *décret-loi*) was created. With the return of ministerial instability after the war, the use of the *décret-lois* became standard. Still, the practice was contrary to the constitution and represented a usurpation of legislative power by the Executive. Consequently, the constitution of the fourth Republic condemned the practice: article 13 stated that legislative power which belongs to the Assemblée nationale cannot be delegated. However, ministerial instability soon crippled the new regime and led to the use of similar mechanisms despite the prohibition.

Interestingly, with the advent of the fifth Republic, the official stance changed. The wish to weaken Parliament led to the authorisation of such delegation: according to article 38, Parliament can delegate to the Executive the power to legislate in specific areas temporarily. The history of this constitutional practice exemplifies the way constitutional change operates at micro-level. In the end, the once-unconstitutional practice was integrated fully into the constitution. Beyond the wish to increase the power of the Executive, there may have been a recognition that resistance against deep-rooted constitutional practices is futile.

Constitutional Cycles and Traditions: The Macro-Level

On the surface, French constitutional history has not had a linear evolution: it has known many stops and starts and has often seemed to lurch violently from one solution to its opposite. The search for meaning and commonality behind the various experiences is a challenge.

Still some lawyers have come to believe that the evolution of French constitutional law could be explained at macro-level as a succession of alternating cycles.[22] Each constitutional cycle creates a dialectical dynamic as it encompasses three distinct periods: a first period recognises the primacy of Parliament, a second reactionary period gives primacy to the Executive and finally, a third and longer period synthesises these experi-

---

[22] See J Gicquel and J-E Gicquel, *Droit constitutionnel et institutions politiques*, Collection Domat (Paris, Montchrestien, 2000) 421.

ences and establishes a period of cooperation of all branches of government. This last era creates a period of comparative stability until another cycle starts again. According to this representation, since 1789 France has already completed two full cycles: while the first cycle started in 1789 and ended in 1848, the second began in 1848 and ended in 1940. Within these cycles, the legislature was a dominant power between 1789 and 1795 and again between 1848 and 1851. By contrast, the Executive had clear primacy in the two periods between 1795 and 1814 and 1851 and 1870. Finally, the two eras of synthesis, stability and cooperation of power spanned the long period of the restoration (1814–1848) and the third Republic (1875–1940).

This representation of French constitutional history has the merit of unearthing a deeper pattern and of bringing order to an otherwise confusing history. Surprisingly, it also highlights an underlying trend in constitutional stability: over the 151-year period covered by the two constitutional cycles (1789–1940), the two periods of synthesis, stability and cooperation of power add up to a total of 99 years. France's constitutional past may not be as troubled as it seems.

A third constitutional cycle began with the 1946 constitution: the recognition of the primacy of Parliament in the fourth Republic was swiftly counteracted by the fifth Republic and its assertion of the Executive's dominance. Although it is early for a clear assessment, one cannot help wondering whether the constitutional reform of July 2008 will help foster a full constitutional cooperation and long-term political stability.

Finally, beyond the constitutional cycles presented above, it is possible to identify three constitutional traditions in the rich tapestry of French constitutional history: the republican, the parliamentary and the caesarian traditions. While the republican tradition was established by the 1789 Revolution, the parliamentary tradition was born out of the experiences of the restoration. These merged with the third Republic and continued into the fourth Republic. By contrast, the caesarian tradition found its expression in the Bonapartist movement and the two empires and is said to inspire the present constitution. These traditions represent a diverging expression of political power: in the parliamentary tradition, sovereignty of the people came to reside in Parliament and expressed itself by way of legislation, while in the caesarian tradition, the strong leadership and authority of the Executive is tempered by the need for popular (if not democratic) support. In the parliamentary tradition, regular elections frame the activities of Parliament and in the caesarian tradition, the leader resorts to plebiscite/referendum to strengthen his legitimacy. These traditions have alternated at regular intervals since 1789.

In Search of Continuity

The analysis has tended to show that constitutional change in France is often synonymous with discontinuity, but this picture is not a true reflection of reality. Behind the political and institutional instability, there is a clear thread of continuity. This continuity has certainly helped the country survive the numerous crises and upheavals and even to maintain some coherence throughout. It is possible to identify three main components of this continuity: longevity of political personnel, permanence of administrative law and structures and a certain vision of society.

Even though many changes of regimes were brutal and followed a revolution or coup, a surprising number of politicians managed to lead successful political careers spanning multiple regimes.[23] Talleyrand is one of the best examples of this political longevity. Of aristocratic extraction, he was a bishop in 1789. A member of the Etats-Généraux, renamed National Assembly, he espoused revolutionary ideas. In 1792 he was sent as a special envoy to Britain (to persuade the Cabinet to support the French cause) and later to the USA. He returned to France in September 1796 and served as minister for foreign affairs during the *Directoire* and under Napoléon Bonaparte until 1809. He played a key role in organising the restoration of Louis XVIII and served as his minister for foreign affairs. After the fall of Charles X in 1830, he was instrumental in arranging for Louis-Philippe to ascend the throne. Under this last regime, he served as ambassador to the United Kingdom and negotiated the Franco-British agreement of 1834.

Similarly, although the third and fourth Republics were plagued by a chronic governmental instability, the personnel staffing these successive governments was remarkably stable.[24] In fact, with governments perma-

[23] There was a continuity of political personnel even during the revolutionary period: for instance, of the 400 deputies of the Convention, 189 had been members of the previous Legislative Assembly and 96 had been members of the Constituent Assembly.

[24] See M Dogan and P Campbell, 'Ministres inamovibles et personnages éphémères dans les régimes à instabilité ministérielle' in Colas, D and Emeri, C (eds), *Mélanges en hommage à Maurice Duverger* (Paris, Presses universitaires de France, 1987) 283.

nently forming and falling, Members of Parliament seemed to be engaged in a political game of musical chairs. For instance, Henri Queuille, whose career spanned two Republics, was member of Parliament from 1914 to 1958; he participated in 33 different governments (three times as head of government and 30 times as minister) and was minister for agriculture for eight years: a formidable record.

Public administration also provided a strong element of continuity throughout French history: many new administrative structures were put in place soon after the 1789 Revolution or under the leadership of Napoléon Bonaparte. Once in place, they continued in existence whatever the regime. For instance, the administrative division of the French territory into *départements* is a lasting legacy of the Revolution. Similarly, the Conseil d'Etat, once the creation of Napoléon Bonaparte, continues to play a key role today. This administrative continuity is further strengthened when it comes to the law: administrative law developed independently and largely unhindered by constitutional change.

Finally, an element of continuity is also found in the adoption and conservation of the basic societal choices and principles established by the Revolution and enshrined in the declaration of 1789. The Revolution led to the adoption of a new organisation of society which remained unchallenged by successive regimes, even after the restoration. Similarly, the political status of citizens may have been unequally protected throughout French constitutional history but the declaration indicated clear goals in this regard; these often served as references and reminders. This created a commonality of vision which remained constant whatever the degree and extent of constitutional change.

The Characteristics of French Constitutionalism

Through these experiences of constitutional change, a certain conception of constitutionalism was gradually adopted in France. This conception has in turn driven constitutional change.

Experimental Constitutionalism

Undeniably, the revolutionary movement of the end of the eighteenth century triggered the birth in France of modern constitutionalism. Although the movement was inspired by political philosophers and constitutional theoreticians, the translation of these doctrines into practice was far from straightforward. This may explain to some extent the repeated failures. For instance, when the first constitutional monarchy came to an abrupt end, the revolutionaries were faced with the task of adopting a new political system. There may have been an abundance of writings and theories on popular sovereignty and representative democracy at the time, but the translation of these theories in institutional terms proved quite challenging, especially as no other republican system was available in Europe to learn from. Constitutionalism had not yet reached a high degree of sophistication and this led at times to a rather naïve interpretation of its requirements: for instance, in the first Republic, drafters believed that popular sovereignty expressed itself in a single and clear voice; they would not contemplate a Parliament with two chambers as they felt it would divide this expression of sovereignty. Ironically, once the desirability of a Parliament with two chambers was recognised, the drafters grappled with other difficulties: the division of labour between the houses and the organisation of their respective legitimacy. The first attempt at such an allocation of power was rather clumsy. The constitution of 1795 aimed to give a clear legislative function to each chamber: the Conseil des Cinq-Cents proposed and drafted the text while the Conseil des Anciens accepted or rejected it with no right of amendment. Although this allocation may have appeared clear and straightforward, it created terrible difficulties and revealed that drafters had a superficial grasp of constitutional realities. The issue of legitimacy also proved a challenge for the *Directoire*. Both chambers represented the French people in strict equality: Members of Parliament were elected by the same electoral system and for the same duration. This meant that the conflicts created by the division of labour mentioned above could not easily be resolved by a reference to separate legitimacies. It is not surprising that deep political conflicts raged throughout the regime.

French constitutional history is in fact riddled with such experiments. Numerous regimes and permutations were tried one after the other: slowly constitutional mechanisms were refined and the understanding of constitutionalism improved. Still, lessons were hard to learn, especially when it came to legitimacy: for instance, although the authors of the second Republic wished to subordinate the President of the Republic to the Parliament, they stipulated that both be elected with direct universal suffrage. The authors did not realise that the recognition of a hierarchy or priority between the two powers would be impossible. Again, although the Sénat of the third Republic was elected with indirect suffrage, it benefited largely from the same powers as the first chamber. This exacerbated greatly the dysfunctions of the regime. In fact, one had to wait for the fourth Republic to see the relative legitimacy of each house match its respective power.

French constitutional history may have lacked continuity but it is partly explained by the need to experiment with new mechanisms and new solutions in a bid to uncover a system that would bring political stability. The French experimented live and this has lasted 200 years. It is hoped that modern constitutionalism and contemporary democracies have benefited from these repeated attempts.

The Historical Paradox of French Constitutionalism

The multiple experiences of drafting new constitutions find their root in the doctrines of the Revolution. The sovereignty of the monarch gave way to the sovereignty of the people and a degree of reverence was attached to the various texts representing the direct expression of this sovereignty. This led to constitutionalism being conceptualised in a rather rigid manner. The written word was seen as having such importance that it needed to be relied upon fully and totally. In this theoretical framework, it is difficult to recognise a place for constitutional practice: any practice outside the text of the constitution cannot be countenanced. This should have ensured the triumph of law over facts. However, throughout French constitutional history, practice was repeatedly at variance with the constitution itself. This created a fundamental paradox in French constitutional law: while constitutional instruments were revered and placed at the top of the hierarchy of norms, constitutional practice often went against them.

Furthermore, as constitutions were meant to frame the strict exercise of political power, those ridden with contrary practices tended to lose their legitimacy and be replaced. Little value was attached to the continuity of constitutional regimes and few were given the chance to transform themselves. On the contrary, successive constitutions founded their legitimacy on clean breaks from the past. This created a chronic inability of regimes to evolve. Again, this may be explained by the rigid conception of constitutionalism adumbrated above: normally the process of constitutional change is inscribed in a dialectical relationship between a constitutional provision and its interpretation and practice. Often, a constitutional amendment aims to provide an acceptable synthesis between the two. However, this dialectical interaction between fact and law was not fully understood in France. Even though one after the other, written constitutions were misapplied and distorted, no one questioned whether this frenzy of constitutional drafting was opportune. French people seemed to believe that there was a regime and constitution out there which would match their needs; it was simply a case of finding it. French constitutionalism became synonymous with this search for constitutional perfection.

Finally, little attention was given to the protection of the primacy of constitutions. To begin with, there was no clear distinction between constitutions and ordinary statutes: both categories of text were often adopted by an elected assembly which embodied the expression of the will of the people. Arguably, there were few legal techniques to ensure a clear superiority of constitutions over statutes: it was difficult to annul a statute for breach of a text which had been adopted in the same manner as the statute it purported to review. Furthermore, as statutes were seen as an expression of the sovereign people, the introduction of any form of control over them would seem controversial in practice and unwarranted in theory. Consequently, it took a long time for a control of constitutionality to emerge and for statutes to be made to respect the constitution. In fact, the 1958 constitution is really the first to ensure that its provisions are not contravened.

Constitutional Symbolism

The multiplicity of constitutional documents and the long history of constitutional upheavals have led to the creation of constitutional symbols and taboos.

Indeed, some constitutional experiences were so painful that they resulted in constitutional taboos: for instance, today, it would be difficult to convince the French people that a single chamber parliament is a viable option. There is a diffuse belief that the single chamber parliament of both the Convention and the second Republic resulted in those regimes becoming dictatorships. This seems to be deeply rooted indeed: for many, it explains in part the rejection of the 1946 draft constitution and the failure of the 1969 referendum (it aimed to transform the Sénat into a consultative body).

Similarly, constitutional history has created some positive symbols. The most famous of all is the Declaration of the Rights of Man of 1789. This text has become such a point of symbolic reference that it is cited in the constitutions of the fourth and fifth Republics. Again, the attempt to adopt a new declaration of rights (ostensibly to replace the declaration of 1789) in the 1946 draft constitution is said to have sealed its fate. The Conseil constitutionnel made full use of this symbolic status when it decided to incorporate the declaration of 1789 into the present constitution.[25] Although momentous, the legitimacy of this move was barely questioned.

CONCLUSION: THE MERGER OF CONSTITUTIONAL TRADITIONS?

The 1958 constitution seems to break from the troubled constitutional history presented above: the fifth Republic has lasted longer than most regimes and more importantly it has fostered constitutional stability and continuity.

Interestingly, the present regime is not modelled on an easily identifiable constitutional system: although the constitution originally established a parliamentary system, the subsequent evolution of the regime bolstered the position of the President of the Republic. In fact, when writers first wished to classify the present system, they had to coin a new category: the French regime is labelled a 'presidentialist' or 'semi-presidential' system. This emphasises its mixed character. The mongrel nature of the regime is also revealing when analysed against the historical evolution. The presidential character of the regime, which emphasises the leadership of the President of the Republic, is combined with the main traits of a parliamentary regime. The caesarian tradition first encountered in the Bonapartist movement finds its expression in the republican institutions and is tempered by mechanisms of parliamentary democracy. All three major political traditions – republican, parliamentary and caesarian – seem to come together in the present Republic. To paraphrase one commentator, the fifth Republic crowns constitutional history by achieving the synthesis of democracy with authority.[26] The in-depth study of the

---

[25] See chapter 2.
[26] See J Gicquel and J-E Gicquel, (n 22) 487.

regime which follows will help us decide if these constitutional traditions have indeed been reconciled and if the French have found their constitutional Elysium at last.

FURTHER READING

G Antonetti, *La monarchie constitutionnelle* (Paris, Montchrestien,1998)

G Berlia, 'Le projet de constitution du 19 Avril 1946' (1946) *Revue du droit public* 209

M Bonnard, 'Les pratiques parlementaires sous le Directoire' *Revue française de droit constitutionnel* (1990) 213

R Chartier, *The Cultural Origins of the French Revolution* (trans L Cochrane) (USA, Duke University Press, 1991)

C-A Colliard, 'La pratique de la question de confiance sous la IV ème République' (1948) *Revue du droit public* 231

H S Jones, *French State in Question: Public Law and Political Argument in the Third Republic* (Cambridge, Cambridge Universiy Press, 2002)

La IVème République (1996) 76 *Pouvoirs*

F Luchaire, *Naissance d'une constitution: 1848* (Paris, Fayard, 1998)

M Morabito, *Histoire constitutionnelle de la France (1789–1958)*, 11th edn, (Paris, Montchrestien, 2010)

P Pactet, 'La IIIe République et la mise en oeuvre de l'héritage républicain' in P Gélard, M Ameller, P Avril and R Ben Achour (eds), *Mélanges en l'honneur de Jean Gicquel* (Paris, Montchrestien, 2008) 403

M Troper, 'La constitution de 1791 aujourd'hui' (1992) *Revue française de droit constitutionnel* 3

M van Nifterik, 'French Constitutional History, Garden or Graveyard' (2007) *European Constitutional Law Review* 476

G Vedel, 'La continuité constitutionnelle en France de 1789 à 1989' RFDC (1990) *Revue française de droit constitutionnel* 5

2

In Search of the Constitutional Fundamentals

———

The Legitimacy of the 1958 Constitution – The Integrity of the 1958
Constitution – The Efficiency of the 1958 Constitution: The Political
System – Conclusion: Something Old, Something New

THE PREVIOUS CHAPTER clearly showed that French constitutions repeatedly failed to engineer political and constitutional stability. In this regard, the 1958 constitution represents a
real break from the past: France has known constitutional stability for
the last 50 years and all the indications are that this state of affairs will
last. The present constitution is responsible for the advent of a robust
and lasting constitutional order. Therefore, an analysis of the present
constitutional document may explain this longevity.

Furthermore, over the last 200 years, French constitutions have been
unsuccessful on other counts: many failed to protect their integrity and
unconstitutional practices flourished; others were unable to ensure
their efficiency with a barely functioning political system, and finally,
few were able to engineer much, if any, legitimacy. As the stability and
success of a constitution will often hinge on its legitimacy, integrity
and efficiency, the 1958 constitution will be examined in light of
these attributes. This investigation may provide a deeper understanding
of the present constitutional order and reveal the reasons for its
success.

THE LEGITIMACY OF THE 1958 CONSTITUTION

The beginnings of a constitution will often determine the degree of
legitimacy the constitution has at first. After that, constitutions must

continue to engineer legitimacy throughout their lifespan. Although the 1958 constitution was adopted quickly and in the midst of a deep crisis, it was held in surprisingly high regard from its inception. Normally, constitutions written in haste and against a difficult political background do not manage to generate much legitimacy and often do not fare well. In fact, the third Republic met its end on 10 July 1940 in alarmingly similar circumstances to those of the fourth Republic. In June 1958 history could have repeated itself. Instead, politicians took great care to pave the way for the fifth Republic and to provide the new regime with as much legitimacy as possible in the circumstances. Also, the adoption of the new constitution stopped France from being engulfed by civil war; at the time, this must have scored a great many points with the French people.

The Adoption of the Constitutional Document

The process by which a constitution is drafted, the reasons why it is written, and the way in which the final draft is approved will go a long way to determine the legitimacy of any constitutional document. Indeed for a constitution to be placed at the top of the hierarchy of norms, its mode of creation and adoption is paramount.

In the past, these questions had not been fully understood in France and the necessary concepts and mechanisms were not researched and developed enough. Happily, the constitution of 1958 fares better than most French constitutions on this count. At the time, politicians were aware of the possible pitfalls and they guided closely the introduction of the new constitution. A law passed on 3 June 1958 by the Parliament of the fourth Republic aimed to guide both substantively and procedurally the production of a new constitution. It hoped to demonstrate that the regime change was taking place within the confines of law and democracy and that it had legitimate beginnings.

A Guide to the Content

The law of 3 June 1958 listed the principles that were to be included in the new constitution: ministerial responsibility, separation of legislative and executive powers, universal suffrage and independence of the judiciary to protect the fundamental rights contained in the Preamble to the

1946 constitution and the 1789 Declaration of the Rights of Man. However, the statute did not go into any details. Parliament had not wished to dictate the precise implementation of the principles. Clearly, the statute aimed to frame the work of the drafters of the new constitution, ensure its democratic content and provide the whole process with a label of constitutional legitimacy. The Algerian war of independence, the insurrections in both Algeria and Corsica and the imminence of a military coup did not create favourable conditions for the drafting of a democratic and liberal constitution. These circumstances could have led easily to the emergence of an authoritarian regime.

Also, the insistence on substantive requirements is revealing of French constitutionalism. From the revolutionary period, French constitutionalism has often linked the constitutional nature of a regime with the presence or absence of a number of principles. Indeed, article 16 of the 1789 Declaration concludes starkly that a regime that does not guarantee individual rights and freedoms and the separation of powers does not have a constitution. A document that did not contain these key components would be denied the very status and label of constitution. The attention in the law to the substantive content was not only meant to enhance the legitimacy of the future constitution, it was meant to reflect a long-held understanding of constitutionalism.

The Constitutional Procedure

In addition, the law of 3 June 1958 established the exact procedure for writing and adopting the new constitution. The initial draft was to be produced by a consultative committee, two-thirds of which was to be made up of Members of Parliament of the fourth Republic. At the time, professional politicians did not trust de Gaulle and made sure that they played a key role in the establishment of the new regime. The statute was thus signalling a clear continuity with the previous regime.

The draft was then to be forwarded to the Conseil des Ministres (Council of Ministers) after consultation with the Conseil d'Etat. These requirements have become standard for all legislation in France. Finally, the statute of 3 June 1958 dictated that the final version be approved by referendum. The requirement for a referendum allowed the expression of the sovereign – the French Nation – and was the most complete seal of legitimacy that could be given. The constitution was adopted by referendum on 29 September 1958 by a majority of 82.6 per cent. This result was strengthened by the fact that 98.9 per cent of the registered voters chose to cast their vote. The constitution began its life on 4 October 1958 with overwhelming support from the French people. There is no doubt that the legitimacy of the present constitution was enhanced by these arrangements.

Still, the circumstances of the period forced all those involved in the drafting of the constitution to act quickly. In effect, the constitution was drafted, scrutinised and approved by referendum in the space of four months. This is a remarkable achievement when one takes into account the complexity of the task and the immense political pressure of the time.

The Construction of a Constitutional Identity

A constitution may have had legitimate beginnings, but unless it establishes a constitutional order respectful of the principles which are held essential by the people, this state of affairs will not continue. Indeed, the principles, ideals and values promoted by a constitution will contribute greatly to the creation of a separate constitutional identity and will enhance any original legitimacy.

As seen above, French constitutionalism tends to combine both institutional and substantive principles. However, unusually, the drafters of the 1958 constitution did not include any declaration of rights and freedoms. The law of 3 June 1958 did not require that such a text be written and the circumstances surrounding the adoption of the constitution made the drafting of such a declaration difficult. The consensus on a draft declaration would have taken time and delayed the adoption of the new constitution. Still, the 1958 constitution had a clear substantive content from its inception. In fact, the principles contained in the constitution project a certain vision of French society and establish a constitutional status for its citizens. The constitution thus resorts heavily to constitutional symbolism.

The French Republic in the 1958 Constitution

The Republic is the constitutional expression of French society and as such it is strongly value laden. Indeed, article 1 of the constitution lists the characters of the French Republic: it is unitary, secular, democratic and social.[1] This phrasing was adopted for the constitution of the fourth Republic and reproduced in 1958.

The Unitary Republic

The constitution of 1958 has internalised a long-standing representation of the French Republic: unitary and, until recently, strongly centralised.[2] This unity was regarded as the corollary of the indivisibility of national sovereignty.[3] The unitary character of the Republic is inferred from the sovereignty of the French Nation: since sovereignty cannot conceivably be divided, neither can the sovereign Nation. This has implications for the rights of individuals and for the organisation of the French territory. Territorially, this means that a federal organisation would be unconstitutional and that territorial entities can never be granted complete autonomy; they cannot have such power that would in effect divide national sovereignty. The principle of unity has implications for the content of citizenship also. The assertion that the sovereign Nation cannot be divided has led to the lack of recognition of specific subgroups and communities (even when these are clearly identifiable by cultural, social or economic markers). This explains the rejection of minority rights and the lack of status of many intermediary bodies.

The Secular Republic

Again the principle of secularism has its origins in the Revolution of 1789 when State and church were separated for the first time. However, this separation was short lived and the church was finally separated from the State during the third Republic after a long and protracted political battle between republicans and church. The statute of 1905, which imposed a complete and radical break, was seen as the triumph of progress and democracy over conservative ideology and church hierarchy. This victory of republicanism was a defining and constitutional moment in France. Unsurprisingly secularism became a central republican value

---

[1] See article 1 § 1: 'France shall be an indivisible, secular, democratic and social Republic. It shall ensure the equality of all citizens before the law, without distinction of origin, race or religion. It shall respect all beliefs. It shall be organised on a decentralised basis.'

[2] See chapter 7.

[3] Commentators rightly point out that this was also a long-standing monarchical tradition, see D Roux, 'Une république une et diverse?' in B Mathieu (ed), *Cinquantième anniversaire de la constitution française* (Paris, Dalloz, 2008) 147.

and was given constitutional recognition for the first time in the constitution of the fourth Republic. Recently, secularism has come under serious attack[4] and it is important to know the origins of this character of the French Republic to understand the context of the present discussions and controversies.

The Democratic Republic

If for a long time Republic and democracy may have been considered interchangeable – a Republic could only be conceived as democratic – reality demonstrated that the two concepts may be linked but are not synonymous. Indeed, while many democracies are not republican, some Republics are not democratic. The assertion that the French Republic is democratic can be found for the first time in the constitution of 1848. In the present constitution, this announcement is supported by the use of universal suffrage for all elections and by the inclusion of mechanisms of direct democracy.

The Social Republic

Soon after 1789, the revolutionaries realised that, beyond political rights and individual freedoms, the Republic ought to provide a minimum of social guarantees to its citizens. Indeed, the constitution of 1793 contained a number of provisions pertaining to the provision of welfare and economic support to citizens in need. However, this constitution was replaced before it was applied and with it disappeared the first attempt to set up a social Republic. Although the adoption of a more social Republic was debated in France at regular intervals, it was only given constitutional recognition in the constitution of 1946 with the incorporation in its Preamble of many social and economic rights.

Citizenship: A Constitutional Status

Ultimately, the Republic aims to serve its sovereign, the French people. To this effect, the constitution of 1958 contains a number of statements regarding citizens and their rights. Although the 1958 constitution did not contain any declaration of rights, the first article states that the Republic ensures the equality of all citizens before the law without any distinction

---

[4] See the controversial statute of 11 October 2011 which makes a criminal offence of covering one's face in public spaces.

on the ground of origins, race or religion. The principle of equality, which emphasised the break from the structural inequality of the monarchical society, is the founding principle of the French Republic. However, the principle referred to is one of formal equality. Indeed, the constitution itself seems to rule out the possibility of any special or preferential treatment: the principle is applied without any distinction on any ground. Still, courts have had to adapt their interpretation of this principle and have allowed a move away from a strict interpretation of formal equality in two cases: when the public interest or the specific circumstances justify it. More recently, controversies arose when Parliament tried to ensure a better representation of women in public life. Methods of positive discrimination met repeatedly with the censure of the Conseil constitutionnel.[5] In the end, a revision of the constitution was necessary to overcome the perceived constitutional obstacle.[6]

Liberty is another core principle of the 1958 constitution. Although reference to the freedom of citizens is more diluted in the constitution, it is clearly there: it is cited in the motto of the Republic, which is reproduced in article 2, and in article 66, which provides that the private law courts are to act as guardians of individual freedom.[7] In fact, the tandem of equality and liberty combines together to establish the foundations of a constitutional status for citizens, a status that was strengthened considerably by the case law of the Conseil constitutionnel and the more recent constitutional reforms.[8]

The Symbols of the 1958 Constitution

In 1958, the constitution did not refer to any national symbols but cited two iconic statements. Article 2 refers to both the motto of the French Republic: 'Liberty, Equality, Fraternity' and its guiding principle: 'the Government of the people, by the people, for the people'. The motto goes back to the Revolution and was first coined by Robespierre in 1790. It has been cited in previous constitutions, it is reproduced on the

---

[5] See C cons no 82-146 DC 18 November 1982, Quotas I and C cons no 98-407 DC 14 January 1999, Quotas II.

[6] This was done by the constitutional reform of 8 July 1999. Also, the reform of 23 July 2008 strengthened the constitution in this regard.

[7] See article 66: 'No one shall be arbitrarily detained. The judicial authority, guardian of the freedom of the individual, shall ensure compliance with this principle in the conditions laid down by statute.'

[8] For further information, see chapter 6.

walls of many French public buildings and its revolutionary heritage is world famous. Although the exact meaning of each term is the subject of debates, the expression has strong symbolic and historic resonances that transcend the definition of its terms.

The expression 'the Government of the people, by the people, for the people' was coined by Abraham Lincoln in 1863 and appeared for the first time in the 1946 constitution. This guiding principle is placed in the part of the constitution concerned with sovereignty and aims to reinforce the democratic foundations of the constitutional order. By 1946, it was felt that the 1790 motto, which concentrated mainly on citizens and their status, was no longer sufficient. It had become apparent that Republic was not always synonymous with democracy: it was necessary to emphasise that the institutions of the French Republic needed to be truly democratic.

In 1992, during the revision of the constitution prior to the ratification of the Maastricht Treaty, the Parliament insisted that a reference to the flag, the national anthem and the French language be added to article 2 of the constitution. This was a reaction to the perceived loss of sovereignty. Of these three national symbols, the anthem and the flag are the only revolutionary ones: the Marseillaise and the tricolour flag were both adopted in 1792 after the constitutional monarchy had ended.

However, the recognition of French as the official language has pre-revolutionary roots. The monarchy fought to impose French as the only language of the country at the expense of regional and minority ones, as early as the sixteenth century. The renewed interest in the protection of the French language stems from the growing use and influence of the English language not only around the world but also in France. However, this recognition had weakened even further the status of regional and minority languages. Indeed, this culminated in the declaration by the Conseil constitutionnel of the unconstitutionality of the European Charter for Regional Languages,[9] and to this day, the Charter has not been ratified. During the revision of July 2008, an amendment was put forward to recognise regional languages as part of French heritage. Originally, this reference was simply added to article 2 of the constitution. However, the Sénat, concerned for the primacy of the French language, insisted that this reference be moved to the title dealing with territorial government. So far, this constitutional recognition has not

---

[9] See C cons no 99-412 DC 15 June 1999, European Charter for Regional or Minority Languages.

strengthened the position of regional languages much. The Government has already declared that it will not ratify the Charter for Regional Languages and the framework legislation giving effect to article 75-1 is still to appear despite numerous announcements to this effect. More recently, the Conseil constitutionnel declared that article 75-1 did not recognise a right or a freedom to citizens and consequently it was not actionable under the new preliminary ruling of constitutionality.[10]

The reference to constitutional symbols in the 1958 constitution contributes to the creation of a constitutional identity.[11] Many of these symbols link the 1958 constitution directly to the ideals of 1789 and provide historical legitimacy to the present regime. Indeed, this contributes to the creation of a symbolic history remote from reality and to a political identity rooted in a sanitised revolutionary ideology.

The Delineation of the 1958 Constitution

The content of the French constitution should be easily determined: after all, it is enshrined in a clearly identifiable document. Still, constitutions may be consigned to paper, but they are nonetheless inscribed in a dynamic and evolve with time. If they do not, their legitimacy may dwindle.

In fact, the French constitution has been markedly dynamic and its very content has been extended far beyond the constitutional document itself. Indeed, the text of the constitution has been interpreted in such a way that the confines of the French constitution have changed. It is important to explain this new delineation and the reasons for its occurrence.

The Conseil constitutionnel and the Bloc de constitutionalité

In light of the practices of the fourth Republic, the drafters of the constitution had imagined that the Executive would need to be guarded against Parliament and originally, the Conseil constitutionnel was conceived as an institutional watchdog for the benefit of the Executive. However, by the mid 1960s the Executive had emerged as the dominant power and the Conseil constitutionnel was left with little to do. Furthermore, the 1958

---

[10] See C cons no 2011-130 QPC 20 May 2011, Mme Cécile (regional languages).
[11] See A-M Le Pourhiet, 'Les symboles identitaires dans la constitution de 1958' in B Mathieu (ed) (n 3) 133.

constitution suffered from a congenital weakness: no declaration of rights was attached to it. The longer the constitution survived, the more incongruous this omission would appear. In a country which still resounds with the revolutionary struggle and the recognition of rights and freedoms to all citizens, this failure may have undermined in the long run the whole constitutional effort. In this context, the change undertaken by the Conseil constitutionnel is easily explained.

In 1971, the Conseil was faced with the perfect case to perform a deep constitutional change.[12] Controversial new legislation was referred to the Conseil constitutionnel: it purported to amend legislation of 1901 and to curtail freedom of association dramatically. The statute of 1901 recognised freedom of association for the first time in France and specified that all associations would have legal personality from the moment of their declaration to a State official. In 1971, new legislation sought to change this: associations would only acquire legal personality after a control by the State. Freedom of association would in effect be lost. The Conseil constitutionnel had to overcome a series of constitutional hurdles to declare the bill unconstitutional.

The Conseil constitutionnel has jurisdiction to control the compatibility of bills with the constitution prior to their coming into force. However, in the absence of a declaration of rights, the freedom of action of the Conseil constitutionnel was seriously reduced. Before the Conseil could intervene, it would have to find a way to import some rights and freedoms into the 1958 constitution. Fortunately, the Preamble of the 1958 constitution cites two texts: the Declaration of the Rights of Man of 1789 and the Preamble of the 1946 constitution. Both texts are constitutional charters: while the declaration of 1789 protects first-generation freedoms, the Preamble of the 1946 constitution recognises second-generation rights. In one interpretative stroke, the Conseil constitutionnel incorporated these texts into the 1958 constitution. Unfortunately, freedom of association is not listed in either of these texts. A further interpretation of the provisions of the 1946 Preamble was required before freedom of association could be recognised as a full constitutional principle. In its opening paragraph, the 1946 Preamble reasserts solemnly the rights and freedoms contained in the Declaration of 1789 and in the 'general principles recognised in the

---

[12] For an analysis of this decision, see L Favoreu, and X Philippe, *Les grandes décisions du Conseil constitutionnel*, 15th edn (Paris, Dalloz, 2009) 180.

legislation of the Republic'. The Conseil constitutionnel deduced from this that there existed constitutional rights and freedoms other than those contained in the Declaration of 1789 and in the 1946 Preamble. These other freedoms were simply embodied in laws passed by past republican regimes. As freedom of association was recognised in 1901 by legislation of the third Republic, the Conseil constitutionnel had no difficulty in declaring it to be a 'general principle recognised in the legislation of the Republic'. Once this was done, the Conseil declared the bill to be in breach of this principle and therefore in breach of the constitution. The attempt to amend the legislation pertaining to freedom of association was dropped forthwith.

Since then, the French constitution has been defined as a composite or bloc de constitutionalité ('block of constitutionality'). The original constitution is only one component of this whole: the Declaration of the Rights of Man of 1789, the Preamble of the constitution of 1946, the general principles recognised in the laws of the republic and, since 2005, the Charter for the Environment are all fully part of this redefined French constitution. In one single decision, the Conseil constitutionnel increased drastically the provisions against which an Act of Parliament could be reviewed.

Arguably, the incorporation of extrinsic documents into the constitution was necessary if the constitution was to continue to benefit from an appropriate degree of legitimacy. The majority of modern constitutions have charters of rights and a constitutional court to ensure their protection. This unusual incorporation seems to have been accepted by all: the Charter for the Environment, which was meant to complete this bloc de constitutionalité, was annexed to the constitution by formal constitutional amendment in March 2005. Also, the Preamble of the 1958 constitution was amended to include a reference to the Charter alongside the Declaration of 1789 and the Preamble of the 1946 constitution. By way of conclusion, it is important to point out that a double revolution was operated by the Conseil constitutionnel: it redesigned the boundaries of the French constitution and redefined its role – two audacious moves, in one single stroke.

A Representation of Historical Continuum

The protection of rights that is included in the bloc de constitutionnalité needs to be described in more depth so as to provide a better understanding of the environment for the protection of rights in France.

It is interesting to note also that in France rights protection is often portrayed to be a permanent dynamic towards a better system of protection. The development of rights and freedoms is inscribed in an historical continuum: the Declaration of rights of 1789 which preceded the general principles recognised by the law of the Republic, was updated by the Preamble of the 1946 constitution and more recently was completed by the Charter for the Environment.[13] However, the representation of this evolution largely disregards the reality of French constitutional history.

The Declaration of the Rights of Man of 1789

The Declaration of 1789 was meant to act as a preamble to the first revolutionary constitution. It was supposed to establish the foundations for a new society. Arguably, the provisions were never meant to be used directly to control the activity of governments.

The influences over the text are numerous: as far as rights and freedoms are concerned, the theory of natural law and the individualism of Christian doctrines can be easily traced. Also, the ideas of the physiocrats clearly influenced the provisions of the Declaration giving pride of place to the right to property.[14] Other constitutional theories found their translation into important principles: the writings of Montesquieu clearly led to the inclusion of the principle of separation of powers, while Rousseau's writings were responsible for the idea that parliamentary legislation is the expression of the will of the people. Finally, the American Declaration of Independence also had some influence on the French text.

The influence of natural law means that these freedoms were not bestowed on citizens by the new Declaration; they existed already. Freedom is inherent in human nature: it is only a case of reasserting its existence. This leads logically to the declaration that all men are equal as they benefit equally from the same natural state.

---

[13] President Sarkozy set up a committee chaired by Madame Veil to study how the 1958 Preamble could be amended to take account of present concerns: diversity, equal opportunity, multi-culturalism . . . However, the report 'To rediscover the Preamble of the Constitution' recommended that no change be made.

[14] Article 17 of the Declaration of the Rights of Man describes the right to property as inviolable and sacred.

Secondly, the text of the Declaration is quite abstract. This can be explained by the fact that the Declaration was supposed to be implemented further by the constitution of 1791. The abstraction was also a reflection of the universal character of the rights and freedoms: any man around the world could claim the same rights and freedoms. This abstraction and universalism has been reproduced in other texts aiming to protect rights and freedoms – for instance, the Universal Declaration of Human Rights of 1948.

The Declaration consequently consists of a list of individual rights and freedoms: equality, freedom from arrest, freedom of conscience, freedom of expression, freedom of religion, right to property, presumption of innocence in criminal proceedings etc. An image of citizens is projected by this Declaration: society is made up of individual citizens, whose freedom finds a territorial expression in the right to property. Facing individual citizens, the Declaration establishes a strong but benevolent State with various powers such as taxation, public power, compulsory purchase etc. These, however, are to be used solely for the protection of citizens' freedoms and the promotion of the general interest of society.

The Preamble of the 1946 Constitution

This Preamble was adopted after the rejection of the first draft constitution by the French people in April 1946. The first project contained a new declaration of rights which replaced previous ones (and among them the Declaration of 1789). It is widely believed that one reason for the failure of this draft was the inclusion of a new declaration of rights. Consequently, the second project chose instead to complete the Declaration of 1789: the long Preamble referred to the Declaration of 1789 and proclaimed new social and economic rights by way of modernisation.

The rights expressly listed in the Preamble denote an evolution from those of the Declaration of 1789: right to work, right to strike, right to the protection of family life, right to social welfare, right to the protection of children, mothers and the old, right to education, equality of men and women, right to political asylum for those fighting for political freedom etc. It is clear that the Preamble addresses the social and economic parameters necessary for the freedom of each individual to flourish. Individual citizens are no longer in a static relationship with the State, but they interact in dynamic and complex interrelationships within society. The State is actively called upon to provide and organise their welfare so as to give real meaning to the individual rights and freedoms recognised by the 1789 Declaration. These second-generation rights realised that the neutral attitude of the State when it came to individual freedom and political equality was insufficient; political equality would remain an empty promise if economic and social inequalities were not addressed. Also, to ensure that the State had the necessary finances to promote social welfare, the Preamble of 1946 grants further economic powers: taxation is reasserted but is levied in proportion to earnings and the need for a State economy is recognised. The social Republic is finally given a constitutional foundation. Again, these rights are written in a rather abstract manner and might not have created a great burden for either the Executive or Parliament had the Conseil constitutionnel decided not to review them.

The 'fundamental principles recognized in the laws of the Republic'

As seen above, this expression can be found in the opening paragraph of the 1946 Preamble. The 1946 Preamble constitutionalised a number of new rights but it did not include systematically all rights and freedoms which had been recognised since the 1789 Declaration. The period of the third Republic had been particularly rich in this regard and it is commonly thought that the 'fundamental principles recognised in the laws of the Republic' was meant to be a reference to the great advances of that period. Indeed, it would have been difficult to ignore this legacy altogether: for instance, among the great reforms of the third Republic one finds freedom of association, right to education, municipal freedom, right to strike etc. As mentioned above, it has allowed the Conseil constitutionnel to use this open-ended category to (re)discover many a right and freedom and to perfect its control of constitutionality.

The Charter for the Environment of 2004

Concerns for the environment have led to the addition in 2005 of a Charter for the Environment to this bloc de constitutionalité. The charter is formally annexed to the 1958 constitution and is listed in its Preamble.[15]

---

[15] See B Mathieu, 'La portée de la Charte pour le juge constitutionnel' (2005) *Actualite Juridique: Droit Administratif* 1170.

This Charter contains 10 articles and represents the first attempt to introduce third-generation rights into the French constitution. It proclaims the right to live in a healthy and protected environment, promotes sustainable development and creates a constitutional duty for citizens to take active part in the protection of the environment. Also, it creates a principle of liability stating that anyone responsible for damaging the environment must contribute to its repair. Finally, the State can intervene in the name of the precautionary principle to prevent possible environmental damage. Although the Charter is written in relatively general terms, the Conseil constitutionnel has already relied on its provisions to control the constitutionality of laws.[16]

THE INTEGRITY OF THE 1958 CONSTITUTION

Although constitutions are consigned to paper, they need to be dynamic and they invariably evolve with time. If they do not, they are in danger of becoming irrelevant and of losing their legitimacy. At the same time, the integrity of the constitution must be protected and its supremacy ensured. Mechanisms have been perfected to make sure that constitutions reign supreme and that they impose a hierarchy of norms that reflects their values and choices.

The Protection of the Present Supremacy

The supremacy of a constitutional document triggers the need for protection. In the early years after the Revolution, it was not felt necessary to do more than declare the new guiding principles; reason, truth and logic would triumph. Also, the first constitution did not contain any amendment or revision procedure: in a fit of optimism, the authors of the first constitution thought that they had produced the ideal constitutional document; no amendment would ever be necessary.

Nowadays, it is felt necessary to protect the integrity of constitutions but at the same time, to allow them to change; this is achieved by establishing a system of constitutional review and by specifying an amendment procedure.

---

[16] See C cons no 2005-514 DC 28 April 2005 French international registration.

A Strict Amendment Procedure: The Rigidity of the Constitution

Many constitutions provide a compulsory procedure for altering their provisions. If the procedure to be followed differs from the ordinary legislative procedure, then the constitution is characterised as rigid. The distinction between rigid and flexible constitutions is relevant to the protection of the integrity of the constitution: the more rigid the constitution, the less likely a loss of integrity. The amendment procedure of the 1958 constitution is reproduced in article 89 and establishes a complex and distinct procedure from the standard legislative procedure. The French constitution is therefore categorised as rigid.[17]

Constitutional Review

Modern constitutions frequently use constitutional review to protect their integrity. A specialised constitutional court ensures that the constitutional document remains an effective legal text. It will have jurisdiction to enforce the constitutional provisions and regulate the activity of the institutions and actors of the political system. In fact, the addition of a constitutional court has come to be regarded as standard in modern constitutions.

However, constitutional review was certainly not mainstream thinking when the first revolutionary constitutions were drafted. Although some thinkers had started to investigate this possibility,[18] ideas on the enforcement of constitutions had not really taken hold to contemplate the creation of a constitutional court. One has to remember that France was breaking from centuries of tradition and treading new paths. No one seriously believed that the sanctity of the new constitutional document needed to be protected with a series of mechanisms and institutions, or that democracy could be diverted so easily from its course. Ideas and experiences had not yet developed the need for an armoury of this type.

Also, the revolutionaries were extremely wary of judges and courts in general. After all, the 1789 Revolution had been triggered by the systematic opposition of the old *Parlements*. Also, soon after the Revolution, France was facing the difficulties of most systems in transition: a new elite of lawyers and judges needed to be trained. Even though checks as

---

[17]   See chapter 8.
[18]   See chapter 7.

regards loyalty to the revolutionary cause were made, politicians did not trust the judicial personnel much. This certainly would have been reason enough to refuse the creation of a supreme or constitutional court.

Furthermore the principle of sovereignty of legislation impeded the control of constitutionality: the legislation voted by Parliament was meant to be the expression of the will of the people, of the constitutional sovereign. In the circumstances, control by a court is inconceivable. This explains why even in 1958, the authors of the constitution opted for a rather lame control of constitutionality.[19]

By 1958, politicians were still reluctant to resort to such a court, even though the need for it seemed to have been amply demonstrated by the regime of the fourth Republic. In fact, the new Conseil constitutionnel was mainly created to ensure that the new 'rationalised' Parliament would remain within its constitutional boundaries. There was no suggestion that the new institution would play the role of a constitutional court. Indeed, during the debates and negotiations which led to the adoption of the 1958 constitution, the Preamble, which refers to the Declaration of 1789 and the 1946 Preamble, was denied any legal status: it was feared that it may lead to government by judges.[20]

This choice of purpose is reflected in the institution itself; many are surprised when studying the Conseil constitutionnel by its composition and organisation in light of its importance. One needs to remember that the Conseil was never meant to assume such a central position.[21]

The Organisation of the Hierarchy of Norms

The expression 'hierarchy of norms' is associated with an understanding of legal orders promoted by Kelsen. Each legal rule finds its foundation in and must respect a superior rule, starting with the constitution at the top and cascading down to individual administrative decisions, thus creating a hierarchical and pyramidal order. In this organisation, all rules

[19] There had been a timid attempt to create such a review in the 1946 constitution but it was difficult to trigger and legislation could not be reviewed against the rights and freedoms listed in the constitution. In fact, unconstitutional practices continued to flourish during the fourth Republic.

[20] See D Maus, *Documents pour servir à l'histoire de l'élaboration de la Constitution*, vol 2 (Paris, La Documentation française, 1989) 256.

[21] See chapter 5.

are derived from the constitution and it is the constitution which ranks the various sources of law in order of importance, thereby creating a hierarchy of norms. This constitutional ranking reflects the choices and values of the constitutional order. Accordingly, the French constitution establishes a clear, but one might say heretical, ranking of the sources of law. For this reason, it is important to describe this constitutional hierarchy in detail.

The Constitution or bloc de constitutionalité

The top rung of the hierarchy of norms is the constitution, which means in effect the bloc de constitutionalité as constructed by the Conseil constitutionnel. Although in the French legal order case law is only a persuasive source of law, in reality, the case law of the Conseil has completely redesigned the content of the French constitution. For this reason, the bloc de constitutionalité is somewhat controversial, especially as the content of the constitution expands with each new 'discovery' of the Conseil constitutionnel.

Article 55: A Decidedly International Outlook

According to article 55 of the 1958 constitution, the French constitution establishes a monist system. International treaties and agreements have direct effect in the French legal order so long as these treaties and agreements meet three constitutional conditions: they must have been regularly approved or ratified, they must have been published, and finally, their obligations must be respected by the other signatories. Once these conditions are met, there is no need for a specific process of incorporation. On first assessment this choice, which favours international law over ordinary legislation, seems to reflect the growing importance of the international and European legal orders. However, in practice, Article 55 was 'revolutionary' to a limited extent only: important international treaties or agreements need to be officially ratified and to do so these international documents must be annexed to a statute and passed according to the ordinary legislative procedure. Although there is no formal process of incorporation in the French constitution, the practical difference between this monist solution and other dualist ones is minimal.

Although the meaning of Article 55 is perfectly clear, it gave rise to diverging case law, dissensions and controversies between the French supreme courts: the Conseil constitutionnel, the Conseil d'Etat and the Cour de cassation. Nowadays, both the Conseil d'Etat and the Cour de cassation give precedence to international treaties and agreements over ordinary legislation as a matter of fact.

The Organic Laws: Implementing the Constitution

The organic laws[22] have a distinctive role in the 1958 constitution; they are used to complement the provisions of the constitution. As the constitution cannot address all points of detail in the text itself, a special category of statutes is provided for in Article 46 of the constitution to carry out this task. The legislative procedure is mostly the same as for ordinary statutes with a few exceptions explained by the subject matter of these statutes. For instance, even when the Government has declared the urgency of adopting an organic bill, Parliament must wait at least 15 days after its introduction before the bill can be read for the first time.[23] This protects the time that Members of Parliament have to grapple with the content and import of the proposal. Also, article 46 makes it more difficult for the Assemblée nationale to by-pass the *Sénat*.[24] For an organic law to be adopted by the Assemblée nationale in a final reading, the vote must be carried by an absolute majority; and in the event that the organic law impacts the Sénat, it must be passed in identical terms by both houses.

Finally, all organic laws are referred to the Conseil constitutionnel for control. The Conseil constitutionnel protects the integrity of the constitution by ensuring that its provisions are properly interpreted and implemented by the organic laws.

The End of the Sovereignty of Parliamentary Legislation

This principle of 'souveraineté de la loi' was a creation of the Revolution and resulted from the recognition that sovereignty resided in the people. As it was not possible for the people to express themselves directly all

---

[22] The term 'organic' refers to State institutions or organs of the State.

[23] When there has been no declaration of urgency, a six-week waiting period applies, as is the case for ordinary legislation.

[24] The French Parliament has two chambers: the Assemblée nationale which is elected with direct suffrage and the Sénat which is elected with indirect suffrage.

the time, the principle proclaimed that legislation passed by Parliament was the expression of sovereignty. Consequently, parliamentary legislation, seen as the expression of the will of the sovereign people, was given a quasi-sacred status. Accordingly, statutes could not be controlled nor their jurisdiction and importance reduced. However, the bitter experiences of the third and fourth Republics led the authors of the 1958 constitution to limit this principle considerably.

The provisions that are analysed below demonstrate clearly this departure and as such signal a paradigm change in French constitutional law. Even though the new constitutional framework did not in reality lead to the full revolution that was anticipated, the principle of the sovereignty of the law is not likely to make a full constitutional comeback.

A Divided Legislative Jurisdiction: Articles 34 and 37

After the experiences of the two previous Republics, the authors of the 1958 constitution wished to ensure that the political system would continue to function in the event of a coalition or minority government. Also, the authors of the constitution had come to accept that the sovereignty of parliamentary legislation did not meet the demands of modern times; it was necessary to grant some legislative powers directly to the Executive to facilitate the speed and efficiency of the business of government.

Accordingly, the authors of the 1958 constitution decided that legislative power would be divided between Parliament and the Executive. Article 34 of the constitution lists the subject matters over which the Parliament has jurisdiction; this list is quite long and contains many important topics (for example, the tax system, criminal procedure, succession, French nationality, rights and freedoms etc). Furthermore, this list can be extended by organic law.[25]

Article 37 indicates that all other matters are left to the Executive, which appears to have been given a wider jurisdiction. However, in reality, this revolution never took place. The political phenomenon of parliamentary majority has not made it necessary for any government to act alone. On the contrary, the Government has found it relatively easy to pass legislation through Parliament. The Executive has not needed to

---

[25] However, in order to add formally to the list, it is necessary to amend the constitution. For instance, the protection of the environment was added to the list by the constitutional reform of 1 March 2005.

resort to its autonomous legislative power. The distinction between Article 34 and Article 37 has remained largely a dead letter.[26]

The Delegation of Parliamentary Jurisdiction – Article 38

Article 38 of the constitution contains another mechanism to speed up the adoption of legislative reforms.

Article 38 allows Parliament to delegate temporarily some of its jurisdiction to the Government. This type of delegation had been a recurring practice in the last two constitutions. It helped bypass the hopelessly dysfunctional Parliament and get on with Government's business. However, the practice of *décret-lois* during the third and fourth Republics ran directly against the principle of the sovereignty of the parliamentary legislation and was unconstitutional. Article 38 formally introduces into the 1958 constitution the practices that were banned previously.

A Complex Hierarchy of Implementing Instruments

Parliamentary legislation in Civilian systems has a tendency to be drafted in a much more concise manner than is normally the case in common law systems. In France, statutes contain mainly general principles; only key provisions are drafted in any detail. Implementation is then relied upon to flesh out the parliamentary text. Consequently, there is a relatively complex hierarchy of instruments for the business of implementation; the implementation of parliamentary legislation will normally be done by *décret*.

Successive governments have been accused of delaying, even setting aside, new legislation by not adopting the texts necessary for its implementation.[27] Without these, the will of Parliament stays a dead letter. Indeed, the Conseil d'Etat annuls the refusal of implementation of parliamentary legislation and can issue an injunction to the administration.[28] Also, Parliament has been concerned with the implementation of legislation for some time. To this effect, each chamber has established a committee to keep the implementation of legislation under constant review.

---

[26] See L Favoreu, 'Les règlements autonomes n'existent pas' (1987) *Revue française de droit administratif* 871 and J Bell, *Constitutional Law* (Oxford, Oxford University Press, 1992) chapter 3.

[27] See Assemblée nationale, Rapport d'information, 'L'insoutenable application de la loi' (Paris, 1995).

[28] See CE 28 July 2000, Ass. France Nature Environnement no. 204024.

THE EFFICIENCY OF THE 1958 CONSTITUTION:
THE POLITICAL SYSTEM

The fifth Republic created by the 1958 constitution is on paper quite
different from the regime firmly established in practice. In fact, the present regime reflects an unfortunate tradition of interpretations and
practices away from the strict constitutional text. However, in this
instance, it has allowed the French political system to acquire stability
and foster efficiency. Also, unlike previous regimes, the fifth Republic
has managed to evolve and has succeeded in staying on top of the dysfunctions that have arisen from time to time. Calls may have been heard
for the adoption of a sixth Republic,[29] but the 1958 constitution has just
celebrated its 50th anniversary, and is, arguably, the most successful and
efficient of the French constitutions so far. This efficiency is mainly the
result of an early transformation of the political system, which resulted
in the emergence of a new constitutional system.

A New Constitutional System

On paper, the constitution of 1958 did not contain much originality. The
drafters of the new constitution were constrained by the law of 3 June
1958, which pointed clearly to a parliamentary system.

The Original Constitutional System

As explained above, the law of 3 June 1958 required, among other
things, that ministerial responsibility and the separation of the executive
and legislative powers be organised. This indicated a parliamentary
regime, but a parliamentary regime with a twist, as the separation
between legislature and Executive is not standard in such a regime.
Consequently, the 1958 constitution is original from the beginning, if at
the margins. In fact, the original constitution reproduces to a large
extent the arrangements of the two previous parliamentary regimes.
The Executive is made up of both a President of the Republic and a
Prime Minister and this was definitely inspired by the arrangements of

[29]   See O Duhamel, *Vive la VI ème République* (Paris, Seuil, 2002).

both the third and fourth Republics. In both regimes, the President of the Republic was a head of state with a symbolic role and little power. Indeed, the President of the fifth Republic was destined to be the same and was not given much electoral legitimacy: he was originally elected indirectly by an electoral college made up of holders of local and national mandates. It would be difficult to develop a strong legitimacy on such foundations. As in all parliamentary systems, the Prime Minister is the head of government and as such is responsible before Parliament.

However, there were some interesting innovations in the 1958 constitution. The new constitution engaged in lesson learning, and wished to address the dysfunctions that caused the previous Republic to fail, namely the uncontrolled power of the Parliament. The power of the Parliament was reined in in a number of ways and some of these required a real departure from long-accepted constitutional beliefs and practices. As explained above, the present Parliament can only legislate on those subjects that are listed in article 34 of the constitution; curtailing the jurisdiction of Parliament in such a way was indeed revolutionary, especially in a parliamentary regime. Also, the Executive was given some key powers to control the legislative procedure and ensure the voting of its bills. Finally, the Conseil constitutionnel was created to keep in check this weakened Parliament.

Although the overall organisation of the 1958 constitution was familiar, a few innovations showed French constitutionalism at work. Adaptations were made to the parliamentary regime to ensure the success of the new constitution. It may have been beyond the drafters to imagine a new regime and a complete departure from the past, but seeds of change were clearly planted.

The Emergence of a Semi-Presidential Regime

As demonstrated above, the 1958 constitution was meant to put in place a parliamentary regime, albeit a 'rationalised' one. However, from the start, the interpretation of key constitutional provisions took the regime in a different direction. De Gaulle was elected the first President of the Republic. He had been recalled to power to solve the Algerian crisis and had made the adoption of a new constitution a condition of his return. In October 1958 he had delivered a new constitution but the Algerian problem still needed solving. One might have guessed, however, that the election of such a man to the presidency would mean a departure from the practice of the previous Republics.[30] Indeed, the indirect electoral system was unlikely to create much difficulty for de Gaulle, as he benefited from an unparalleled historical legitimacy. The head of the French government in exile during World War II does not need electoral legitimacy when he returns to office to 'save' France once more. Furthermore, his personality was well known and would reproduce with difficulty the type of behaviour that was expected of a President of the third or fourth Republics. In fact, one might safely argue that de Gaulle would never have been elected President in either Republic: he did not possess the appropriate persona. His election in 1958 was only made possible because of the urgency of the situation. Politicians accepted going along with this novelty so long as necessity required it.

From the very beginning, de Gaulle imprinted his own interpretation on the constitution. Although the constitution does give the President the power to appoint the Prime Minister, de Gaulle read it literally, ie implying a freedom of choice in the appointment. He also decided that the Prime Minister held the appointment at the pleasure of the President and reported directly to him.

Although de Gaulle did have a significant historical legitimacy, he was careful to seek electoral legitimacy too. De Gaulle resorted to referendums to gain popular legitimacy and to have a direct dialogue with the French people. He organised four referendums during his two Presidential mandates and each time he linked his future to the results. A rejection would trigger his resignation (which it did in 1969). Clearly, this practice did not really fit the parliamentary logic of the 1958 constitution.

Also, de Gaulle created a practice of a President of the Republic having decision-making powers, something which had not been experienced in France for a long time.

However, these practices were unlikely to survive the departure of de Gaulle and the resolution of the situation in Algeria. Many thought that once the architect of this Presidential interpretation had departed, a parliamentary reading of the constitution would be reinstated. Only a strong electoral legitimacy could give future Presidents of the Republic the standing to compete with Parliament. Accordingly, de Gaulle led a reform of the constitution in 1962 to introduce direct universal suffrage for the Presidential elections. The referendum was successful and helped

---

[30] The President of the third and fourth Republics played a ceremonial role.

institutionalise the Presidential reading of the constitution. In turn, this ensured a continued efficiency of the political system.

The Evolution: From Constitutional Reform to Political Coincidence and Back

The institutionalisation of the practices that were first adopted by de Gaulle was made possible by the 1962 constitutional reform. However, this constitutional reform led by coincidence to the emergence of a political circumstance which would form the linchpin of the new political regime.

The 'Majority Phenomenon'

The amendment of the constitution of 1962 had an unexpected result which strengthened greatly the Presidential reading of the constitution. In 1958, the President of the Republic was not meant to head a parliamentary majority. In fact, between 1958 and 1962, de Gaulle's Government did not benefit from a real parliamentary majority; de Gaulle was tolerated and his Government supported because of political expediency. Politicians were biding their time; once the Algerian crisis was over, they would have overthrown de Gaulle's Government and returned to a parliamentary reading of the constitution.

However, this changed in 1962: de Gaulle's plans to amend the election of the President of the Republic resulted in the Assemblée nationale rebelling and dismissing the Government. De Gaulle retaliated by dissolving the chamber and the subsequent parliamentary elections gave de Gaulle's party a clear majority in the Assemblée nationale. From then on and for most of the fifth Republic, successive Presidents have benefited from a parliamentary majority and have been in effect their leader. Although many Presidents aspire or claim to be above party politics, this has not been the reality for some time. The emergence of this political phenomenon has been instrumental in securing the future of the new regime. However, in time, the phenomenon of parliamentary majority gave birth to another political phenomenon: 'cohabitation'. Although relatively recent, this political phenomenon had the potential to compromise the Presidential reading of the constitution.

Cohabitation: Experiences and Rejection

The practice of the presidency has diverged from the model identified above in specific political circumstances. Three times, the President lost his supporting parliamentary majority during his mandate.

This situation arose originally because the President was elected for seven years while the Assemblée nationale is elected for five years only. Consequently, parliamentary elections would normally take place five years into the Presidential mandate. No problem arose until 1986 when a right-wing majority was returned in the Assemblée nationale while the socialist President Mitterrand was still in power. Since Mitterand refused to resign, he had no choice but to appoint Jacques Chirac, the leader of the new right-wing majority, as Prime Minister. The first period of cohabitation had begun.[31]

Two further cohabitations would follow: the second one took place between 1993 and 1995, and the third one between 1997 and 2002. The last cohabitation lasted longer and led to a momentous constitutional reform. It was felt that these recurring periods of cohabitation endangered the stability and compromised the efficiency of the 1958 constitution. A referendum was organised in September 2000 to shorten the mandate of the President of the Republic to five years; both Presidential and legislative mandates can now run in parallel. Although not impossible, cohabitation has become unlikely.

Some might wonder why cohabitation was rejected in such a radical manner, especially since it had forced the return of the original parliamentary regime and arguably the proper interpretation of the French constitution. In practice, the cohabitation between President and Prime Minister was often tense and this did not constitute a rational and efficient organisation of power. By 2000, many feared that the repeated experiences of cohabitation would damage permanently the working of the institutions. The constitutional amendment aimed to protect the long-term efficiency of the political system.

CONCLUSION: SOMETHING OLD, SOMETHING NEW

The present French constitution stands apart from its predecessors. It has succeeded where previous regimes have failed: it has managed to

---

[31] See chapter 3.

engineer its legitimacy, protect its integrity, facilitate change and foster an unusual but efficient political system. However, this was often achieved by violating the spirit and sometimes the text of the constitution. Indeed, the cavalier attitude towards the constitutional document in evidence in early regimes is a tradition that has definitely thrived in the fifth Republic, but with drastically different consequences from those experienced in the past. It has allowed the 1958 constitution to take root and to develop into a functioning democracy.

FURTHER READING

G Berlia, 'L'élaboration et l'interprétation de la constitution de 1958' (1973) *Revue de droit public* 485

S Brouard, A Appleton and A Mazur, *The French Fifth Republic at Fifty* (Basingstoke, Palgrave Macmillan, 2008)

A Chandernagor, 'La loi du 3 juin 1958 et sa mise en oeuvre' (2008) 9 *Cahier de l'Académie des sciences morales et politiques* 65.

G Conac, M Debene and G Teboul (eds), *La déclaration des droits de l'homme et du citoyen de 1789* (Paris, Economica, 1993)

G Conac, X Prétot and G Teboul (eds), *Le préambule de la constitution de 1946* (Paris, Dalloz, 2001)

O Duhamel, 'Remarques sur la notion de régime semi-présidentiel' in D Colas and C Emeri (eds), *Mélanges en hommage à Maurice Duverger* (Paris, Presses universitaires de France, 1988) 581

R Elgie, 'Duverger, Semi-Presidentialism and the Supposed French Archetype' (2009) 32 *West European Politics* 248

'La citoyenneté' (2007) 23 *Cahiers du Conseil constitutionnel*

F Lemaire, *Le principe d'indivisibilité de la République: mythe et réalité* (Rennes, Presses universitaires de Rennes, 2010)

F Luchaire, 'Article 38' in F Luchaire, G Conac and X Prétot (eds), *La constitution de la République française*, 3rd edn (Paris, Economica, 2009) 967

D Marrani, 'The Second Anniversary of the Constitutionalisation of the French Charter for the Environment' (2008) *Environmental Law Review* 9

P Morton, 'Judicial Review in France: A Comparative Analysis' (1988) 36 *American Journal of Comparative Law* 89–92

3

The Primacy of the Executive

The Origins – The Search for a Strong Executive – The President of the Republic: From Strength to Strength – A Contested Bicephalous Executive – The Difficult Accountability of the Executive – Conclusion

IN FRANCE, THE primacy of the executive branch can be asserted after a superficial survey of the French constitution: the current text is divided into 17 titles and those concerning the President of the Republic and the Government are respectively the second and third titles. The first title is devoted to sovereignty and the fourth to Parliament. The ranking that is apparent from this structure is also reflected by constitutional practices and conventions.

However, the term 'executive' is a misnomer: it does not exist in the French constitution and it represents inadequately the power that this branch holds in reality. Still, the expression is a useful identifier, especially as the rise of the executive branch has been commented upon in many (if not most) modern democracies. It is well known that nowadays the Executive does not simply 'execute' but drives decision making. It is possible to identify three holders of executive power in the 1958 constitution: the President of the Republic as head of state, the Prime Minister as head of government, and the Government. Each is a separate constitutional entity with specific roles and powers. They will be presented in turn and their relationship to each other analysed. In addition, the accountability of the holders of executive power will be examined closely. Although the regime has evolved notably since its inception, the system of accountability was not altered at first to match this transformation. This has given rise over time to controversies and a perceivable accountability gap which is still debated today.

THE ORIGINS – THE SEARCH FOR A STRONG EXECUTIVE

As mentioned already, the 1958 constitution aimed to address the dysfunctions of the previous parliamentary regimes, namely the third and fourth Republics. In fact, the Executive was one of the main weaknesses of these regimes. While presidents of the Republics were heads of state with no real legitimacy and no real power, Prime Ministers and governments were not in office long enough to govern effectively.[1] Arguably, the business of government was left to the civil service for most of the fourth Republic.[2]

De Gaulle always contended that these dysfunctions would be corrected by a regime with a strong Executive. When World War II ended, it was time to wrestle with the introduction of a new constitution. However, the adoption of a new regime was neither smooth nor straightforward: a first draft constitution was rejected by referendum on 5 May 1946. At this juncture, de Gaulle aired his views in the Bayeux speech of 16 June 1946.[3] Even though these proposals were ignored in the 1946 constitution, they dictated largely the arrangements of the fifth Republic. In the speech, de Gaulle favours a bicephalous Executive consisting of a Prime Minister and a President of the Republic, with the latter benefiting from an increased electoral legitimacy and clearly holding the more important office of the two. Also reading between the lines, the Prime Minister would appear somewhat subordinate if not accountable to the President.

The failure of the fourth Republic to establish a stable system of government and the dramatic events of spring 1958 surrounding the fall of the fourth Republic gave de Gaulle the necessary leverage to incorporate some of these ideas into the new constitution and the French people the necessary impetus to adopt them by referendum. However, the original constitution did not ensure a clear supremacy for the President of the Republic. Only constitutional practice and further constitutional reforms were able to secure a presidential reading of the constitution.

---

[1] See chapter 1.

[2] See C Bigaut, *Les cabinets ministériels* (Paris, Librairie générale de droit et de jurisprudence, 1997) 50.

[3] For the Bayeux speech, see www.charles-de-gaulle.org/pages/espace-pedagogique/le-point-sur/les-textes-a-connaitre/discours-de-bayeux-16-juin-1946.php.

Even after the recent constitutional reform, the provisions of the 1958 constitution concerning the Executive remain ambiguous, especially with regard to the exact role and powers of each component of the Executive.

THE PRESIDENT OF THE REPUBLIC: FROM STRENGTH TO STRENGTH

Originally, the 1958 constitution was not so clearly biased in favour of the President. In fact, many of the provisions reflect a half-hearted attempt to establish a parliamentary system. Consequently, the evolution of the powers and position of the French President of the Republic throws an interesting light on the reliability of written constitutions. Here, political practices and constitutional reforms combined in transforming the regime into a more presidential one.

The Early Constitutional Practices

De Gaulle was elected as first President of the fifth Republic for a period of seven years.[4] From the beginning, he adopted a presidential reading of the constitutional provisions. Arguably this could have been explained by the need to solve the extreme crisis that France was facing. After all, the question of the independence of Algeria had brought France to the verge of civil war. De Gaulle had to have the necessary powers if a solution were to be found. Also, any other President of the Republic elected at he was, by a system of indirect universal suffrage, would have suffered from a weak electoral legitimacy. De Gaulle, however, had great personal and 'historical legitimacy': he had saved France once and could be trusted with power to do it again.[5]

Accordingly, de Gaulle did not hesitate to interpret the newly adopted constitution so as to emphasise the powers of the President of the Republic. First, he created a responsibility of the Prime Minister before the President of the Republic. In parliamentary systems, Prime Ministers

[4] Originally, the President of the Republic was elected for seven years. This reproduced the mandate of the third and fourth Republics.
[5] De Gaulle headed the French Government in exile in London during World War II and participated in the liberation of France in 1944–45.

are commonly responsible for their decisions, actions and policies before Parliament. Indeed, the 1958 constitution organised such responsibility in its articles 49 and 50. However, de Gaulle regarded the appointment and dismissal of Prime Ministers as a prerogative of the President, thereby creating a responsibility and a relationship of subordination of the Prime Minister to the President of the Republic.[6] Barring the cohabitation periods, presidents of the republic have appointed and dismissed their Prime Ministers more or less at will throughout the fifth Republic. It would be an exaggeration to regard the Prime Minister as a 'creature' of the President of the Republic, but strong disagreement between them often ends with the departure of the Prime Minister.

Although de Gaulle transformed the presidency into a key institution, the 1958 constitution gave it few powers and none which allowed day-to-day decision making. It is clear from the constitutional provisions that the Prime Minister was meant to govern. Consequently, de Gaulle resorted to a series of constitutional interpretations and practices in a move to acquire governmental power. It is worth pointing out that some of these practices and interpretations were highly controversial at the time. In January 1961 de Gaulle asked by referendum whether the French people agreed in principle to the independence of Algeria. This referendum in effect empowered him to lead the negotiations aiming to resolve the Algerian question. In April 1962 de Gaulle organised a second referendum; this time the French people were asked to approve the Evian agreements[7] and to empower de Gaulle to implement them. The repeated use of referendums gave the President of the Republic a clear mandate to pursue and implement an extremely important policy. In this way, the presidency acquired a domain of governmental competence. Also, the repeated use of referendums allowed de Gaulle to extract the democratic legitimacy that was necessary to underwrite his policy choices and his presidential reading of the constitution. Although de Gaulle had a strong personal legitimacy, he was not satisfied with relying solely on this reference to past achievements; he was keen to proceed from popular sovereignty. Only this could provide the lasting legitimacy for a 'growing' presidential institution.

---

[6] It is rumoured that de Gaulle required his successive Prime Ministers to sign an undated letter of resignation. He only had to fill in the date when he thought that the time had come to part with his Prime Minister.

[7] These agreements paved the way for the independence of Algeria.

Also de Gaulle made a controversial use of the powers contained in article 16 of the constitution. According to this provision, were exceptional circumstances to arise – eg war, nuclear accident, natural disaster – and 'the proper functioning of the institutions interrupted', the President of the Republic would receive all constitutional power to act and restore the continuity of the political system. On 22 April 1961 four generals fomented a coup in Algeria. After consulting the Conseil constitutionnel as required, de Gaulle decided on 23 April to resort to article 16. However, the coup soon failed and by 25 April all had returned to normal. Accordingly, de Gaulle should have relinquished his powers under article 16. Instead, de Gaulle continued using them until 29 September 1961 and took 26 decisions on the basis of such powers. Moreover, although Parliament sits by right when article 16 is used, de Gaulle interpreted the constitutional provision as prohibiting Parliament to debate any issues or decisions relevant to the use of article 16.

Still, this 'constitutional dictatorship' combined with the repeated use of referendums established a practice of a President of the Republic closely involved in policy making. This was a move away from the traditional conception of head of state.

The 1962 Constitutional Reform: Increasing the Legitimacy of the President

Although de Gaulle achieved his immediate aim and established a strong presidency, it was debatable whether any other President would be able to continue with these practices. The political situation would no longer justify direct interventions of the President of the Republic and few presidents, if any, would benefit from the personal legitimacy that de Gaulle possessed. Many expected that the Gaullist interpretation of the constitution would disappear with the man. Although a new constitution had been adopted, neither political parties nor political personnel had been renewed. Politicians bided their time and thought that, the Algeria crisis over, 'normal' political life and practices would be resumed. There was a real possibility – one may say danger – of a return to the parliamentary regime of the fourth Republic. De Gaulle's real legacy was to try and institutionalise the reading of the constitution that he had favoured and practised. De Gaulle doubted that future presidents would be in a position to stand up to the directly elected first chamber, the Assemblée nationale. A reform of the electoral system of the President of the Republic was therefore required. However, by a curious coincidence, the events surrounding this constitutional reform led to a complete and durable transformation of the French political system. On 2 October 1962[8] de Gaulle announced to the Parliament his intention to have articles 6 and 7 of the constitution amended: the President of the Republic would be elected by direct universal suffrage. As Parliament was strongly opposed to this reform, de Gaulle resorted to the referendum contained in article 11 of the constitution rather than the amendment procedure provided for in article 89. While article 89 requires the approval of any constitutional reform by both houses of Parliament before being submitted to referendum, article 11 allows the use of a simple referendum to approve changes 'to the organisation of public institutions'. Even though a reform of the system of presidential elections can arguably be interpreted as a change in the organisation of a public institution, it is clear that the constitution should only be amended by means of the procedure contained in article 89 and that article 11 should be restricted to reforms other than constitutional ones. However, de Gaulle knew that parliamentary approval would not be forthcoming and resorted to article 11 in an attempt to bypass Parliament. Consequently, on 5 October 1962 the Assemblée nationale withdrew its confidence in the Government, the only means at its disposal to signal its disagreement with the policy pursued by the President of the Republic.[9] The President reacted swiftly by dissolving the Assemblée nationale on 9 October. The two elections that followed combined their political effects to create the system which is in place today. On 28 October the French people approved by referendum the direct election of the President of the Republic by 62 per cent of the votes. It made it difficult thereafter to question the 'constitutionality' of the reform; with sovereignty ultimately resting in the French people, their approval cleansed the reform from any perceived unconstitutionality.[10] However, the most surprising thing was

---

[8] Although de Gaulle was elected for seven years and was not due to face an election for another three years, the question of 'succession' became a hot topic with the assassination attempt in August 1962. In fact, Antoine Pinay, who had been Prime Minister during the fourth Republic, was tipped as a possible successor; it would undeniably have signalled a return to past practices.

[9] The second chamber, the Sénat, was also strongly opposed to the constitutional reform.

[10] The Conseil constitutionnel declared that it did not have jurisdiction to review a statute adopted on the basis of a referendum, see C cons no 62-20 DC 6 November 1962.

still to come: the parliamentary elections triggered by the dissolution returned a clear Gaullist majority in the Assemblée nationale. The phenomenon of parliamentary majority was observed for the first time in France. From then on, with the exception of the cohabitation periods, presidents of the republic would always be supported by a majority of *députés*. This signalled a real break from the unstable coalition governments of the past republics. The events of autumn 1962 firmly established the regime of the fifth Republic as we know it today.

The 2000 Constitutional Reform: Protecting the Presidential Reading of the Constitution

The presidential reading of the constitution was temporarily endangered by the political phenomenon of cohabitation. This phenomenon was made possible by the difference between the lengths of the mandates of the President of the Republic (seven years) and the members of the Assemblée nationale (five years). The discrepancy meant that an election of the Assemblée nationale would normally take place two years before the end of a presidency. The French people could return a different majority party in the first chamber from the one of the President of the Republic. No problem arose in the early part of the fifth Republic as right-wing parties were returned with a majority in every election. In 1981, with the election of a socialist President and a left-wing majority in the Assemblée nationale for the first time, the scene was set for a change. Political parties had begun to 'alternate' in power. In 1986 the inevitable happened: parliamentary elections returned a right-wing majority while Mitterrand was still in power.[11] Two options were left to the President: to trigger a presidential election by resigning or to stay in office and appoint the leader of the new majority as Prime Minister. Mitterrand chose the second solution and 'cohabitated' with Chirac and the new majority Government. Suddenly, the presidential reading of the constitution had to be abandoned in favour of a parliamentary one. From virtual leader of a majority, Mitterrand became overnight the leader of the opposition, but an opposition leader with a presidential mandate, key constitutional powers and some residual electoral legitimacy. However, the President of the

---

[11]   Mitterrand came to power in May 1981. He dissolved the Assemblée nationale soon after his election and a socialist majority was returned then.

Republic could no longer aspire to leadership and policy making. At first it seemed that people were quite content with this temporary shift in regime. It appeared to create a degree of political consensus as majority and opposition had to work together. In May 1988 Mitterrand was re-elected to the presidency and called new parliamentary elections. The elections returned a left-wing majority once again supporting the President of the Republic; the traditional presidential interpretation of the regime was resumed. However, when another cohabitation period began in March 1993, it became clear that cohabitation would be a recurring experience. Consequently, following election as President of the Republic in May 1995, Chirac dissolved the Assemblée nationale in 1997, after two years in office. He hoped that the people would return a right-wing majority, thereby allowing him to complete his presidential mandate without a period of cohabitation. However, Chirac's strategy backfired as a left-wing majority was elected instead and a five-year cohabitation period ensued. The President of the Republic found himself having to relinquish control over governmental policies and decision making after two years in office. Furthermore, this long and tense period of cohabitation highlighted the shortcomings and even dangers of this recurring phenomenon. Negotiations took place across political parties and a consensus emerged: Chirac sponsored a constitutional reform shortening the presidential mandate to five years. Not only would both mandates coincide, but more frequent presidential elections would enhance the democratic credentials of the office. The electoral calendar was also altered to ensure that the presidential election preceded systematically those for the Assemblée nationale. In September 2000 the French people approved an amendment to article 6 of the constitution: the presidential mandate was shortened accordingly. Although it is still possible for the French people to trigger a cohabitation deliberately, it is unlikely. With the constitutional reform of September 2000, the French people have clearly endorsed the presidential reading of the 1958 constitution. A return to a parliamentary reading of the constitution now seems improbable. The fifth Republic has reasserted its break from the constitutional past.

A CONTESTED BICEPHALOUS EXECUTIVE

In the Bayeux speech, de Gaulle had sketched the organisation of the executive branch that he favoured: a President of the Republic as head of state and a Prime Minister as a head of government. It might seem paradoxical to split the Executive if one is hoping to strengthen this very branch of government. At best, a bicephalous Executive could create confusion when it comes to allocation of power and at worst, it could lead to open constitutional and political warfare between the two incumbents. In 1958 de Gaulle might have had no choice but to conform to constitutional tradition. Indeed, the constitutional statute of 3 June 1958, which empowered his Government to draft a new constitution, specified that the Government be responsible before Parliament.

Still, de Gaulle was appointed (and later elected) in clear opposition to the parliamentary regime of the fourth Republic. And if the organisation of the Executive of the 1958 constitution is divided into two offices as of old, the constitutional text indicates that the Prime Ministerial supremacy had ended. This in turn was strongly emphasised by the new constitutional practices and interpretations as demonstrated above. A new allocation of executive power was found alongside a new emerging constitutional system.

However, the powers and the structure of the Executive have been controversial from the start. To understand these controversies, it is necessary to present the holders of executive power and their respective roles.

The Ambiguous Position of the President

The provisions describing the role and powers of the President of the Republic seem similar to those traditionally given to heads of state in parliamentary systems. In fact, it is difficult to imagine a strong presidency emerging from the combination of these constitutional provisions.

The Election of the President of the Republic

As mentioned above, originally the President of the Republic was elected for seven years with indirect universal suffrage. Members of Parliament and a large selection of elected local government representatives convened in a separate college[12] and together they elected the

---

[12] This electoral college, which elected de Gaulle as the first President of the fifth Republic on 21 December 1958 with 78.5% of the votes, had 81,764 members.

President of the Republic. However, this system was far from perfect: it lacked the transparency of direct suffrage – it would be difficult to know what negotiations and compromises, if any, took place within the electoral college, and for anyone other than de Gaulle, it would have been difficult, if not impossible, to derive much legitimacy from it. Still, this was an improvement on the third and fourth Republics as then, presidents of the republic were elected by Parliament. This explains why past presidents were never strong: not only did the method of election bestow little legitimacy but also Members of Parliament had no interest in electing a strong political figure.

Articles 6 and 7 of the 1958 constitution contain the main rules framing the organisation of presidential elections. The system adopted in 1962 is a majority system with two rounds. A candidate can only be elected after the first round of elections if he/she obtains an absolute majority of the votes. In fact, no candidate has ever managed to be elected this way.[13] The second round is organised two weeks later; only the two candidates with the most votes in the first round go forward to the second. In 1962, the authors of the reform rejected the first-past-the-post system. Although more cumbersome, the two-rounds system protects a larger diversity of political parties, a number of which can enter a presidential candidate in the first round of elections.[14] The second round, on the other hand, requires that all parties forge alliances to campaign for one or the other remaining candidate. This allows for a majority and opposition to emerge. Also, the future President benefits from a stronger electoral legitimacy as he/she will always be elected by absolute majority.[15]

The electoral system needs to be described in some detail. To begin with, not everyone can be a presidential candidate. Three conditions need to be met: the candidate must be French, 23 years of age and be sponsored by a minimum of 500 elected representatives – Members of

---

[13] Not even de Gaulle managed this feat during the first presidential election with direct suffrage in 1965. He only obtained 44% of the votes, a record never equaled since.

[14] Although there is an outside chance of going through to the second round, as happened in 2002 with Le Pen, candidate for the National Front. However, this resulted in a formidable majority of 82.21% for Chirac, his opponent in the second round of elections.

[15] 50.8% was the narrowest majority ever registered; it served to elect Giscard d'Estaing in 1974.

Parliament or local government representatives.[16] Once a representative has given his/her support and sent in his/her signature, neither can be withdrawn or transferred. This system of sponsorship is not completely satisfactory. A reform took place in 1976 to increase the number of sponsors from 100 to 500 and to require that the signatures originated from at least 30 *départements*. The number of presidential candidates kept increasing:[17] not only was it felt that that a large number of candidates compromised the clarity of the electoral campaign, but that it was also necessary to ensure that presidential candidacies were truly national. However, this has not solved the issue: there were 16 presidential candidates in 2002 and 12 in 2007. Another filter may be necessary.[18]

Article 7 of the constitution specifies that a new President must be elected at least 20 days and at most 35 days before the end of the mandate of the President in office. In any event, the electoral campaign is officially opened exactly 15 days before the first round of elections and lasts a month. During this time, all candidates benefit from the same access to the media. Furthermore, a reform has attempted to rein in the electoral expenses of each candidate. The legislation stipulates a threshold amount that cannot be exceeded and specifies that each candidate must keep a campaign account during the 12 months previous to the election. The same legislation also prohibits private electoral marketing by press, television or posters during the last three months of the campaign. The Conseil constitutionnel ensures that all these rules are enforced.

---

[16] The record number of local government structures in France ensures that the pool of potential signatories is large – approximately 40,000 people.

[17] There were six presidential candidates in 1965, seven in 1969 and 12 in 1974. In view of this, the Conseil constitutionnel called for more exacting conditions and the legislation was amended.

[18] In 2007, the Conseil constitutionnel expressed its concern regarding the way some of the sponsorships are obtained (negotiations and deals are too often the order of the day). It felt that it was not 'compatible with the dignity that should prevail in all elections'. Also, the Balladur committee favoured another system for the identification of presidential candidates. A large college of elected representatives – 100,000 strong – would be convened some time before the official presidential campaign and designate all the candidates, see Comité de réflexion et de proposition sur la modernisation et le rééquilibrage des institutions de la Ve République, *Une V République plus démocratique* (Paris, Documentation Française, 2007) 24, available at http://www.ladocumentationfrancaise.fr/var/storage/rapports-publics/074000697/ 0000.pdf. This recommendation was not included in the 2008 constitutional reform.

The Presidential Mandate

The presidential mandate has also led to debates and numerous calls for reform. As explained above, the President of the Republic was elected originally for seven years. This may seem a long time, but it followed a constitutional tradition first established during the third Republic and was meant to highlight the continuity of the office. Furthermore, no one imagined that the President would become the leader of the parliamentary majority and the real head of the Executive. Once the presidential reading of the constitution was secured, politicians and commentators began to question the length of the mandate. In fact, in 1973, President Pompidou attempted to shorten the mandate to five years and both chambers adopted a constitutional bill to this effect. However, the reform was abandoned for lack of the 60 per cent majority in the Congrès. For many, the distinctive position of the President, the constitutional tradition and the need for institutional continuity all combined to justify a long mandate.

Later, the experiences of cohabitation reopened the debate and the mandate was finally shortened to five years in 2000. More recently, the mandate of the President of the Republic has been restricted further. Since the constitutional reform of July 2008, presidents of the republic are limited to two consecutive mandates. Some believed that a continuous period of 10 years in office was long enough for any President of the Republic. Although Mitterrand and Chirac had both been in office for 14 and 12 years respectively, their mandates had been 'punctuated' by periods of cohabitation. As the five-year mandate reasserted the presidential reading of the constitution, some argued that a limit should be imposed to the number of consecutive mandates a President should hold. If a period of 10 years was acceptable, one of 15 years was not. Of course, this does not stop a candidate from seeking office after an intervening period.[19]

---

[19] Interestingly, neither the Vedel committee in 1993 nor the Balladur committee in 2007 thought this restriction desirable. This was seen as an unnecessary limitation on the expression of national sovereignty; see also, H Roussillon, 'Article 6' in J-P Camby, P Fraisseix, J Gicquel (eds), *La révision de 2008: une nouvelle constitution?* (Paris, Librairie générale de droit et de jurisprudence, 2011) 37.

The Constitutional Role of the President of the Republic – Article 5

A bicephalous Executive requires that the respective roles and powers of President of the Republic and Prime Minister are clearly defined and the 1958 constitution innovated in this respect. The role of the President of the Republic is described in article 5[20] of the 1958 constitution. Although it is only three lines long, it is said to encapsulate a Gaullist vision of the presidential function. In fact, it reproduces closely the description given by de Gaulle in his Bayeux speech. According to this provision, the President of the Republic is the guardian of the constitution and beyond that of the French State: not only must he strive to protect the constitution, but he must also take the necessary steps to ensure the proper functioning of the institutions and the continuity of the State. Also, he is the guarantor of national independence, territorial integrity and treaty obligations. In its present drafting, article 5 highlights a strong role of guardianship for the President of the Republic; he is the all-important constitutional overseer. The description of this role is supplemented by article 64, which declares that the President of the Republic is the guardian of the independence of the judiciary.

Article 5 indicates also the manner in which the President of the Republic must act to perform his constitutional functions: he must be a referee. This indication needs to be analysed closely as it reveals the original conception of the presidency. The President of the Republic was conceived by de Gaulle as a referee between political actors and institutions, a mediator above the struggle of political parties. The President guarantees the observance of the constitution and to this effect, he is in fact the temporary incarnation of the French State and the depositary of its national sovereignty; in this capacity, the constitution requires of him to bridge divisions and rise above the short-term considerations of party politics. In many ways, the constitution directs him to foster consensus. However, even if this constitutional ideal were to be achieved, one wonders whether the modus operandi matches the reality of the task. The protection of national independence and territorial integrity requires more than a simple mediation from the President:

---

[20] See article 5: 'The President of the Republic shall see that the Constitution is observed. He shall ensure, by his arbitration, the proper functioning of the public authorities and the continuity of the State. He shall be the guarantor of national independence, territorial integrity and observance of treaties.'

it requires a strong leadership with a touch of 'constitutional' dictator-ship. Indeed, to safeguard the independence and integrity of the coun-try, the President needs powers that are likely to be controversial and somewhat divisive: a simple referee will not do. On analysis, article 5 reveals a tension: two representations of the presidential role compete within the confines of this provision even before political practice intro-duces another layer of complexity.

Article 5 reflected de Gaulle's understanding of the presidential role and he was guided by this representation during his 11 years in office. In 1958 he certainly did not emanate from a political party.[21] De Gaulle was given only conditional and limited parliamentary support to extricate France from the Algerian crisis and had little difficulty in rising above political parties. Indeed, political leaders had no wish to be involved in the resolution of the crisis. If the negotiations failed, the responsibility would rest squarely with de Gaulle, thereby screening them from it. Furthermore, the habit of de Gaulle of engaging in direct debate with the electorate via referendums allowed him to bypass political parties and to proceed directly from the French people. Still, even then, de Gaulle had some difficulties in reconciling the various aspects of his role: the use of article 11 to amend article 6 of the constitution and the use of article 16 are indicative of a constitutional tension. While safe-guarding national sovereignty, de Gaulle breached the constitution twice and cannot be said to have acted as a referee.

Furthermore, the decision to resort to direct elections triggered a fundamental change in the role performed by the President. Not only did the political events of 1962 lead to the appearance of a majority in Parliament, but the subsequent presidential elections of 1965 were fought and won by a re-established Gaullist political party. The process of normalisation of the presidential reading of the constitution made it necessary to move away from a President transcending political par-ties; with the advent of direct universal suffrage, the President needed to proceed from one. The complex ideal contained in article 5 had lived. Once elected on the basis of a party manifesto, the President of the Republic had a clear party label. Moreover, he was expected as leader of the majority to play a clear role in defining policies and in governing the country. From refereeing the political arena, the President

---

[21] The first Gaullist party, which had been created by de Gaulle in 1947, was in abeyance since 1955.

was suddenly hurled into the middle of it. The constitution, however, had never been written to provide governmental power to the President. This series of political and constitutional events contains a serious threat to the balance of power between the President of the Republic and the Prime Minister. The constitutional text no longer defines realistically the relevant roles of each institution and the risk of power struggle between the two heads of the Executive has increased dramatically since 1962.

In view of this, one would have thought that the description of the respective roles and powers would have been amended in the constitution at the first available opportunity. However, this was never done. Recently, the Balladur committee proposed some amendments: while a third paragraph specifying that '[the President] defines the policies of the Nation' was to be added to article 5, in article 20, the Government would no longer 'determine' the policies of the Nation. For the first time, the constitution would have reflected political practice. However, the amendment did not find its way into the Government draft for lack of cross-party support. As the July 2008 constitutional reform was to adjust the institutional balance in favour of Parliament and to frame the powers of the President of the Republic, it might have been politically sensitive to sponsor such an amendment. Still, it is a missed opportunity: there may not be another chance of reconciling the constitutional text with political reality for a long time to come.

The Constitutional Powers of the President of the Republic

The constitutional powers of the President of the Republic reflect a literal interpretation of article 5. However, they do not match the present political practices and presidential reading of the constitution. In reality, not only have successive presidents of the republic constructed freely the existing constitutional provisions but they have yielded powers beyond the confines of the constitutional text.

According to article 8, the President of the Republic appoints the Prime Minister and on proposal of the Prime Minister, appoints the other members of government. In many systems, the head of state appoints but does not necessarily choose the head of government. In France, with the exception of the three cohabitation periods, the President of the fifth Republic appoints a Prime Minister of his own choosing; then, they decide jointly on the governmental team.[22] Furthermore, article 8 specifies that the President dismisses the Prime Minister when the latter tenders the resignation of the Government. However, from the beginning, the provision received a presidential reading: de Gaulle made clear that the Prime Minister owed his position to, and held it at the pleasure of, the President. By assuming the right to appoint and dismiss, the President of the Republic in effect created a new system of accountability: the Prime Minister is responsible to the President of the Republic for his/her actions and decisions. This has turned out to be a more significant responsibility for the Prime Minister than the one organised before Parliament. While the Assemblée nationale has triggered the fall of a government only once, presidents of the republic of all political persuasions have replaced their Prime Ministers freely and at regular intervals.[23] This interpretation has deep implications for the system of government as it inverts the lines of accountability: the Prime Minister looks to the President and not the Parliament when adopting and implementing government policy. The original parliamentary system is turned on its head.

The President can also dissolve the lower chamber, the Assemblée nationale (article 12). Unlike the previous constitution, no condition is to be met before pronouncing a dissolution. This was meant to allow the President to act and solve a political deadlock. However, once a dissolution has taken place, it is not possible to dissolve the house again for another year. This delay is dissuasive and protects the Assemblée nationale from repeated and undemocratic dissolutions.

The President chairs the Council of Ministers. It is a key institution as by law all government bills and much secondary legislation must first be approved there (article 9).

All bills adopted by Parliament and cleared by the Conseil constitutionnel (if reviewed) are to be 'promulgated'[24] by the President within 15 days of their reception. However, the President is entitled to return

---

[22] The negotiation between the two heads of the Executive depends largely on their individual political strength and their relation to the parliamentary majority. However, presidents of the republic have been known to impose a minister on their Prime Minister: in 1971, Chirac was appointed by Pompidou as minister in charge of the relations with Parliament without consulting the Prime Minister, Chaban-Delmas.

[23] In a break from tradition, Fillon served as Prime Minister during the whole of Sarkozy's presidency.

[24] The '*promulgation*' is the procedural equivalent of the royal assent. The President has no discretion in the matter.

the bill to Parliament for a further reading. This may happen when the President has great misgivings concerning the legislation. However, normally the President has either agreed to legislation or even decided its adoption beforehand. The request for another reading is therefore used exceptionally. In practice, it has been used to amend a drafting defect or to allow Parliament to evaluate the effects of a declaration of unconstitutionality by the Conseil constitutionnel.

Article 11 specifies that the President decides on holding a referendum. Although the constitution requires that the proposal comes originally from the Prime Minister, in reality the President is often the prime mover behind the call for a referendum.

According to article 13 § 1, the President is responsible for the appointment to all army and civil service positions. The most important of these appointments are listed in article 13 § 2 and are made in the Council of Ministers: members of the Conseil d'Etat and the Court of auditors, ambassadors and extraordinary envoys, State representatives for the *départements* and overseas territories, generals, heads of government departments and heads of the education districts. While these appointments are still at the discretion of the President, the reform of July 2008 has introduced a procedure to frame other presidential appointments. If a position is key to the protection of rights and freedoms or relevant to the country's social and economic life, the President's choice must be confirmed by the relevant permanent parliamentary committees of both houses.[25] No appointment is possible if it is rejected by 60 per cent of the votes cast by the members of both committees. This procedure is used to approve other important appointments of the President: the members of the Conseil constitutionnel (article 56) and the new defender of rights (article 71-1). This parliamentary control is meant to ensure a more democratic system of appointment. Indeed, the choice of Dominique Baudis for the position of the defender of rights was confirmed by Parliament after a hearing before the relevant permanent committee of each chamber on 15 June 2011.[26]

Also, article 16 contains the most important presidential power ever granted to a President of the Republic in France. In case of exceptional

---

[25] The organic law of 23 July 2010, which implemented this provision, listed 50 such positions.

[26] He was supported by 49 votes (with 17 votes against). See the interview of Dominique Baudis in *Le Monde* of 26 June 2011.

circumstances (such as war, natural catastrophe, major nuclear accident etc) and if the political institutions, the integrity of the territory, the independence of the Nation or the respect of international obligations cannot be secured, the President of the Republic (after the consultation of key institutions and officials) is entitled to assume all constitutional powers until the circumstances have returned to normal. The idea was to create a constitutional framework should a similar situation to the one experienced in June 1940 arise. Had these powers existed in the constitution of the third Republic, the constitutional crisis which led to the appointment of Pétain and the infamous Vichy regime may have been averted.[27] However, article 16 has been criticised, particularly in view of the use that de Gaulle made of it in 1961. The original provision did not contain any mechanism to check the continuing need for these exceptional powers. On the basis of this experience, calls to remove article 16 from the constitution were heard repeatedly. However, in view of the recent surge of international terrorism, it was felt that article 16 may still have a role to play. Instead, the provision was amended by the reform of July 2008 to rectify the original failure: the Conseil constitutionnel reviews the need for article 16 after a certain period.[28] The constitution is now protected against a repetition of the abuses of 1961.

Finally, the constitution recognises that the President has a special role to play when it comes to international relations. Article 52 specifies that the President negotiates and ratifies relevant international treaties and that he is informed of any negotiations regarding international agreements which do not require his intervention. Furthermore, he receives and accredits ambassadors and special envoys (article 14).

In addition, to the powers presented above, the President enjoys also the following powers: he signs all secondary legislation approved by the Council of Ministers; he is the head of the army (article 15); and he has discretion to grant pardon in individual cases (article 17).[29] Finally, the President has a right to have a message read to each house of Parliament and since the reform of July 2008, to address directly both houses convened together in the Congrès (article 18). A debate can follow a

[27] See chapter 1.
[28] See chapter 5.
[29] Prior to the reform of July 2008, the President was entitled to grant collective amnesty for minor offences. Traditionally, the President would grant such amnesties on becoming President and on the national day (14 July). This discretion was felt increasingly unjustified in a modern democracy.

presidential declaration to the Congrès but it cannot end with a vote. This ensures that the new provision is not used to create a responsibility of the President of the Republic before Parliament. It is worth noting that this amendment was portrayed by opposition parties as a marked extension of presidential powers, a label that this change hardly warrants.

The list of these powers is impressive. The President is indeed required or empowered to act with regard to important constitutional events; this matches his role as guardian of the constitution and reflects his incarnation of the French State. However, none of these powers are appropriate to govern the country and or even direct the work of the Government. In fact with the exclusion of the periods of cohabitation, the President of the Republic yields considerably more power that what might be extrapolated from the list above; some of the Government's powers are in fact diverted for the benefit of the President. By contrast, the various experiences of cohabitation demonstrate that when not supported by a parliamentary majority, the President experienced difficulties when using his strict constitutional powers.

The Prime Minister: A Head of Government?

The Prime Minister is appointed by the President of the Republic according to article 8 § 1 of the constitution. With the exception of the periods of 'cohabitation', the President of the Republic appoints a Prime Minister of his choosing. In doing so, he will be guided by personal and political considerations. In 1974, although Giscard d'Estaing was the newly elected President of the Republic, he only headed a small centre-right party: the *Indépendants Républicains*. Arguably, he reached the second round of the elections because Chirac, who was rising fast in Gaullist circles,[30] endorsed Giscard's candidacy, thereby disowning the Gaullist candidacy of Chaban-Delmas. Unsurprisingly, on being elected, Giscard d'Estaing chose Chirac for his Prime Minister. This was also a necessary gesture towards the party which was the main right-wing party of the parliamentary majority. The disagreements and struggles that ensued between the two men, and which ended with the resignation of

---

[30]   In fact, Chirac assumed the leadership of the Gaullist party soon after that.

Chirac in summer 1976, highlight the political tension that can exist between the two incumbents of the Executive.[31]

The Role and Powers of the Prime Minister

While the President of the Republic has become the true leader of the parliamentary majority, the position and role of the Prime Minister is more difficult to fathom. Article 21 of the constitution sets out the role of the Prime Minister: he directs the action of government. Thus, he is proclaimed and assumes the constitutional role of head of the government. Article 21 allocates to him some specific duties and powers in accordance with this position. He is responsible for the implementation of laws and he is given a general regulatory power to this effect. The regulatory power rests in its entirety with the Prime Minister[32] but it can be delegated to individual ministers. Finally, the Prime Minister can deputise for the President of the Republic when chairing the Council of Ministers and various other committees. The former can only be chaired by the Prime Minister on an express mandate and specific agenda.

Unfortunately, the constitutional reform of July 2008 did not amend any of the provisions defining the role of the Prime Minister. Although the Balladur committee had recommended that the main provisions defining the respective roles of the President, Government and Prime Minister – articles 5, 20 and 21 respectively – all be amended, only a proposal concerning article 21 found its way into the Government bill. The draft bill aimed to clarify the respective roles and powers of both President and Prime Minister in relation to the armed forces as they appear to compete: while article 15 states that the President of the Republic is Commander in Chief and chairs a number of committees on national defence, article 21 specifies that the Prime Minister is responsible for national defence. The amendment, which attempted to clarify the division of power between President and Prime Minister, was abandoned during the legislative process. Although the involvement of both heads of the Executive may appear superfluous, this ensures that

---

[31] Similar deep-seated tensions and disagreements led to the 'departure' of other Prime Ministers: although Rocard was appointed Prime Minister by Mitterrand at the beginning of the second presidency in May 1988, their relationship broke down so completely that Mitterrand requested Rocard's resignation in May 1991.

[32] This excludes the powers of appointment granted to the President of the Republic in accordance with article 13.

the Prime Minister is clearly accountable for defence matters. Were the President solely in charge, these matters would escape parliamentary control. Still, this arcane division of power is unclear and has led to real difficulties in relation to the deployment of armed forces in periods of cohabitation.[33]

The Role and Powers of the Government

According to article 8 § 2, each member of Government is appointed by the President on proposal from the Prime Minister. If the opinion of the President is often decisive,[34] neither President nor Prime Minister can afford to create a government that ignores the balance of parties within the majority.

The French constitution recognises a collective identity to the Government. It is a constitutional actor with a defined role. Article 20 § 1 specifies that the Government determines and conducts the policy of the Nation. According to this provision, the Government is identified as the main decision maker in the Executive. To this end, the Government is not given powers as such – these rest with the Prime Minister – but institutional tools. Article 20 § 2 states that the Government has at its disposal both the administration and the armed forces. These ensure that government policies are implemented and effective.

Finally, article 20 § 3 organises the responsibility of the Government by reference to articles 49 and 50 of the constitution. Accordingly, confidence can be withdrawn from the Government by the Assemblée nationale. This reproduces a system of accountability typical of a parliamentary system. However, as was intimated above, the emergence of a parliamentary majority in conjunction with a presidential reading of the constitution has led to a complete transformation of the system of accountability.

Interestingly, from the beginning the French constitution implemented a parliamentary system with a twist: according to article 23, a

---

[33] On these difficulties see B Chantebout, 'Le Président de la République' in *Mélanges en l'honneur de Pierre Pactet* (Paris, Dalloz, 2003) 569.

[34] In fact, even in periods of cohabitation, events have demonstrated that the President has some residual power in relation to appointments. The powers of President of the Republic in matters of defence and international relations have given him the edge to influence the appointment of the foreign affairs and defence secretaries.

Member of Parliament (of either chamber) cannot be concomitantly in the Government.[35] Although many (but not all) members of the Government are appointed from the Assemblée nationale, they have a month to choose between parliamentary seat and government office. This divide between the Government and Parliament was felt necessary to try and break the vicious circle of government instability which had marred the previous two republics. Then, Members of Parliament had few scruples in bringing a government down if they were promised a ministerial appointment in the next one. Furthermore, there was no danger in accepting a government's portfolio: in the event of the government falling, there was always a seat in Parliament to return to. In an attempt to 'cure' the political system of past problems, the drafters of the fifth Republic wished to sever the link between Parliament and the Government. It was hoped that by adopting the prohibition between ministerial office and parliamentary seat, Members of Parliament would think twice before accepting a ministerial position as they would have no seat to return to. However, the evolution of the political system rendered this prohibition obsolete and soon political practice circumvented it. When a member of the Government, with a seat in Parliament prior to accepting a portfolio, lost his/her Government position, the incumbent of the parliamentary seat would often resign, thereby triggering a by-election. This gave the opportunity to the former member of Government to regain his/her seat in Parliament. This became so common a practice that the Balladur committee recommended that it be adopted. Since July 2008, Members of Parliament who accept a ministerial portfolio are allowed to return to their seat on leaving the Government.[36] Ironically, it was felt that it would help strengthen the link between Parliament and Government, so necessary in a democracy.

The Advisors to the Government

The 1958 constitution has given the Government access to two advisors in the form of two councils.

---

[35] A member of Government cannot have any other professional activity while in office.
[36] With each elected Member of Parliament is also elected a spare member who steps in if and when the original Member of Parliament resigns, dies or accepts a governmental position. This avoids the organisation of by-elections.

The Conseil d'Etat

The Conseil d'Etat was created by Napoléon Bonaparte in 1799. It was to give advice on the drafting of primary and secondary legislation and on solving disputes between citizens and the administration.[37] Although the institution has evolved into an independent court when fulfilling it judicial functions, it has remained an advisor to the Government. The 1958 constitution requires that it be consulted for all government bills (art 39 § 2), the ordinances of article 38 and some secondary legislation. Individual ministers can ask its advice on any administrative issues. Finally, the Conseil d'Etat can suggest legislative and administrative reforms to the Government on its own initiative. The Conseil d'Etat is a powerful institution and a great asset for the Government.

The economic, social and environmental council (art 71)

This council is of more recent creation as its first incarnation dates from 1924. It is a consultative body representing civil society. Its members are chosen by professional organisations (trade unions, guilds etc) or appointed for their qualifications and experience. It advises on all programming laws (art 34 § 6) and can be consulted by the Government or Parliament on any social, economic or environmental issue. It receives the petitions of citizens (art 69 § 2) and advises both the Government and Parliament on the pursuant action to be undertaken.

Constitutional Reform and the Bicephalous Executive

As shown above, all attempts to clarify the respective roles of the two heads of the Executive during the last wave of constitutional reform have failed. The fear of a return to a period of cohabitation was presented as the main obstacle to the adoption of the constitutional reforms adumbrated above. The new distribution of power would not have had the necessary flexibility to allow a parliamentary reading of the constitution: were a cohabitation to happen again, the new distribution of power would create insoluble and dangerous constitutional tensions. Although a period of cohabitation would indeed be a problem, commentators have exaggerated the danger of possible recurrence of this constitutional phenome-

---

[37] A law of 16–24 August 1790 prohibited ordinary courts from reviewing administrative action.

non. With the reduction of the presidential mandate to five years and the organisation of parliamentary elections to coincide with this mandate, another cohabitation is extremely unlikely. Therefore, the inability to adopt the necessary constitutional amendments in July 2008 is a missed opportunity that may have far-reaching consequences for the future. By failing to reflect political reality and to end the endemic confusion with regard to the distribution of executive power, the system invites criticisms. These criticisms may grow in strength and trigger a larger constitutional reform than is for the moment necessary. There is already a strong movement demanding that the position of the Prime Minister be abolished and favouring the adoption of a presidential-style system of government.[38] Had a sensible reform been adopted, the feeling of urgency in this matter may have disappeared.

THE DIFFICULT ACCOUNTABILITY OF THE EXECUTIVE

The system of accountability of the Executive has been at the centre of debate and controversy for some time in France and a process of constitutional change is underway. This is partly explained by the presidential reading of the constitution and by the relative failure of the traditional methods of control. Furthermore, accountability is undergoing a more global cultural change which is clearly noticeable when it comes to the Executive and its powers. Constitutional reform in this domain is only the tip of the iceberg of this discourse of constitutional change.

The Relative Failure of the Traditional System of Accountability

Traditionally in parliamentary regimes, the government is responsible to Parliament. The constitution or the constitutional practices ensure that mechanisms are in place to monitor the activity of the government and ultimately to censure it, if the Parliament is not satisfied with its findings.

The 1958 constitution is no exception: while article 50 specifies that in the eventuality of a vote of no confidence, the Prime Minister will

---

[38] See J Massot, 'Faut-il encore un Premier ministre?' *Les Petites Affiches*, 22 May 2008, 5.

tender the resignation of the Government to the President of the Republic, article 49 identifies three possible routes for the Assemblée nationale to withdraw its confidence.[39]

First, article 49 § 1 empowers the Prime Minister to request a vote of confidence from the Assemblée nationale on the presentation of the Government's programme and on an announcement of general policy. This is often used by the Prime Minister to bind a new parliamentary majority to a newly appointed government (eg Mauroy in July 1981), to gather the support of the parliamentary majority on an essential reform (eg Mauroy in June 1982), to strengthen a weakened Prime Minister (eg Juppé in 1995), or even to allow Members of Parliament to voice their opinion on a policy originating in the Presidency (eg Rocard in January 1991 and the Gulf War). No government has ever had to resign having triggered this constitutional provision. The interpretation of this provision has given rise to a number of commentaries in academic literature. Some commentators have argued that the drafting of the provision suggests an obligation on the part of the Government when first appointed to trigger a vote of confidence on its programme or general statement of policy. However, the practice is far from constant: while some Prime Ministers did seek such a vote, others did not. This refusal by some Prime Ministers seems to signal that they proceed from the President of the Republic rather than the Parliament and it contributes to the general uneasiness regarding the accountability of the Executive. If the Government does not have to present its programme – even in outline and even as a matter of courtesy – when it takes office, then the role and position of Parliament is clearly undermined.

The second possible challenge to the Government is contained in article 49 § 2 and allows one-tenth of the *députés* of the Assemblée nationale (ie 58 members) to table a motion of censure. The motion of censure, if passed by a majority after a cooling-off period of 48 hours, triggers the resignation of the whole government.[40] However, only one such motion was ever successful during the fifth Republic. As mentioned above, the Assemblée nationale tabled and passed a motion against the first Pompidou Government in 1962. Interestingly, this

---

[39] The Sénat cannot force the government to resign.

[40] The provision imposes restrictions on the number of motions of censure that each member of the Assemblée nationale can vote for in a single ordinary sitting: no more than three motions per member and in the event of an extraordinary sitting, it is restricted further to one single motion.

political episode exemplifies one of the main problems for the accountability of the Executive in the fifth Republic. The *députés* were trying to bring de Gaulle to account for using article 11 to amend the constitution. However, with no political accountability of the President, the *députés* did the only thing opened to them: to bring the Government down. Since then, political context and constitutional requirements have combined to make it impossible to pass such a motion. In both 1990 and 1992, Prime Ministers Rocard and Bérégovoy succeeded in surviving such a motion (the motion was lost by five votes in 1990 and by three votes in 1992). This procedure is often resorted to, not to challenge the Government but to allow the *députés*, especially those in the opposition, to voice concerns they might have. With the emergence of a parliamentary majority, this mechanism of accountability has been somewhat perverted.

The third mechanism, which is reproduced in article 49 § 3, combines fiendishly both parliamentary roles of legislation and control which would be better separate. The mechanism, which was used at the discretion of the Prime Minister until the reform of July 2008, considers a bill adopted unless a motion of censure is passed by an absolute majority. Originally, this provision was meant to overcome the absence of a majority in the Assemblée nationale and give a tool to the Government to force legislation through Parliament. It was assumed that the Assemblée nationale would think twice before withdrawing confidence because of the threat of dissolution. This was meant to avoid a return to the continual inefficiency of the Parliament in the fourth Republic. However, the advent of a parliamentary majority meant that the provision was commonly used not only to muzzle the opposition but also 'to convince' the parliamentary majority. In this context, article 49 § 3 is not a mechanism of accountability in the hands of the Assemblée nationale, but a tool of coercion in the hands of the Prime Minister. Furthermore, successive Prime Ministers have not hesitated to resort to this mechanism: between October 1958 and May 2006 article 49 § 3 was used 82 times;[41] it was even combined with other coercive provisions[42] such as article 44 § 3 (the blocked vote)[43] or the delegation of legislative powers of article 38.[44]

---

[41] Socialist Prime Ministers resorted to article 49 § 3 50 times in 179 months in contrast to right-wing Prime Ministers who used it 30 times in 397 months.

[42] See chapter 4.

[43] This combination was used to pass the legislation on social security in 1995.

[44] This combination was used to pass the legislation on privatisation in 1996.

Finally, with the emergence of a parliamentary majority, no Government was ever dismissed on the grounds of article 49 § 3. It is not surprising that the reform of July 2008 curtailed its use dramatically.

The new drafting specifies that article 49 § 3 can only be used for financial and social security finance bills and for a single ordinary bill per parliamentary sitting. It is a considerable improvement in terms of parliamentary democracy.[45] This was felt a necessary change as overall the use of article 49 was not contributing greatly to the accountability of the Executive. With the Prime Minister feeling under no legal obligation to present the Executive's programme to Parliament, the phenomenon of parliamentary majority compromising the working of the governmental responsibility, and the coercive use made of the mechanism of article 49 § 3, the picture painted was more of the Government controlling the Parliament rather than the reverse.

Accountability and Incremental Constitutional Change

One reason for the perceived failures of the system of accountability is that the initial system of government was transformed by the combination of constitutional practices and reforms as presented above.

In the original system, the President of the Republic was not meant to be the real head of the Executive. However, once the President was directly elected and the institutionalisation of the early practices was under way, some attention should have been given to the organisation of accountability.

As mentioned above, the new practices resulted in the creation of a new line of accountability between Prime Minister and President of the Republic. However, this accountability competes with the responsibility of the whole Government to Parliament. The Prime Minister is conceivably at the centre of a tension between two models of accountability: a parliamentary and a presidential one. Although it would be perfectly conceivable for both lines of accountability to function in equal balance, the emergence of a parliamentary majority tipped the scale in favour of the presidential line of accountability to the detriment of the parliamentary one. Arguably, the constitution was only altered recently to try and rectify this imbalance.

---

[45] However, this is not the feeling of some commentators, see: P Jan, 'Une réforme dangereuse' in J-P Camby, P Fraisseix and J Gicquel (eds) (n 19) 281.

Furthermore, the presidential line of accountability ends with the President: he can only be sanctioned by the people in presidential elections. For this reason, the reduction of the presidential mandate was indeed a way to increase the accountability of the office. Although it is too simplistic to claim that there is no accountability of the President of the Republic, there is a noticeable gap. This has been accentuated by the change of attitude of later Presidents with regard to referendums. While de Gaulle engaged in a direct and repeated dialogue with the people, his successors have resorted to referendums sparingly. Also, the absence of formal political responsibility has been quoted by past Presidents to justify a number of pernicious refusals. In September 1984, Giscard d'Estaing, three years after the end of his mandate, refused to appear before a committee of enquiry investigating the scandal of the sniffer planes.[46] Again, the creation of a committee of enquiry into the financial affairs of the Mitterrand family was not authorised on the ground that there was no political responsibility of the President of the Republic.

Finally, it is important to note that the analyses presented above do not apply during the periods of cohabitation. The President of the Republic is not able to appoint or to dismiss the Prime Minister of his choice, and no relationship of accountability exists between the two incumbents. Interestingly, the parliamentary reading has not resulted in an increase of the responsibility of the Government to the Parliament. As the Government is supported by a parliamentary majority, the mechanisms of articles 49 and 50 appear to be neutralised still.

The Adoption of New Mechanisms of Accountability

The relative failure of ministerial responsibility has led to the search for other forms of accountability. One such evolution is somewhat paradoxical: constitutional responsibility seemed to have come round a full historical circle. Modern constitutionalism had tended to replace or transform the mechanisms of criminal liability (eg impeachment) into mechanisms of political responsibility. The more recent trend in French constitutional law to criminalise political behaviour seems to indicate a return to old times. Still, these mechanisms need to be examined in detail and their suitability assessed.

[46] Public money had been wasted on research and development of the so-called 'sniffer planes'. Allegedly, these airplanes were able to locate underground oil reserves.

The Criminalisation of Political Behaviour

From its inception, the 1958 constitution contained provisions aiming to define and punish the criminal activity of Presidents of the Republic and government ministers. Originally, both came under the jurisdiction of the High Court of Justice as described in title IX of the constitution. The High Court of Justice was a specialised court staffed by Members of Parliament in equal numbers from both chambers. It was understood that the principle of separation of power required that members of the Executive be judged by their peers and not by the ordinary courts, so as to protect them from unjustified judicial attacks. However, the procedural requirements to introduce a case were so difficult to comply with that the original High Court of Justice was never convened. Indeed, 10 attempts were made to convene this court between 1958 and 1992 and all failed. When it proved impossible to convene the High Court of Justice even in the affair of the contaminated blood, it was felt that the constitutional threshold was too high and the provisions of the constitution inadequate to deal with the criminal liability of government ministers.

The Creation of the Court of Justice of the Republic

As a consequence of the perceived inadequacy of the constitutional provisions, a constitutional amendment was adopted in 1993. It created clear principles of criminal liability and a new court – the Court of Justice of the Republic[47] – to deal with members of Government and their actions in office. Also, prosecution is no longer triggered by Parliament but by individual citizens. A judicial committee reviews the seriousness of the allegations and the overall case before allowing the prosecution to proceed. Following this constitutional reform, the Prime Minister, Laurent Fabius, and two ministers in office at the time of the contaminated blood scandal, Georgina Dufoix and Edmond Hervé, were prosecuted: they were accused of being responsible for the continued distribution of contaminated blood after it was scientifically established that the Aids virus was being transmitted to patients in this way. While Laurent Fabius and Georgina Dufoix were cleared, Edmond Hervé was found guilty of two actions: the failure to contact the patients who had been given contaminated products and the failure to organise

---

[47] The Court of Justice of the Republic is staffed by 12 Members of Parliament (six from each chamber) and three judges of the Cour de cassation – the court heading the ordinary court system.

the control and destruction of products which were already stocked after the introduction of systematic testing. However, no sentence was pronounced against him; the court explained that the facts of the case were 15 years old and that the presumption of innocence had never been really secured for any of the three ministers charged.

The Court of Justice of the Republic has had to judge a few other cases since.[48] In 2000, the minister Ségolène Royal was prosecuted for having made slanderous accusations against the academic staff of the Veterinary School by criticising their attitude (ie passive support) during the hazing activities at the school in 1997. She was cleared after the investigation found her allegations to be true. In 2004 the minister Michel Gillibert was accused and found guilty of embezzlement of 1.3 million euros. State subsidies to a few fictitious charities were in fact used to meet some of his personal expenses and the expenses of his advisors. In 2010 Charles Pasqua was condemned for misuse of company assets in the Sofremi affair when he was Minister of the Interior.[49] More recently, the Court of Justice of the Republic has decided to open an investigation into Christine Lagarde's decision in the Tapie affair when she was Minister of the Economy. Still, the number of cases before the Court of Justice of the Republic has remained low and its effectiveness is debated regularly.[50]

The Steady Flow of 'Politico-Financial Affairs'

The number of cases before the Court of Justice of the Republic may seem to contradict the existence of a trend tending towards the criminalisation of political behaviour in France. However, many criminal prosecutions in so-called politico-financial affairs involving government ministers have been conducted before the ordinary courts. The most famous of these cases concerned the then state-owned company Elf-Aquitaine and involved an ex-foreign affairs minister, Roland Dumas. The top executives of the company and a number of politicians were accused of misappropriation of company funds. Fictitious employments

---

[48] In a case against a minister, Noir, the Court of Justice rightly judged that the facts did not relate to his ministerial activity and held the ordinary courts to have jurisdiction instead.

[49] The company Sofremi, which exported security material and services, was 35% state owned and under the control of the Ministry of the Interior. Commissions paid to the company were transferred to family and friends of Charles Pasqua.

[50] See O Duhamel and G Vedel, 'Le pénal et le politique', *Le Monde*, 3 March 1999.

were created as well as illegal commissions paid. Dumas was condemned in the first instance but cleared on appeal. Many of the actors in this scandal were also involved in the affair of the Taiwanese frigates.[51]

Beside this, there have been a number of similar scandals through the years and they involve politicians on both sides of the political spectrum. To cite but a few, the affair of the association 'Carrefour du développement'[52] involved Christian Nucci, then minister of international cooperation, and the Clearstream 2 affair involved de Villepin, then Prime Minister,[53] and although the very long-running saga of the various affairs of the Paris Town Hall and the financing of the Gaullist party involved (among others) Alain Juppé, as leader of the Gaullist party, and Jacques Chirac, as Mayor of Paris, and was not concerned with their actions while in office, the scandals highlight the pervasive culture and depth of the problem at the time.[54] It also raised the question of the immunity of the President of the Republic. A number of reasons may explain this trend: judges are increasingly active in affairs of political corruption, legislation was late in regulating the financing of political activities and parties[55] and, as mentioned above, criminal liability acts as a peripheral substitute for political responsibility.

[51] A consortium of French companies was contracted to build six frigates for the Taiwanese navy in August 1991. However, some Chinese and Taiwanese officials received large illegal commissions, part of which were returned to France as retro-commissions. An arbitration tribunal ordered France to reimburse 591 million dollars to Taiwan in May 2010; an appeal against this decision was rejected by the Court of Appeal on 9 June 2011.

[52] Charged with the organisation of some international cooperation, this association received state subsidies. A large amount was used to cover the personal expenses of both minister and advisors. Surprisingly, Parliament passed a statute granting Christian Nucci criminal immunity. However, he was ordered in a civil action to repay 20 million francs jointly with two other State officials.

[53] Prime Minister de Villepin was accused of having attempted to manipulate the justice system to compromise Sarkozy, his political rival. Forged documents implicating him and many others were sent to the judge investigating a financial scandal. After the forgery was discovered, de Villepin was accused of having orchestrated the whole affair and was prosecuted. The court gave a verdict of 'not proven' in January 2010.

[54] Among other things, some Gaullist party personnel were fictitiously and illegally employed by private companies or the Paris Town hall. Alain Juppé was condemned for illegal conflict of interests in January 2004 to an eighteen months suspended sentence and the loss of all political rights for one year; Jacques Chirac was condemned in December 2011 to a two years suspended sentence.

[55] See E Phélippeau, 'Genèse d'une codification' (2010) *Revue française de science politique* 519.

The Difficult Immunity of the President of the Republic

Originally, article 68[56] in title IX specified that the President of the Republic was not accountable for any acts or decisions taken while in office with the notable exception of high treason. Not only did this provision create some tensions with regard to the accountability of the Executive, but the interpretation of its scope led to a serious disagreement between the Conseil constitutionnel and the Cour de cassation. Both courts handed down decisions against a highly charged political background: Jacques Chirac, then President of the Republic, was seemingly entangled in various politico-financial affairs, all concerned with his previous mandate as Mayor of Paris.[57] While the Conseil constitutionnel in a decision of 1999[58] had interpreted article 68 as granting in effect complete immunity to the President in office with the exception of high treason, the Cour de cassation held in a decision of 2001[59] that with the exception of high treason, ordinary courts had jurisdiction regarding events pre-dating the presidential elections and over acts outside the President's official capacity. However, the Cour de cassation qualified this by specifying that the President of the Republic in office could not be prosecuted, charged or even forced to appear as a witness in criminal proceedings, since he embodies the continuity of the State. Such proceedings are authorised only after the President has stepped down. Under strong political pressure, Jacques Chirac promised during the presidential campaign of 2002 that he would seek advice on amending the constitution and on clarifying the immunity of the President of the Republic. An expert committee, which was convened in July 2002, recommended a number of changes.[60] The constitutional reform of February 2007 clarified the scope of the presidential immunity by indicating in article 67 that while in office the President of the Republic cannot be charged,

[56] See the former article 68 of the constitution: 'The President of the Republic shall incur no liability by reason of acts carried out in this official capacity with the exception of High Treason.'

[57] Chirac refused to appear as witness in the affairs concerned with the finances of the Gaullist party on the ground of his presidential immunity.

[58] See CC 98-408 DC of 22 January 1999, International Criminal Court. In this decision, the Conseil constitutionnel expressed concerns about the fact that heads of state did not have any immunity from prosecution for crimes against humanity or war crimes during their term of office.

[59] C. Cass. Plen. 10 October 2001 *Breisacher* [2002] *RTDCiv* 169 note Molfessis.

[60] See *Le statut pénal du Président de la République* (Paris, *La Documentation française*, 2003).

prosecuted or asked to appear before any administrative authority or court (other than the High Court), but that such proceedings can be started or resumed one month after the end of the President's mandate. Furthermore, article 68 attempts to define the circumstances in which the President can be prosecuted before the High Court: the reference to high treason is deleted and instead the provision now requires the President to have acted in breach of his duties in a way manifestly incompatible with the presidential mandate. Although the new arrangement excludes any prosecution or legal action while the President is in office, the immunity is only temporary. With the clarification of the circumstances in which a President of the Republic can be prosecuted, the trend of criminalisation of political behaviour appears strengthened.

The Coming of Age of Financial Control

Even before the constitutional reform of July 2008, a trend had been established to strengthen the financial control of government departments, public bodies[61] and political life. Unsurprisingly, these concerns were also reflected in the 2008 constitutional reform. The introduction of a complex system of financial accountability has brought to light a number of dubious financial practices. For this reason, the Balladur committee highlighted two areas of improvement when it comes to the financial accountability of the Executive.

The Financial Control of the Presidency

Like other French constitutional institutions, the Presidency is financially autonomous; it determines its budget independently. However, until 2008, many expenses were not covered by the budget of the Presidency and various ministries were required to cover a share of the Presidency's expenses – for instance, the special advisors to the President were rarely remunerated from the Presidency's budget, but continued to be paid by their original government department or state institutions. Furthermore, the Presidency did not come within the remit of the Court of Auditors. Consequently, the Balladur committee, following the wish expressed by Sarkozy in his speech at Epinal, recommended that the salary of the President of the Republic be determined by statute, that the Presidency be granted a budget to cover the whole of its

---

[61] See chapter 4.

expenses and that, along with all other constitutional institutions, it be controlled by the Court of Auditors. These recommendations were all put into effect: in December 2007, the legislation determining the salary of the members of Government was amended to include the salary of the President of the Republic[62] and since 2009, the Presidency has benefited from a proper budget which is approved by Parliament and subjected annually to the control of the Court of Auditors.[63]

The Controversial Ministerial 'Entourage'

For a number of commentators, many of the financial scandals discussed above were made possible because of a specific governmental structure: the *cabinets ministériels*.[64] These represent a light and flexible structure consisting of ministerial advisors (often top civil servants) recruited for their expertise and/or their political allegiance to serve, advise and inform the minister in policy and decision making.

However, this rather bland definition hides a reality of power and controversy: even though the *cabinets ministériels* have existed for a long time and are important players in government, they are barely regulated by law and function on the basis of complex and obscure budgetary arrangements. These are held partly responsible for the practices of 'creative accounting' which are necessary to support the activities of the *cabinet* and its minister and which sometimes degenerate into financial corruption. Accordingly, the Balladur committee felt it necessary to suggest changes with regard to the personnel of the *cabinets*.[65] Having noted that attempts to control the *cabinets* by curbing their personnel had all but failed, the Balladur committee recommended instead that the budgetary arrangements for paying these advisors be altered. For historical reasons, the *cabinets* have a weak financial autonomy and many advisors are civil servants on secondment from a government department or other public body; often, these continue to pay the salary of their 'former' employee. The Balladur committee noted that this solution flies in the face of the new rules and principles of financial accountability and should be abandoned. New positions of *cabinet* advisor and a new salary scale

---

[62]   See article 106 of the financial law of 24 December 2007.

[63]   In its report for 2010, the Court of Auditors noted that the Presidency had improved its management and reduced its expenses, but that further improvement was required.

[64]   See C Bigaut, (n 2) 130.

[65]   See the Balladur report (n 18) p 27.

should be created to facilitate the financial accountability and transparency of these structures. Also, a list detailing these positions and their salaries should be annexed to the budget for Parliament to see. In practice the Prime Minister, Fillon, has continued to oversee the number of positions attached to the *cabinets* of each minister, but legislation has not been amended to include all the proposals mentioned above. While more information is made available to Parliament via the financial legislation, it has required a parliamentary question[66] to each and every ministry to establish the average salary of their *cabinet* advisors.

The Era of the Technocrats: The Need for Further Change?

According to article 20 of the constitution, the administration is subordinate to the Government. Indeed, it would be surprising in a democracy to find the administration recognised as a separate, independent and competing power. With the exception of article 20, no provision specifies the constitutional position and status of the *fonctionnaire* (or civil servant) in the 1958 constitution. Traditionally, government ministers in office (and not civil servants) are held politically accountable for policy-making. In fact, the law defining the rights and duties of civil servants[67] organises their political neutrality carefully: for instance, they must respect a duty of reserve when expressing their personal and political views. Otherwise, the public may come to regard them as biased and begin to doubt the fairness of their decisions. Although the official position in France appears clear cut, on investigation, further analysis is required. Some commentators have even wondered whether it is possible to talk of a separate administrative power.[68]

Cabinets ministériels *and Accountability of the Executive*

Beyond the issues of financial accountability and transparency mentioned above, the *cabinets ministériels* represent another challenge to the accountability of the Executive. The *cabinets* are accused of concentrating considerable power in a small group of people and of competing

---

[66] This written question was addressed to all ministers by the *député* Rosière on 27 July 2010.

[67] While the law of 13 July 1983 listed many of the duties of civil servants, the duty of reserve is still based on the case law of the Conseil d'Etat.

[68] See P Bon, 'Peut-on parler de pouvoir administratif?' in B Mathieu (ed), *Cinquantième anniversaire de la Constitution française* (Paris, Dalloz, 2008) 385.

with the ministry itself.[69] Not only does this create confusion with regard to allocation of power, but as a result, ministries tend to be deprived of their role of advice and conception of new policies. With little consultation or participation of interested parties, this creates a technocratic culture in which decisions are increasingly detached from the reality of ordinary citizens. The *cabinets* are thus seen as a threat to the traditional mechanisms of political accountability: any number of important policy decisions originate from the *cabinets ministériels* themselves, while their members eschew any political responsibility. Finally, this engenders a process of politicisation of the civil service, thereby potentially compromising its neutrality and endangering the very foundations of the system of accountability.

A Contested Process of Elite Creation

Civil servants play an important role in French politics and make up a large proportion of the political personnel. Indeed the rules governing the political activity of civil servants facilitate the development of a political career. While it is not possible to continue to work in the civil service when holding a parliamentary mandate or a ministerial office, it is not necessary to resign either: civil servants are simply placed on detachment during the term of their mandate or office. At the end of it, they are entitled to rejoin the civil service. However, this practice and its effects have come under strong criticism in recent times.

The phenomenon which has come to characterise the fifth Republic was triggered by a combination of factors. In the early days of the Republic, not only were a number of ministers with no prior political experience appointed by de Gaulle directly from the civil service,[70] but these appointees were given key ministerial positions: interior, foreign affairs, army etc. In 1962 even the Prime Minister, Pompidou, was appointed with no prior parliamentary experience. This choice is easily understandable: at the time, de Gaulle did not have a pool of experienced men at his disposal. Interestingly, the first civil servant appointees who crossed over to the world of politics later reasserted their choice by seeking a parliamentary seat. The next generation of top civil servants who were attracted by a career in politics sought a top political party

---

[69] In practice, access to the minister is often regulated by and/or limited to the members of his/her *cabinets ministériels*.

[70] Consistent with the fact that de Gaulle did not trust the political personnel inherited from the fourth Republic.

position early in their civil service career (eg Chirac in the Gaullist party and Jospin in the socialist party). Still, to this day, some ministers are appointed straight from the civil service. Consequently, the mixing of politicians and top civil servants is now well established, whatever the party in office. To cite but a few, Pompidou, Giscard d'Estaing, Chirac, Juppé, Fabius, Jospin and Hollande are all examples of politicians who straddled both worlds of administration and politics.

The practice adumbrated above is supported by the *cabinets ministériels*. Indeed, the *cabinets* represent a border territory where the worlds of politics and administration come together. The appointment of a civil servant to a position in a *cabinet* often opens up for him/her the option of a political career: for a few, it may come later in the form of a ministerial appointment, but for many, the election to a parliamentary seat will be required to strengthen their political credentials first. In effect, a phenomenon of elite creation can be clearly observed in this process.

However, the elite that emerges from this system has come under particularly strong criticism in the last few years. Critics have pointed out at length that the political elite emerging from this process was not representative of French society, whatever the political party of origin. In fact, the majority of top civil servants themselves are educated at some of the most prestigious French *grandes écoles*: the Ecole Nationale d'Administration (ENA) or in the case of experts and engineers, at the Ecole Polytechnique. Furthermore, their studies completed, the most successful are appointed to prestigious but small State institutions: namely the Conseil d'Etat, the Court of Auditors and the tax and revenue service. It is often from this small pool that the *cabinets* recruit their staff. Accordingly, a number of accusations have been levelled at the system beyond the issue of representation mentioned above. First, the elite so created is composed in the main of technocrats who are not known for their imagination and clarity of decisions. Their ability as political decision makers is thereby strongly contested. Secondly, similarity in backgrounds, education and professional experience creates a commonality of mannerisms, principles and beliefs among the members of this elite, which is seen to transcend party politics and gives rise to concerns with regard to policy making. Finally, the system does not foster a culture of personal accountability: these appointees will often return to their administration of origin, once their appointment or mandate comes to an end. These criticisms are indicative of a tension between ordinary French citizens and the ruling class.

CONCLUSION

The transformation of the Executive has been largely responsible for the success of the fifth Republic, but this may have been secured at a cost: parliamentary democracy has come out decidedly weakened. As the organisation, powers and accountability of the Executive have come under increased criticism, reforms have been adopted. However, it is doubtful whether the criminalisation of political behaviour is a real solution to the accountability gap. A review of the prosecutions and sentences of politicians over the last two decades shows rather mixed results: Christian Nucci, although sentenced, was granted immunity by Parliament; Edmond Hervé, although found guilty in the contaminated blood affair, received no sentence; Roland Dumas was cleared on appeal; Alain Juppé, although sentenced, was re-elected Mayor of Bordeaux soon after the end of his disqualification and he was appointed Minister for Foreign Affairs from February 2011 to May 2012. Finally, although Jacques Chirac has been given a two-year suspended sentence, the main plaintiff, the Paris Town Hall, dropped all charges after agreeing to an out-of-court settlement in which Jacques Chirac and the Gaullist party jointly are rumoured to have agreed to pay 2.2 million euros by way of compensation. On balance, neither the decisions of the Court of Justice of the Republic nor those of the ordinary courts strengthen much the accountability of the Executive.

Similarly, the attempt made by the constitutional reform of 2008 to shift the balance of power in favour of Parliament may fall short of what is needed. Arguably the whole system of accountability would need to be redesigned so as to fit with the presidential reading of the constitution. As the regime that emerged in the early 1960s both borrows and departs from the presidential and parliamentary models, the new organisation of accountability would need to strive for creativity and originality.

FURTHER READING

P Ardant, 'L'article 5 et la fonction présidentielle' (1981) 41 *Pouvoirs* 37
D Baranger, 'Executive Power in France' in PP Craig and A Tomkins (eds), *The Executive and Public Law* (Oxford, Oxford University Press, 2006) ch 7

B Branchet, *La fonction présidentielle sous la Vᵉ République* (Paris, Librairie générale de droit et de jurisprudence, 2008)

A-M Cohendet, *La cohabitation. Leçons d'une expérience* (Paris, Presses Universitaires de France, 1993)

J-E Gicquel, 'Article 6' and 'Article 7' in F Luchaire, G Conac and X Prétot (eds), *La constitution de la République française* Economica, 3rd edn (Paris, Economica, 2009) 298, 328

E Grossman, 'The President's Choice? Government and Cabinet Turnover under the Fifth Republic' (2009) 32 *West European Politics* 268

J Massot, 'Quinquennat et présidentialisation' in *Mélanges en l'honneur de Pierre Pactet* (Paris, Dalloz, 2003) 703

J Massot, *Chef de l'Etat et chef du Gouvernement*, 2nd edn (Paris, La Documentation française, 2008)

B Mathieu, 'La responsabilité pénale des ministres devant la Cour de justice de la République' (1993) *Revue française de droit constitutionnel* 601

Numéro spécial, 'Quinquennat' (2000) 4 *Revue française de droit constitutionnel*

K Oellers-Frahm, 'Italy and France: Immunity of Prime Minister of Italy and the President of the French Republic' (2005) *International Journal of Constitutional Law* 107

J Robert, 'La candidature présidentielle' (2006) *Revue de droit public* 3

F Saint-Bonnet, 'Réflexions sur l'article 16 et l'état d'exception' (1998) *Revue de droit public* no spécial 1699

J-M Sauvé, 'Le conseil des ministres' in P Gélard, M Ameller, P Avril and R Ben Achour (eds), *Mélanges en l'honneur de Jean Gicquel* (Paris, Montchrestien, 2008) 497

J-M Sauvé, 'La responsabilité du chef de l'Etat' (2009) vol 12, Société de législation comparée 9

O Schrameck, *Dans l'ombre de la République: les cabinets ministériels* (Paris, Dalloz, 2006)

Relevant Websites

President of the Republic: www.elysee.fr/president/accueil.1.html
Prime Minister: www.gouvernement.fr/premier-ministre
Government: www.gouvernement.fr/

4

Towards a Renewal of the Parliament

——◦◦◦——

A Return to Institutional Autonomy? – The Constitutional Status of Members of Parliament – Parliament's Work: A Great Improvement – Conclusion: Further Reform?

I N LIGHT OF the experiences of the previous republics, the drafters of the 1958 constitution were not well disposed towards the legislative branch. Consequently, they established a modified parliamentary regime with a 'rationalised' Parliament – a euphemism signalling that strict limitations were imposed on the legislature. Indeed, many constitutional provisions aimed to keep the Parliament in check. Unfortunately, political practices and successive constitutional reforms ensured the unrivalled supremacy of the Executive, compounding further the demise of Parliament.

Once the survival of the regime was secured, the weakness of the French Parliament became a serious concern: it threatened the legitimacy of the entire system. A first attempt to correct this situation was made in 1995 but the revision achieved too little. The issues came to a head with the constitutional reform of 2000: the end of cohabitation signalled the end of the parliamentary reading of the constitution. Arguably, the chronic institutional imbalance should have been addressed then. Instead, the problem continued to grow and many commentators and politicians were beginning to call for the adoption of a sixth (and more democratic) Republic.[1] Indeed, constitutional reform was at the heart of the campaign for the presidential elections of May 2007 and the main candidates – Royal (the Socialist party candidate) and Sarkozy (the Gaullist party

---

[1] See O Duhamel, *Vive la VIème République* (Paris, Seuil, 2002); A Montebourg and B François, *La Constitution de la 6ème République* (Paris, Odile Jacob, 2005).

candidate) – made constitutional reform their priority. It is therefore not surprising that two months after his election, Sarkozy began the process of major constitutional reform. It was completed successfully in July 2008 and aimed for a large part to give more power to Parliament. For many, the reform has allowed the regime to survive into the twenty-first century and may trigger a renewal of parliamentary democracy in France. To assess this eventuality, an investigation into the impact of the reform on the Parliament's institutional structure, membership and work is called for.

A RETURN TO INSTITUTIONAL AUTONOMY?

Arguably, the principle of separation of powers requires that the legislative branch organise its parliamentary work independently. In fact, a long-established French constitutional tradition entitled each chamber of the French Parliament to organise itself freely and adopt its own rules of procedure. However, the fifth Republic has departed from this: not only does the 1958 constitution regulate closely the internal organisation of each chamber but it resorts to an external body – the Conseil constitutionnel – to enforce it.

Unequal Bicameralism

Not only has the French Parliament been divided into two chambers continuously since 1875 but prior to that, the large majority of regimes resorted to a bicameral parliament. The 1958 constitution simply continued an established tradition. In fact, the French people had signalled their attachment to a bicameral system when they rejected the first project of constitution in 1946. In truth, two regimes since 1789 have resorted to a single chamber and both evolved into dictatorships: the Convention (1792) and the second Republic (1848). French citizens may have reason to believe that a bicameral parliament is essential to a functioning democracy. For this reason, article 24 § 2 of the constitution states that the French Parliament is comprised of the Assemblée nationale and the Sénat.

The difficulty with a bicameral parliament lies with the distribution of power and the allocation of functions between the two chambers. History has also taught the French that when both chambers fulfil the same role and have the same power, conflicts often ensue.[2] Democracy may require a bicameral parliament but for it to function, each chamber must not be granted equal power. This reality is recognised by the present constitution: article 3 may consider all Members of Parliament as equal representatives of the sovereign people, but the constitution puts the chambers on an unequal footing. In doing so, the authors of the constitution understood the necessity of giving priority to one chamber and avoiding insoluble political conflicts between them. To differentiate one from the other, the constitution bestows a separate electoral legitimacy on each chamber and identifies a specific role for the Sénat – the second chamber represents the various territorial governments of the Republic.

The Assemblée nationale

According to article 24, the Assemblée nationale is elected by direct universal suffrage and its membership cannot exceed 577 *députés*.[3] This number was reached in 1985 after demographic growth required an increase in the number of representatives. There are 108,000 inhabitants per *député*. Mainland France has 555 seats and 22 are overseas. *Députés* are elected for a mandate of five years.

Following a long constitutional tradition, the electoral system itself is not contained in the constitution and this absence may be surprising: politicians and commentators alike agree that the electoral system for the Assemblée nationale is a key factor in the success of the present political system. The rejection of proportional representation[4] and the adoption of a majority system with two rounds have allowed the emergence of a parliamentary majority since 1962. As the presidential reading of the constitution and the stability of the political system rests on the continuation of a parliamentary majority in the Assemblée nationale, one may be excused for thinking that the electoral system itself ought to be cited in the constitution. In fact, in 1985, the Socialist Government changed the electoral system to proportional representation following a party manifesto commitment (also, they were about to lose the coming parliamentary elections and may have wanted to limit

[2] See chapter 1.
[3] *Député* or deputy is the name given to members of the Assemblée nationale. It underlines clearly the idea of popular mandate.
[4] The first house of the fourth Republic was elected by a system of proportional representation. It is widely believed that this was responsible for the fragmentation and multiplication of political parties.

the damage). A right-wing majority was returned in the Assemblée nationale, along with 35 members of the National Front. It is ironical that the Socialists' electoral reform was responsible for the National Front's unprecedented electoral success. Soon after, the new Government reverted to the previous electoral system. It has not been altered since. Still, in its report, the Balladur committee restated that such inclusion was superfluous.[5]

Furthermore, the legitimacy of this electoral system is questioned still. The Balladur committee noted that the return to full proportional representation may not be desirable but recommended that the present system be altered to allow for a more equitable representation, with 20 to 30 seats being elected by proportional representation.[6] This became a major point of disagreement during the constitutional revision of July 2008 and was not included in the final bill. Indeed, the socialists refused to endorse the constitutional revision in part because of the lack of electoral reform.

At present, *députés* are elected by a direct, majority, and uninominal electoral system with two rounds. This system has the double advantage of allowing for a majority to emerge but also of ensuring that smaller parties are represented in Parliament. In the first round of elections, all candidates who are entered in the constituency can receive votes. It is possible for a candidate to be elected after the first round of elections if he/she receives an absolute majority of the votes cast. Most of the time, no such majority emerges and a second round is required. Only the candidates who obtained the first and second position in the first round can compete in the second. In the second round, the candidate with the majority of the votes is elected. Negotiations often take place between the first and the second rounds as parties on each side of the political divide decide on the candidate to run in the second round. For instance, a socialist candidate may step down to let the communist candidate continue to the second round. The socialist electors will be asked to vote for the chosen left-wing candidate. The same negotiations take place among right-wing parties, with the exception of the National Front.[7]

---

[5] See the Balladur report, p 69, http://www.ladocumentationfrancaise.fr/var/storage/rapports-publics/074000697/0000.pdf; in contrast, see the personal statement of Professor Casanova at p 102.

[6] See Balladur report (n 5) proposal no 62, p 69.

[7] To this day, all parties have refused to enter into negotiations with the National Front.

The Sénat

According to article 24, the Sénat is elected by indirect universal suffrage and aims to represent local communities and territorial governments: towns, *départements*, regions and overseas territories. There are 348 *sénateurs*, all elected with a two-tier electoral system. Elected representatives for the various territorial governments are convened in an electoral college for each senatorial election. This college elects the *sénateurs*: the chamber is renewed by half every three years. This partial renewal avoids swings of political allegiance and ensures a certain continuity of the French Parliament. Some have argued that this undermines its institutional legitimacy. Still, it has not hindered the Sénat in developing a clear identity and establishing a role for itself.[8] In any event, the use of indirect suffrage was designed to bestow a lower legitimacy than the one granted to the Assemblée nationale.

The electoral system is complex and changes according to the size and demography of the constituency.[9] The majority system with two rounds is used for smaller constituencies which elect at most three *sénateurs*. A system of proportional representation is used in the constituencies which return four *sénateurs* or more. At present, 52 per cent of the seats are elected by proportional representation.

However, the representation of the Sénat is discussed at regular intervals and is often seen as compromising its legitimacy. Small towns and villages are over-represented in the Sénat as they make up 95 per cent of the electoral college. Arguably, this ensured until recently that a Conservative majority be returned systematically in the second chamber. The Sénat is also criticised for the average age of its members (too high) and its female membership (too low). To address these criticisms, the Sénat sponsored a reform in 2000: it altered the composition of the electoral college to ensure a more equal representation of the population.[10] However, the Conseil constitutionnel[11] found this to be unconstitutional. Prompted by this decision, the Sénat sponsored another reform in 2003

---

[8] Although Conservative, the Sénat contested many of de Gaulle's initiatives and policies; see also, A Delcamp, 'L'affirmation du Sénat' in B Mathieu (ed), *Cinquantième anniversaire de la constitution française* (Paris, Dalloz, 2008) 281.

[9] The *département* is the constituency.

[10] In the *communes* (ie towns and villages), the reform planned one delegate to the electoral college per 300 inhabitants. This reform would benefit particularly large towns and urban areas.

[11] See decision C cons no 2000-431 DC, 6 July 2000.

which aimed to improve the legitimacy of its membership:[12] the age for eligibility was lowered from 35 to 30 years, the number of *sénateurs* was increased to allow for a better representation of urban constituencies, and finally, the timing of the elections was altered to ensure a shorter mandate and a more frequent renewal: *sénateurs* are now elected for six years instead of nine.[13] Still, many commentators argued that this was insufficient. Consequently, the Balladur committee recommended that article 24 of the constitution be amended to ensure the equal and demographic representation of the population. Although included in the constitutional bill, it was not included in the final text. For many, this issue needs to be resolved. Still, the senatorial elections of September 2008 and September 2011 tend to show that the reform of 2003 is having the intended effect: not only has the average age lowered[14] but the number of female *sénateurs* has increased.[15] Indeed, the elections of 25 September 2011 saw the election of a left-wing majority in the second chamber. While a left-wing Sénat is indeed a first in French political life, it may signal a renewal of this institution. Even though the left-wing parties have a tight majority of three seats, parliamentary practices will need to adapt to this state of affairs. In view of this development, one wonders whether the lack of constitutional reform in 2008 may be overlooked.

The Internal Organisation of Parliament: A Constitutional Straitjacket

A study of the constitutional provisions concerning the internal organisation of Parliament sheds light on the rationalisation of the institution which was attempted by the drafters of the 1958 constitution. Although the reform of July 2008 has begun to lift some of the more controversial limitations, the French Parliament's freedom of action is still impeded by some serious restrictions.

---

[12] See the organic law of 30 July 2003.

[13] This mandate was too long and a reduction was agreed in exchange for an increase in the number of *sénateurs*.

[14] The average age was 65 years after the 2008 elections and it is now 62 years.

[15] It has risen to 22, 13%.

The Règlements d'assemblée *and their Control*

Each house adopts *règlements d'assemblée* or regulations of the house to organise and conduct its parliamentary work. In the past, these regulations were at the complete discretion of the house. The process of rationalisation mentioned above has led to the freedom of Parliament being seriously curtailed in this domain. Still, it is difficult to find fault with the desire of the authors of the 1958 constitution that the constitutional document be respected.

The Conseil constitutionnel was given the task of controlling automatically the constitutionality of these regulations and ensuring their compliance with the constitution. Still, much depended on the stance taken by the Conseil constitutionnel. From the start, the Conseil constitutionnel intimated that it would impose a strict and in-depth control over these. The Conseil constitutionnel annulled a number of provisions in the first *règlement d'assemblée* ever drafted by the Assemblée nationale.[16] Among other things, the first house had attempted to recreate the possibility of ending a parliamentary debate with the adoption of a resolution expressing a wish, an orientation or a reserve regarding a government's policy. This was judged to be unconstitutional by the Conseil constitutionnel: according to article 20 of the constitution, the Government is solely responsible for policy making. The Conseil constitutionnel construed the move as an early grab for power. Also, resolutions had been abused during the fourth Republic and had been partly responsible for the ministerial instability which plagued the regime. Allowing these to flourish again may have seriously compromised the strict system of ministerial responsibility contained in articles 49 and 50 of the constitution.

More recently, the Conseil showed the same sternness when it reviewed the amended regulations of the Assemblée nationale[17] and the Sénat[18] following the reform of July 2008. While the Conseil was obviously concerned that the control by both houses should stay within the confines of the constitution, one may wonder whether this control may in fact hinder the transformation of the French Parliament: for instance, it declared unconstitutional a number of provisions relating to the new committee of evaluation of public policies, thereby limiting markedly its

[16] See C cons no 59-2 DC, 17, 18, 24 June 1959.
[17] See C cons no 2009-581 DC, 25 June 2009.
[18] See C cons no 2009-582 DC, 25 June 2009.

powers and impact. This is surprising in view of the recognition of the new role of control and assessment included in article 24 of the constitution. Similarly, the Conseil stopped the Sénat from organising a general debate on a new bill prior to the committee stage; this may, however, have helped to achieve a better examination in committee and overall rationalise parliamentary work. Finally, the insistence by the Conseil constitutionnel that the large majority of constitutional provisions be implemented by laws rather than directly by the regulations will make it more convoluted for each chamber to experiment in the implementation of their new powers. One may fear that in the circumstances, both houses may establish practices outside of any laws or regulations to achieve flexibility and allow experiments. If these mechanisms were to continue, they may in turn create constitutional conventions. This tendency would not be to the advantage of the rule of law and would undermine ultimately the control of the Conseil constitutionnel.

Indeed, the control of the Conseil constitutionnel has not been enough to check the propensity of the French Parliament to apply 'creatively' the constitution. For instance, according to article 27, the right to vote is personal and individual, and it can only be delegated in very specific circumstances. Although the texts implementing this provision are consistent with the constitutional requirement, the parliamentary practice has not always reflected the letter or the spirit of the provision. Both chambers have suffered from high levels of absenteeism and Members have tended to delegate their right to vote systematically. Indeed, there were frequent scenes in the Assemblée nationale of formal votes being taken by a few individuals for the whole house. It has needed the sustained effort of successive presidents of the Assemblée nationale to ensure that Members are actually there to vote the final text. Furthermore, the requirements of article 27 are still largely ignored in the Sénat.[19]

The Key Internal Structures

The Parliament's key internal structures are cited in the constitution. Only one such structure was created outside this text. Arguably constitutions should describe the general organisation of Parliament but in the 1958 constitution, this was often used to impose limitations.

---

[19] See J Gicquel and J-E Gicquel, *Droit constitutionnel et institutions politiques*, 25th edn (Paris, Montchrestien, 2011) 680.

The President of the House

The president chairs the debates in the house and heads the secretariat. Furthermore, the president is invested with considerable constitutional powers: both are consulted by the President of the Republic before a dissolution of the Assemblée nationale and before using the emergency powers of article 16. Also, each is entitled to refer a bill or a treaty to the Conseil constitutionnel for review. Finally, the president of the Sénat is the third most important State official (after the President of the Republic and the Prime Minister) and he replaces the President of the Republic temporarily when the office falls vacant.[20] As the President of the Republic incarnates the continuity of the republic, it is important that the presidential office be filled at all times.[21]

The Secretariat

The *bureau* or secretariat is only referred to briefly in three articles of the constitution: articles 26 § 2, 39 § 2 and 89 § 3. However, this does not reflect the central role played by this institution: the *bureau* supervises the work of the house in plenaries and committees. It is also responsible for the various administrative departments of the house. The secretariat is elected by each chamber and is composed of 22 members for the Assemblée nationale[22] and 26 for the Sénat.[23] The president chairs the debates in the house but as he/she cannot physically sit through all the debates, he/she shares this task with the vice-presidents. The secretaries ensure that the debates are properly recorded and the minutes accurate. Finally, the *questeurs* head the various administrative departments in each chamber. Personnel, finance and purchasing are all managed independently in each house.

The secretariat is renewed every three years in the Sénat and every year in the Assemblée nationale. Although the secretariat is elected for a year in the Assemblée nationale, tradition dictates that the same team is renewed for the five years of the legislature. In both chambers, the secretariat reflects the balance of power in the house.

[20] This can happen in case of resignation (eg de Gaulle in 1969) or death (eg Pompidou in 1974).
[21] It is revealing that this role was not given to the Prime Minister by the authors of the constitution.
[22] The *bureau* of the Assemblée nationale is composed of: the president, 6 vice-presidents, 3 *questeurs* and 12 secretaries.
[23] The *bureau* of the Sénat is composed of: the president, 8 vice-presidents, 3 *questeurs* and 14 secretaries.

The Conference of the Presidents

The conference of the presidents is so called as it is composed of the president of the house, the vice-presidents, the presidents of each permanent committee, the president of the committee for European affairs, the president of each parliamentary party and the general reporter of the finance committee. In short, the most influential Members of the house sit on this committee.

The conference of the presidents meets weekly in each house and plans the work of the house and the timing of the sittings. The reform of July 2008 has changed the manner in which the agenda of each house is determined and therefore the role and importance of the conference of the presidents has increased considerably. The new drafting of article 48 of the constitution specifies that each house is responsible for determining its agenda. When the constitution was originally drafted, article 48 was a clear example of the 'rationalisation' of parliamentary work: priority was given to the bills chosen by the Government. Each house had little autonomy in the organisation of its legislative work as little time was left for the residual agenda.

Political groups

Political groups were given recognition by the reform of July 2008 in article 51-1 of the constitution. In each house, the main political parties organise themselves into parliamentary parties called political groups. Each group must issue a political manifesto endorsed by all its members and have a minimum membership: 20 in the Assemblée nationale and 15 in the Sénat. At present, there are four parliamentary parties in the Assemblée nationale and five in the Sénat.

In fact, political groups have always participated actively in the work of the house and benefit from a number of prerogatives and powers: for instance, the president of each political group belongs to the 'conference of the presidents', the right to speak during parliamentary debate is largely reserved to political groups, and political groups put forward names for membership of parliamentary committees. Furthermore, the new article 51-1 has created the categories of opposition and minority parliamentary parties, and states that each house grants them specific rights. Indeed, the constitution itself indicates in article 48 § 5 that opposition and minority political groups determine freely the agenda of the house one day a month. Finally, the new article 50-1 allows a political group to demand that the government explain itself on a specific question. This explanation can be followed by a debate and a vote, but it cannot be used to trigger a vote of confidence.

Legislative committees

Parliamentary committees of the fourth Republic were held partly responsible for the parliamentary dysfunctions of this regime. Permanent committees were specialised and powerful and intervened frequently in the work and decisions of government departments. Not only did this compromise the efficiency of public administration but it contributed to increasing the imbalance of power to the detriment of the Executive. With this in mind, the authors of the 1958 constitution decided that a 'rationalisation' of the Parliament's committee system was needed if political practices were to be reformed successfully. As a consequence, the constitution created a very restrictive system of parliamentary committees. This has only been alleviated marginally by the constitutional reform of July 2008.

Article 43 of the constitution distinguishes between two types of committee: temporary and permanent ones. The authors of the constitution envisaged that most bills would be examined by a special (and temporary) legislative committee. The use of permanent committees was to be exceptional and originally the constitution limited their number to six. In practice, temporary committees are rarely created[24] and the great majority of bills are entrusted to one of the permanent committees. Indeed, the creation of a new committee for each bill is not a rational use of Parliament's time and resources. Since the 1990s, special legislative committees have been resorted to when the bill proved important, complex, controversial and required the expertise of a number of permanent committees.[25]

Of late, the limitation to six permanent committees has impacted negatively on the work of Parliament, which has had to deal with an ever-growing number of bills. Also, permanent committees have gone beyond their strict constitutional mandate and increasingly assess public policies within their remit. The limitations to six permanent committees

---

[24] Only 3% of bills are examined by a special legislative committee. Between 1958 and 2004, only 123 special legislative committees had been set up, with two-thirds of these in the Assemblée Nationale; see P Jan, *Les assemblées parlementaires françaises* (Paris, *La Documentation française*, 2006) 66.

[25] For instance, a special committee was convened in the Assemblée nationale for the bill on bio-ethics in October 2010.

compromised the quality of their legislative work and impeded the evolution of their role.

To circumvent these constitutional limitations, each house has resorted to creating other parliamentary structures: parliamentary missions, parliamentary delegations etc. For instance, in view of the growth of Community legislation, both houses had wished to create a separate committee for European affairs, but were not able to set up a permanent committee until the reform of July 2008.[26]

Members of Parliament had also long advocated and campaigned for a constitutional revision to increase the number of permanent committees. The reform of July 2008 has raised the number of permanent committees to eight and has transformed the delegation for the European Union into an additional permanent committee. Although Members of Parliament wanted the number of permanent committees to be increased to 10, the Government managed to convince a majority that the lower figure would be sufficient. One cannot help but feel that this change falls short of what was needed. The demand for 10 permanent committees was not excessive if one considers that many parliaments in Europe have a much higher number of permanent committees.[27]

The permanent committees are divided along similar lines in both chambers. In the Assemblée nationale, the eight committees are: foreign affairs, cultural affairs, social affairs, economic affairs, legal affairs, finance, defence and sustainable development. In the Sénat, the second chamber has not increased the number of its permanent committees from six to eight; these have the following remit: foreign affairs, defence and the army, cultural affairs, economic affairs and sustainable development, social affairs, legal affairs and finance.

Finally, the membership of permanent committees, which is large (with a maximum of 73 in the Assemblée nationale and an average of 50 in the Sénat), respects the political balance of each house. It is renewed annually for the Assemblée nationale and every three years for

---

[26] See S Boyron, 'The "new" French Constitution and the European Union' (2008–9) 11 *Cambridge Yearbook of European Legal Studies* 321.

[27] See the comparative data put forward by the Balladur report (n 5) p 46. Interestingly, some commentators warn that a notable increase in the number of committees may create its own problems; see P Türk, 'Le statut des commissions permanentes: une évolution sans révolution' in J-P Camby, P Fraisseix and J Gicquel (eds), *La révision de 2008: une nouvelle constitution?* (Paris, Librairie générale de droit et de jurisprudence, 2011) 210.

the Sénat. Every Member of Parliament is necessarily a member of one permanent committee.

Time Management

The most controversial provisions to be adopted in the 1958 constitution must surely be the limitations originally imposed on the timing of parliamentary work: the French Parliament could not decide freely when to sit nor could each house really establish its own agenda. Although the principle of separation of powers should dictate that Parliament organises the timing of its work independently, the French constitution erected formidable obstacles in this regard. Successive constitutional reforms have tended to return some autonomy to Parliament in this matter, but there is still some way to go.

The Parliamentary Sitting

According to articles 28, 29 and 30 of the constitution, there are three categories of parliamentary sittings: ordinary, extraordinary and compulsory.

Ordinary Sitting

In France, according to the 1958 constitution, Parliament does not decide when it sits during the year. The constitution has always made such a determination and although some improvements have been made with the constitutional revision of August 1995, the situation is still not optimal.

Originally, article 28 of the constitution specified that Parliament could only sit during two periods in the year. The first ordinary sitting would start on 2 October (or on the first working day thereafter) and would last a maximum of 80 days and the second would start on 2 April (or on the first working day thereafter) and would last a maximum of 90 days. This provision had devastating effect: the first sitting was invariably dedicated to the discussion and adoption of the budget and little other parliamentary work was being achieved beyond that. Then, Parliament would rise and only resume its work in spring. Not only was the adoption of legislation in abeyance, but little control of the Executive took place during these winter months. Parliament was not convened during one of the most financially and economically active times of the year. In a parliamentary democracy, this seemed at best absurd and at worst dangerous. Furthermore, the period covered by the ordinary sitting was not long enough to complete all parliamentary work and by the end of June an extraordinary sitting was convened systematically every year.

Numerous presidents of house requested that the ordinary sitting be altered so as to cover the whole year (with a recess during the summer months). This reform was finally achieved in 1995. Since the constitutional reform of August 1995, the French Parliament can sit from the first working day of October to the last working day of June. This long-awaited reform created an annual parliamentary sitting of nine months. Paradoxically, the total number of days that the Parliament can sit has been reduced by the 1995 reform to a maximum of 120 days – a reduction of 50 days from the previous arrangement. This reduction aimed to contain and even curb the increase in legislation. In practice, the single parliamentary sitting has not had the effects hoped; many believe it to be responsible for the increase in legislation witnessed over the last decade. Also, the practices which existed prior to 1995 have returned: long night sessions[28] and extraordinary sittings in July[29] are still common. Both presidents of house were committed to addressing these issues and the Government promised to reduce the amount of legislation introduced in Parliament, but so far little has happened. On a positive note, since the reform of August 1995, the Assemblée nationale has devoted more time than before to the control of the Government.[30]

Extraordinary Sitting

The issues discussed above show that the Government does not hesitate to convene an extraordinary sitting when required. According to articles 29 and 30 of the constitution, the Prime Minister or the majority of *députés* of the Assemblée nationale can request an extraordinary sitting. There are two conditions: the sitting must be on a predetermined agenda and cannot last longer than 12 days.

---

[28] For instance, in October 1998, members of the Assemblée nationale sat 200 hours, an average of 50 hours of plenary debate a week.

[29] An extraordinary sitting was also convened on 6ᵗ September 2011 to discuss and adopt the financial discharge law. This implemented the agreement reached on 21st July 2011 by the governments of the Eurozone to ease the Greek financial crisis.

[30] See M Ameller, 'Article 28' in F Luchaire, G Conac and X Prétot (eds), *La constitution de la République française*, 3rd edn (Paris, Economica, 2009) 822.

One would have thought that the limitations in place were sufficient to protect the Executive against possible abuses. However, as the sessions are opened and closed by a decision of the President of the Republic, successive Presidents of the Republic have regarded this as a discretionary power. In 1960 De Gaulle refused to convene an extraordinary sitting although it was formally requested by a majority of the Assemblée nationale and in 1987, during the first period of cohabitation, Mitterrand refused such a request by Chirac, then Prime Minister. Prior to the revision of August 1995, 60 extraordinary sittings had been convened with one only at the request of the Assemblée nationale.

Compulsory Sitting

The constitution requires that in circumstances when democracy may be particularly vulnerable, Parliament sits as of right. Parliament must be convened when the emergency powers of article 16 are in use and also immediately following an election triggered by a dissolution of the Assemblée nationale (art 12 § 3). Finally, if not in session, the Parliament is recalled to hear a message of the President of the Republic (art 18 § 3).

Regaining Control of its Agenda

Originally, article 48 specified that the Government had priority when drawing up the agenda of both houses: this was another example of the rationalisation of Parliament. Again the organisation of the daily work of Parliament was in the hands of the Government with only the possibility for each house to decide on the residual agenda. This provision was criticised for its implications concerning the autonomy of Parliament; it was particularly detrimental with regard to the control of the Government's decisions and policies.

When the constitution was amended to allow a single parliamentary sitting in 1995, Members of Parliament argued and campaigned for a change of the rules relating to the agenda. Both houses sponsored amendments to article 48 and a paragraph was added to the original provision: each house was given the freedom to decide on its agenda one day a month. This option has been fully utilised by both chambers and in practice the time devolved to government bills has been reduced by more than a strict application of the reform required.

Still, for many, the amendment of August 1995 was too limited; calls for Parliament to decide freely on its agenda were heard repeatedly. By

2008, it had become clear that Parliament needed to be given more autonomy. To achieve this, article 48 was completely redrafted to give to each house a larger degree of control. The first paragraph now specifies that the agenda is the responsibility of each house. The new provision creates a complex system of various agendas and priorities but begins by stating that two weeks of sitting out of four are reserved by priority to the Government. In addition, article 48 § 3 lists the texts or debates that must be put on the agenda when required by the Government: constitutional bills, organic bills, the annual budget, the social security budget, the bills adopted by the other house, and debates regarding a state of emergency, a state of siege or a declaration of war.

The combination of these two provisions recognises a degree of control over the agenda by the Government. However, the remaining paragraphs of article 48 contain noteworthy innovations aiming to strengthen the function of control of the Parliament: in paragraph 4, it directs that one week in four must be reserved to the 'monitoring of Government action and to the assessment of public policies'. This provision attempts to curb a tendency of Parliament to concentrate too much of its time on the legislative function. Two other provisions strengthen the mission of control: in paragraph 5, one day a month is reserved to opposition parties and in paragraph 6, one day a week is reserved to the organisation of Government's question time. While this last requirement has been in the constitution since 1958, the revision of July 2008 extends it to extraordinary sittings.

Although the constitution continues to recognise important prerogatives to the Government and still directs each house as to the use of its parliamentary agenda, there is no doubt that the new drafting of article 48 has changed the working environment of each house for the better. Indeed, it contributes to the creation of a fairer institutional balance.

THE CONSTITUTIONAL STATUS OF MEMBERS OF PARLIAMENT

Constitutions often try to reconcile two considerations when it comes to Members of Parliament. On the one hand, most parliamentary democracies impose certain limitations on Members of Parliament to ensure that they fulfil their mandate with the necessary integrity, commitment and dignity and on the other hand, provision is also made for their protection. It would be too easy to compromise the functioning of parliamentary democracies by obstructing Members of Parliament or the performance of their duties.

The Protection of Members of Parliament

According to article 26 of the constitution, both the individual freedom and freedom of expression of Members of Parliament receive protection. Indeed, as representatives of the sovereign Nation, they need these freedoms to perform their duties effectively.

Beyond their personal protection, the constitution ensures their financial independence.

The Privilege of Members of Parliament

According to article 26 of the constitution, Members of Parliament cannot be held liable for any action performed or opinion expressed pursuant to their parliamentary duties. For instance, they cannot be sued for libel for opinions expressed during parliamentary debates. This strong immunity is necessary to allow Members to express themselves in Parliament without fear of retaliation from an arbitrary Government or a vengeful citizen.

This privilege covers all activities within the legislative chamber itself, and also everything outside of Parliament that is done or said pursuant to parliamentary business (reports, missions etc). Members of Parliament remain responsible for their private actions and any actions which can be separated from their parliamentary duties: public meetings, press conferences, television interviews etc.[31]

The Immunity of Members of Parliament

As a matter of principle, Members of Parliament should not be removed from Parliament before the end of their mandate. Accordingly, article 26 of the constitution regulates strictly the manner in which the criminal liability of Members of Parliament can be triggered. This protection has been in place since 1789 and concerns facts or events which are not

[31] A Member of Parliament can be prosecuted for libel on the basis of a newspaper interview, even when he/she aimed to discuss a parliamentary report for which he/she was responsible. (eg C cass 30 September 2003, *Jean-Pierre B, Stakim B & Sté. I*).

related to parliamentary business. The mechanisms to ensure the respect of this immunity were altered during the constitutional reform of August 1995. Since then, no Member of Parliament can be arrested without the authorisation of the secretariat of his/her chamber.[32] Similarly, the secretariat must agree to any custodial or semi-custodial measure taken against a Member of Parliament. The house can request that detention, prosecution, custodial and semi-custodial measures be lifted until the end of the sitting. The secretariat plays no role when the culprit is caught red-handed or the prison sentence is definitive.

The Parliamentary Indemnity

As will be explained below, Members of Parliament are often required to leave their professional occupation in order to take up their seat. Consequently, they need to be compensated for this loss of earnings and paid for the work that their mandate requires. This was not really understood in revolutionary France despite the pronouncements on citizens' equality. Until the Second Republic, it was not felt necessary to provide financial support for Members of Parliament. Only the independently wealthy could envisage a political career. The revolution of 1848 reflected the demands of the working class to participate fully in the political system and resulted in the adoption of universal suffrage. This made it necessary for a system of financial compensation to be created so as to enable the less wealthy to serve as Members of Parliament too.

Financial compensation is also important to ensure the integrity of Members of Parliament. The parliamentary indemnity brings a degree of financial independence and makes Members less susceptible to bribes and corruption. Since 1938 the indemnity has been calculated by reference to the salary scale of top civil servants.[33]

The Incompatibilities

The activity of Members of Parliament is also restricted, essentially to protect the legitimacy of their office and to avoid abuses and corruption.

---

[32] Before the constitutional reform of 4 August 1995, the house had to grant this authorisation.
[33] See the organic law of 13 December 1958.

To this end, Members are required to choose between different electoral mandates or between their parliamentary mandate and other activities (professional, commercial etc) which might compromise the performance of their duties.

The Professional Incompatibilities

As required by article 25 of the constitution, the electoral code lists the occupations strictly prohibited for Members of Parliament: top management positions in companies floated on the financial market, or public procurement and public works companies under contract with the State/public body. In these cases, conflicts of interest may arise between the public and private interests of the Member of Parliament. Finally, even though not all professions are systematically prohibited, in practice, combining a parliamentary mandate with a full-time occupation is difficult. Furthermore, it is strictly prohibited for all Members of Parliament to fulfil some public functions: they cannot be a member of the Government, Civil Service, Conseil constitutionnel or Social, Economic and Environmental Council or hold a top management position in a public corporation. Only two categories of civil servants are allowed to combine their professional activity with a parliamentary mandate: university professors and ministers of religion living in Alsace and Moselle.[34]

Finally, according to article 23 of the constitution, Members of Parliament cannot be in Government. If they accept a government position, they must vacate their parliamentary seat. Originally, this separation of personnel was conceived as a remedy for the ministerial instability of the previous regime. However, since the reform of July 2008, on leaving the Government, a Member will be able to return to his/her parliamentary seat.[35]

The Conseil constitutionnel is charged with deciding whether there is an incompatibility between the parliamentary mandate and the specific occupation of the Member of Parliament. If the Conseil finds that there is one, the Member of Parliament must choose between his/her seat and the continuation of the professional activity concerned.

---

[34] Ministers of religion living in Alsace and Moselle can sit in Parliament because of a concordat in effect in these regions.

[35] See chapter 3.

More recently, both houses have been concerned with the issues arising from the conflict of Members' interests. In the Assemblée nationale,
it has been proposed that a declaration of interests be submitted to the
secretariat by all *députés* at the start of their mandate. A code of deontol-
ogy has been drafted and a position to ensure its enforcement has been
created.[36] The Sénat made similar commitments but went further and
proposed that an independent authority be created to ensure the
enforcement of these new rules.

The Two Mandates Restriction

Since 1985[37] the trend has been to prohibit French politicians from
holding too many electoral mandates concomitantly. As a result of this,
Members are only allowed to keep two electoral mandates and are
required to make a choice on entering Parliament. The rule was adopted
to curb past excesses; many politicians hoarded a great number of mandates (eg mayor of a town, president of the regional council, Member
of the French Parliament and MEP). Not only was this controversial in
itself, as it tended to concentrate elected positions in the hands of a
small elite, but it created dysfunctions in Parliament. Absenteeism was
rife and important legislation was often debated with only a handful of
députés or *sénateurs* present. This did nothing to enhance the image of
politicians and damaged considerably the standing of Parliament.
Unfortunately, absenteeism in Parliament is still endemic and commentators fear that it may be a formidable obstacle to the renewal of the
function of control.[38]

Still, the reform met with a strong resistance from politicians and
more particularly from the *sénateurs*. They argued that their position
should be differentiated as they represent territorial governments: their
local government mandates provide them with first-hand knowledge
and experience and help them perform their parliamentary office.

[36] Emeritus Professor Gicquel was appointed to that position on 15 June 2011.
[37] See the organic laws of 30 December 1985 and 5 April 2000.
[38] See R Dosière, 'Le contrôle ordinaire' (2010) 134 *Pouvoirs* 37. In fact, he notes
that absenteeism has increased with the week now reserved for the control of the
Government!!

PARLIAMENT'S WORK: A GREAT IMPROVEMENT

Parliaments are meant to fulfil a number of functions in a constitutional system: they vote legislation and bring the Executive to account. Overall the French Parliament fulfils these same functions, but the weight of history was such at the time of drafting the original constitution that Parliament was restricted in all its functions. However, a clear evolution in this regard has started to bear fruit.

A Matter of Definition

The original title IV of the 1958 constitution on the Parliament contained the most revealing oversight: although it contained 10 provisions, no definition of the role of the legislative branch was to be found therein. This is surprising (not to say suspicious) considering that the constitution included a definition of the role of all the actors of the Executive branch. Obviously, it was not judged necessary to give a constitutional definition of the work of Parliament.

However, this omission may have hidden an ulterior motive: of the two functions of legislation and control, the 1958 constitution clearly favoured the former. Not only was the legislative procedure covered in great detail but article 34, which determines the jurisdiction of Parliament, stated in the first paragraph that 'the law is passed by Parliament'. While a legislative role was recognised expressly to the French Parliament, the existence of a role of scrutiny was only implicit. In fact, the legislative procedure may have imposed restrictions on the legislative freedom of both houses, but the tools for the control of the Government left a lot more to be desired.

With the evolution of the regime, the French Parliament struggled for its role and place in the institutional framework. Not only was the Government granted formidable powers to ensure the adoption of its legislation, but with the evolution of the regime, the function of control withered. Soon, the role and legitimacy of the French Parliament was questioned and commentators and politicians were calling for a renewal of the legislative branch.

The movement gained momentum and by 1993, the Vedel committee recommended (among other things) that the function and role of

Parliament be included in the constitution. However, the reform of August 1995 did not do this. With the reform of July 2008, it was felt that the time had finally come to spell out the functions of a modern parliament. It was hoped that it would provide the institution with the necessary impetus to transform itself. To this effect, article 24 of the constitution was amended. In the first paragraph, it lists the three functions of the French Parliament: it passes legislation, it controls Government's actions and it assesses public policies. While the first two functions are straightforward, the assessment of public policies needs to be explained in more detail. Since the 1980s Parliament has widened its conception of accountability and focused on the assessment of public policies. This aims to establish whether the legal framework, administrative structures and financial support are appropriate to achieve the public policy ends contained in the legislation. This assessment highlighted a shift in the culture of parliamentary control and may yet herald a renewal of the French Parliament.

Legislating in the French Parliament: A Gained Independence

Until recently, it was possible to argue that the French Parliament was acting somewhat at the dictation of the Government. Indeed, the Government had (and to a lesser extent still has) important powers to ensure the successful completion of the legislative procedure. However, the reform of July 2008 has improved the position of the French legislator.

Conflicting Demands

The reform of July 2008 had two aims regarding the legislative role of Parliament. First, Parliament was to regain some independence and be put on a more equal footing with the Executive. In doing so, it was believed that advantages would be drawn from it: for one thing, the legislative process would be more efficient (eg the increase of the role of permanent commissions). Both houses would spend less time passing legislation and would have more time to devote to the control of the Government. The independence of the institution was presented as a necessary condition for the required evolution of Parliament's role.

However, the Balladur committee, politicians and commentators all agreed that there was another worthy aim of the reform of July 2008: to improve on the quality of the legislation adopted by Parliament. Not only did the exponential growth of legislation alarm politicians and practitioners and baffle citizens, but the issue of the quality of the texts adopted by Parliament had become a 'crusade' of the Conseil d'Etat,[39] the Conseil constitutionnel[40] and commentators.[41] To this effect, the new mechanism for a presentation of a new bill, with its requirement for an impact assessment, was meant to contribute to this search for quality. Similarly, the new obligation to ratify expressly all the ordinances taken by the Government on the basis of a delegation provided for in article 38 should result in better texts. Finally, a better control over the agenda by both houses should deliver an improvement in the working conditions of both houses and should inevitably benefit the content of the legislation (fewer over-night debates should yield some results).

If the objectives of institutional independence and quality of output have been mostly reconciled in the reform of July 2008, one reform is indicative of tensions between the two objectives. Article 34 determines the jurisdiction of Parliament by listing the topics that are its exclusive domain.[42] If one is really determined to improve the quality rather than quantity of the legislation, one does not propose to widen the jurisdiction of article 34 further; this is only likely to result in an increase in the volume of legislation. However, the reform of July 2008 made some changes to article 34: it introduced a new topic – the freedom and plurality of the media; it widened an already existing provision – the representation of French citizens abroad; and the status of local government representatives is added to the provision which referred to the elections to the national and local assemblies. Also, article 34 gives constitutional recognition to the multiannual programming laws. Although the later change pertains to the function of financial control, it still demonstrates a trend to increase the jurisdiction of Parliament. Finally, in view of the discussion above, article 34 could have been amended further and included provisions putting down markers with regard to the quality of

---

[39] See the report of the Conseil d'Etat, 'Sécurité juridique et complexité du droit' (2005) EDCE no 57.

[40] See C cons no 2009-580 DC HADOPI 10 June 2010 and the constitutional objectives of clarity, accessibility and comprehension of legislation.

[41] See B Mathieu, *La loi*, 2nd edn (Paris, Dalloz, 2004).

[42] See chapter 2.

the legislation. However, this was not done.[43] When it came down to it, Members of Parliament may have been more concerned with strengthening their legislative power than controlling the quality of legislation.

The Right of Initiative

According to article 39 of the constitution, the right of legislative initiative belongs equally to the Prime Minister and to Members of Parliament. However, as is common in many Western democracies, the great majority of draft legislation introduced in the French Parliament originates from the Government; Government bills are called 'legislative projects' by contrast with 'legislative proposals', which are sponsored by Members of Parliament. On average only 10 per cent of all draft legislation is introduced by Members of Parliament.[44] Furthermore, only 10 per cent of these legislative proposals will survive the legislative procedure and be enacted. It is true that the right of initiative of Members of Parliament is limited by article 40 of the constitution: legislative proposals (and amendments) which increase public spending or entail a loss of revenue are prohibited. However, this cannot explain the limited use that Members of Parliament make of their right of initiative. The constitutional reform of July 2008 has attempted to redress this inequality where possible.

In reality, Members of Parliament wishing to put forward a legislative proposal were at a marked disadvantage as they seldom received the necessary technical and administrative support to draft a robust legislative proposal. Consequently, the reform of July 2008 attempted to redress this inequality: article 39 was amended to allow the president of each house to put forward a legislative proposal authored by a Member of his/her house to the Conseil d'Etat.[45] This will ensure that Members of Parliament receive the same expert advice as the Government. Hopefully, a greater number of legislative proposals will reach the statute book.

---

[43] In fact, the debates in Parliament on the reform of article 34 were not concerned at all with the quality of legislation.

[44] By contrast, Members of Parliament of the second Republic drafted 70% of all legislation.

[45] Already, the Conseil d'Etat has been consulted for a bill on simplifying the law. In fact, the opinion of the Conseil d'Etat was quoted extensively in the report of the committee. The law was adopted on 22 March 2011.

Also, the right of initiative of Parliament can be altered by the delegation of article 38: on a request by the Government, Parliament can delegate temporarily part of its jurisdiction to the Government. The delegation can only take place for a limited period of time[46] and for a clearly defined topic. The Conseil constitutionnel controls these limitations and does not allow a delegation that is not specific enough.[47] However, delegations with a wide remit are still authorised. Finally, Parliament must ratify the texts or *ordonnances* adopted on the basis of the delegation before the end of the period.

The use of article 38 is hotly debated among politicians and lawyers alike. It is often argued that governments resort to it too readily (especially since 2000)[48] and that it reduces unnecessarily the legislative prerogatives of Parliament. Criticisms also extend to the content of the legislation adopted in this way: the drafting is often found to be wanting because of the lack of parliamentary debates. In an attempt to address these issues, article 38 was amended during the revision of July 2008: all *ordonnances* need to be expressly adopted by Parliament before the end of the period of delegation. Prior to that, the authorisation could be (and often was) implicit.

The Pre-legislative Stage

According to article 39, all legislative projects must comply with two procedural requirements prior to their introduction in Parliament: Government bills must be submitted to the Conseil d'Etat for advice and they must be adopted by the Council of Ministers.

The Opinion of the Conseil d'Etat

When it comes to Government bills, the Conseil d'Etat must be consulted by the Government. Its opinion contains a detailed analysis of the draft legislation. First, it ensures that the constitution, treaties and organic laws are all respected. The case law of the Conseil constitutionnel and the permanently expanding European Union legislation makes this task increasingly onerous. Any incompatibility will be highlighted.

---

[46] In practice, the period has ranged from one month to three years depending on the topic, but the majority of the delegations are for a period of three to six months.
[47] The Conseil requires the Government to indicate to Parliament the aim of the delegation, see C cons no 2003-473 DC 26 June 2003.
[48] For instance, there were 83 *ordonnances* adopted in 2005.

Also, the Conseil d'Etat checks the quality of the legislative drafting: in formal terms, it looks at the structure, the style and the clarity of the text. Then, the Conseil d'Etat goes further and analyses the merits of the draft legislation. It will question the need for new legislation when a change in administrative practice would be sufficient. Also, the Conseil reminds the Government regularly that general statements devoid of normative effect should be avoided and that the creation of new legal concepts should be driven by legal necessity and not fashion. In its opinion, the Conseil d'Etat drafts its version of the text with an explanation for the changes. If the Conseil has serious objections to the draft legislation, it can reject it without even submitting a version of its own. This is not a frequent occurrence.

On receiving the draft of the Conseil d'Etat, the Government has a choice: it can accept the text of the Conseil or keep its original draft. The Government cannot, however, pick and mix between the two versions. This is important as the Government tends to follow the opinion of the Conseil d'Etat on issues of legality and constitutionality. In the event that the Government amends its original draft after consulting the Conseil d'Etat, the draft needs to be submitted anew.[49] The Council of Ministers has the full opinion of the Conseil d'Etat to assess the bill adequately. This opinion is not made public.

The Council Of Ministers

Once a final text is agreed, it is put on part A of the agenda of the Council of Ministers.[50] During the Council of Ministers, the minister responsible for the bill will be called to defend his/her text. Once adopted, it can be introduced in one of the houses of Parliament.

The Introduction of Legislation in Parliament

Generally, legislative projects can be introduced in either house: it depends mostly on their workload. However, there are exceptions: according to article 39, finance bills and social security financing bills must be introduced in the Assemblée nationale, while bills concerned with the organisation of territorial government must be introduced in

---

[49] If not, the Conseil Constitutionnel will annul the relevant provisions; see C cons no 2003-468 DC, 3 April 2003, elections of MEPs and regional councillors.

[50] Part A of the agenda concerns items which have the support of the President of the Republic and require little discussion.

the Sénat. Finally, proposals of Members of Parliament must be introduced in the house to which they belong.

Furthermore, two new paragraphs were introduced into article 39 by the constitutional revision of July 2008. Politicians and commentators expressed misgivings with regard to the massive growth of legislation in France. Consequently, a new stage was added to the legislative process: the presentation. Prior to being formally introduced, bills must comply with the requirement for presentation and in particular, the Government must submit an in-depth impact study. According to the organic law of 15 April 2009, this study describes the aims of the legislation, presents the reasons for resorting to a new Act of Parliament, reviews the state of law, studies the integration of the bill with European Union law, evaluates its economic, social, financial and environmental implications, and specifies the necessary implementation legislation and its consequences. No government bill can be formally introduced without it. If, in one house, the conference of the presidents finds that the requirements were not adhered to, it can refuse to put the bill on the agenda. Any disagreement between the house and the Government on this point can be referred to the Conseil constitutionnel by the Prime Minister or by the president of the house. This new procedure gives the possibility to challenge the right of legislative initiative of the Government and exemplifies the evolution that the reform of July 2008 is trying to trigger.

The Committee Stage

Once a legislative proposal or project is handed over to the *bureau* of either chamber and, in the case of a project, its presentation is accepted by the conference of the presidents, it is sent directly to one of the permanent committees for examination. Prior to the reform of July 2008, the work in committee was already crucial.[51] With the constitutional reform, the committee stage has become the linchpin of the legislative process: the amended article 42 of the constitution now provides that the plenary will debate the version of the bill adopted in committee (rather than the original text submitted by the Government). This is a welcome change: not only does the reform increase the autonomy of

---

[51] Research shows that amendments adopted in committee represented the largest category of amendments adopted in plenary, See J-L Hérin, 'Article 44' in F Luchaire, G Conac and X Prétot (eds) (n 30) 1064.

Parliament but it helps clarify and rationalise greatly the legislative work of each house, particularly with regard to amendments. For one thing, the careful work of the committees is now properly harnessed.

On reception, the committee appoints a reporter; he/she is responsible for drafting the report on the bill and will be speaking to the report in the plenary. The committee begins by organising a series of hearings to understand the aims of the legislation and the context in which it will operate. The committee hears the government minister or the Member of Parliament responsible for the text and any experts or interest groups it chooses. Following the reform of July 2008, the relevant minister is present in committee throughout its work.

The committee then analyses each provision in detail and all the amendments that have been put forward at this stage. Once provisions and amendments have been examined, the report and the resulting text are drafted and are submitted to the committee (the new draft is annexed to the report). Once adopted by the committee, the report is printed and distributed.

However, in view of the endemic growth of the number of amendments debated and the changes described above, the rules relating to the right of amendment needed to be overhauled. While the new role of the committees grants more autonomy to Parliament, it may not help reduce the unsustainable numbers of amendments witnessed in the Assemblée nationale since 1981,[52] nor address the practices of obstruction by the opposition.[53] While article 44 § 2 remains unchanged and prescribes that the Government can oppose any amendment that has not been submitted to the committee, it is rarely used. Consequently, article 44 § 1 was amended to require that an organic law determined the exercise of the right of amendment.

The organic law of 15 April 2009 adopted a liberal solution: in addition to amendments being submitted to the committee, Members of Parliament are free to submit amendments for discussion in the plenary until the start of the debate. To ensure that this right does not degener-

---

[52]   During the 11th legislature (1997–2002) 50,851 amendments were put forward in the Assemblée nationale, with only 16,800 adopted and during the 12th legislature (2002–2007), the number of amendments put forward in the Assemblée nationale rose to 243,000.

[53]   From time to time, the opposition would flood committees with amendments, so as to bring the legislative process to a standstill. In September 2006, during the debate on the energy bill, over 100,000 amendments were received.

ate, the organic law introduces two mechanisms to frame the debate in plenary: the simplified legislative procedure[54] and the programmed legislative time.[55] So far, these reforms, which have been put to good use in the Assemblée nationale, have proved successful: obstruction has mostly disappeared and the number of amendments has returned to a normal level.[56]

The Agenda

In the past many legislative proposals failed to proceed further than the committee stage. Finding time for them on the agenda was difficult. However, with the reform of article 48, each house has regained some control over its agenda and more legislative proposals are already tabled, debated and adopted. In fact, the reform is likely to have a notable impact as the previous reform of August 1995, which allowed each chamber to control its agenda one day a month, had led to a clear rise in the number of successful legislative proposals.[57]

The reform of July 2008 has also been innovative when it comes to the timing of the plenary: according to article 42, draft legislation can only be tabled for debate in plenary after a period of six weeks from its introduction in the house. Similarly, draft legislation can only be tabled for debate in plenary after a period of four weeks from the time of its transmission by the other chamber. These time-management provisions aim to strengthen the position and work of committees: they are assured a minimum time to examine and report on the draft legislation. Their work is not to be curtailed by unrealistic timetabling and the pressure of a looming plenary. Again, the concern for better legislation is at the root of this change.

[54] According to article 16, the right of amendment is limited to the committee and the Government during the debate in plenary of a bill.
[55] According to article 18, a bill is debated in plenary with a strict timetable. When time has run out, amendments are put to the vote without any debate.
[56] See the speech given by Accoyer, president of the Assemblée nationale, on 13 January 2011 regarding a round-table of the *Association française du droit constitutionnel*, www.assemblee-nationale.fr/13/dpr/dpr0089.asp#P3_0.
[57] With the 1995 reform, the number of legislative proposals had risen from 10% to 20%.

The Debate in Plenary

The debate in plenary is divided into two parts: the general debate and then the detailed discussion of each provision and amendments. One must remember, however, that the debate may follow the simplified legislative procedure or follow a strict timetable.

The general debate aims to address the aims, philosophy and content of the draft legislation. The minister or Member of Parliament sponsoring the bill will speak first. Then will follow the reporter of the legislative committee and a speaker for each political group.[58]

At the end of the general debate, a number of motions can be put to the vote to strike out the draft legislation. There are three such motions: the prohibition of financial incidence of article 40, the lack of jurisdiction of article 41 and the return to committee (provided for by the regulations of both houses). These are often used by the opposition to delay the legislative process but they rarely succeed and a detailed discussion of the draft legislation ensues: the text is gone through clause by clause and amendment by amendment with the representative of the Government, the reporter of the committee and the author of the amendment intervening briefly. A vote is taken on each clause and on each amendment. Finally, a general vote is taken on the whole text. Once adopted, the draft legislation is forwarded to the other house, where it is passed in the same way.

Furthermore, to ensure that the text is adopted without delays, article 44 § 3 gives the Government the power to demand that a house adopt the draft legislation in whole or in part with the sole amendments agreed to by the Government. This procedure, which is called the 'blocked vote', is strongly resented by Members of Parliament as it leaves them with little option: the chamber either accepts the Government's text or runs the risk of not adopting any text at all. Nowadays, the provision is only used exceptionally.

Agreement between the Two Chambers: The Three Stages

For a bill to be adopted it must be done in identical terms by both chambers. However, brokering an agreement can be a long and protracted business. To this effect, article 45 of the constitution provides the Government with ways to accelerate the adoption of a final text.

---

[58] The time allotted to each political group is decided by the conference of the presidents.

In case of disagreement between the two houses, the Government has three options. It can leave the Parliament alone and the text will 'shuttle' between the two chambers until the disagreement it resolved.[59] Secondly, the Government can ask the Assemblée nationale to adopt the text in a final reading after two readings in each chamber. Finally,[60] it is possible for the Government to convene an optional conciliation committee according to article 45 § 2. The committee is composed of seven Members of each chamber, a small number to facilitate negotiations. Negotiations in the conciliation committee are often successful and a compromise found. If a drafting is agreed, it is submitted for approval to both chambers; at this late stage, further amendments can only be made with the approval of the Government. Finally, if no agreement is reached in the conciliation committee or if the draft is rejected by either or both chambers, the Government can ask the Assemblée nationale to adopt the text in a final reading. When doing so, the Government can choose either the last text voted by the Assemblée nationale or the text agreed to in conciliation.

Agreement with the Government

Tensions between the Government and the parliamentary majority can be disruptive too. Until recently, the French Government had at its disposal such an array of weapons that it did not need to coax, threat or negotiate much. A disagreement with the Sénat is less important as the Government can always ask the Assemblée nationale to adopt the text in a final reading and in effect bypass the second chamber (see article 45 § 4). However, a political impasse with the Assemblée nationale may force the Government to resort to article 49 § 3 of the constitution. As explained in chapter three, the provision combines fiendishly the adoption of legislation with ministerial responsibility. This most powerful weapon was extremely controversial, especially as successive governments have not hesitated to use it.[61] Indeed, a simple threat was often enough to resolve any disagreements with the Assemblée nationale.

---

[59] This is canvassed in article 45 § 1 of the constitution.

[60] If the Government declares the urgency of the adoption of the text, the number of readings drops to one in each chamber.

[61] Article 49 § 3 has been used 82 times since the beginning of the fifth Republic. On 15 December 1989 the Socialist Prime Minister, Rocard, used it three times to facilitate the adoption of three different pieces of legislation before the Christmas recess.

Unsurprisingly, the reform of July 2008 has limited the remit of article 49 § 3 considerably: according to the new drafting, the provision can only be used for the adoption of a finance bill, a social security financing bill and for one other bill per year. This will foster a more exceptional and therefore more acceptable use of article 49 § 3.[62]

A Better Scrutiny of the Executive

Traditionally, the scrutiny of the Executive was undertaken in Parliament with the help of three mechanisms: questions in the house, investigations by committees and vote of confidence. As there were considerable problems with the scrutiny of the Government during the fourth Republic,[63] the authors of the 1958 constitution spared no thought on improving the traditional methods of parliamentary scrutiny. They only sought to restrict it.

However, with the evolution of the constitution came the need to increase the scrutiny of the Executive. The demand by Parliament for a better scrutiny of the Government's activity became more pressing with the growing integration of the European Union and the financial difficulties of the social security system. However, it was soon clear that little could be achieved outside a constitutional reform. To this effect, the reform of July 2008 has created an environment more favourable to the control of the Government's activity: it sets aside parliamentary time, adds a few weapons to the Parliament's arsenal and increases the Parliament's existing powers of control. This goes a long way to strengthening a growing culture of parliamentary control.

Creating a Culture of Control and Assessment

'Culture' is a concept with a definite meaning: it describes the tradition, customs, morals, knowledge, belief system, language etc of a community. The concept is not referred to randomly: in the last two decades, the French Parliament has seen the emergence of a new culture of con-

---

[62] Some commentators expressed their concern at the limitations imposed on the use of this provision: see M Ameller, P Jan and J Gicquel, 'Trois voix sur l'article 49, alinéa 3' in J-P Camby, P Fraisseix and J Gicquel (eds) (n 27) 277.

[63] Traditionally, parliamentary questions were often followed by a vote of confidence; many governments of the third and fourth Republic fell in this way.

trol and assessment. This change expressed itself in two ways: control came to be regarded as equally important as legislation and parliamentary control underwent a process of normalisation. Both changes combined together to engineer a real cultural shift.

Prior to 1958, Parliament expressed its opinion and control by the common use of an extraordinary tool: it withdrew its confidence and brought governments down repeatedly. It was an impossibly narrow and rather 'final' understanding of the mission of control. Questions and debates in Parliament would often lead to the resignation of the government in place. What should have been an extraordinary method of control became all too common, with the consequences that have been explained in earlier chapters. The constitution of the fifth Republic and the subsequent evolution of the regime completely eradicated this conception of control, but in doing so, it also destroyed the cultural foundations for the very notion of parliamentary control. From 1962, the meagre parliamentary tools and their use did little to bring governments to account; the function of control seemed in an impasse and condemned to remain there.

In the last two decades, the growth of the European Union, the deficit of the social security budget and the waning legitimacy of the regime resulted in a major culture shift. A new conception of parliamentary control has emerged: it resorts to more ordinary tools, aims to be less adversarial, tends to focus on information gathering and marks a continuation of the legislative function of Parliament. The aim is no longer to bring the Government down but to check on the implementation of its policies and establish an objective benchmark to assess the effectiveness of its reforms. If the findings require them, recommendations for change are made at legislative and policy levels. The function of control is now inscribed in a logic of continuity: with the adequate information, it aims to shape decision making.

In fact, this new culture has been recognised by the new drafting of article 24: in addition to the legislative function, Parliament controls Government's actions and assesses public policies. The reform of July 2008 seeks to amplify and further engineer this cultural change in both houses of Parliament. It aims to alter the political habits of Members of Parliament by transforming their environment. To this effect, the reform increased the tools at the disposal of each house, elevated the opposition into a new and separate community – the purpose of which is to nurture this culture of control – created new lines of communication and expression of this 'ordinary accountability' and granted Parliament new powers of control. The combination of all these should help the new culture of control to take root and flourish.

Breathing New Life into Old Tools

In parliamentary democracy, parliamentary questions and investigations by committees are traditionally used to bring the governments to account. While their use was restricted in the original constitution, their importance has grown as a result of practices, constitutional conventions and successive constitutional reforms.

Parliamentary Questions: A More Solid Constitutional Foundation

While most constitutions recognised two types of questions: written and oral, the 1958 constitution does not mention the possibility of putting written questions to the Government. Oral questions were always provided for but the original system has required some improvements.

Written Questions

In France, written questions were established by constitutional conventions and tradition. On this point, the 1958 constitution is no different. Written questions are provided for in the regulations of both houses of Parliament and the Government replies fully, but often with some delay. According to Parliament's customary rules and practices, written questions must be answered within a month. If the minister or government department is unable to provide an answer by the deadline, another month can be granted. However, the increase in written questions has required the adoption of a 'signalling procedure': every week, the president of each political group identifies among the unanswered questions those which take priority. They will be answered within a strict 10-day time limit. Generally, written questions elicit detailed information for the benefit of a Member of Parliament or his/her constituents, rather than contributing to the strict control of the Government.[64] A great many questions aim to clarify the meaning of a law or regulation.

---

[64] There are exceptions though: see the use of written questions in the crusade lead by Dosière with regard to the budget of the Presidency, for instance.

Re-inventing Question Time

The constitution always contained provision for parliamentary questions but the system was flawed and met with little success. Consequently, in 1974, a new system of parliamentary questions was introduced in the Assemblée nationale on the initiative of the newly elected President of the Republic, Giscard d'Estaing. Until the reform of August 1995, this system had a conventional basis only (article 48 § 6). Nowadays, in the Assemblée nationale, a session of 'questions to the Government' is organised on Tuesdays and Wednesdays for one hour. Members of the majority and opposition take turns to ask their questions. The questions are not communicated to the Government in advance; only the list of the ministers who are required to attend is provided. The author of the question and the minister have two minutes each.

In 1982 the system was copied by the Sénat. It organises its question time twice monthly on Thursdays. The time is divided proportionately between political groups. Again the author of the question and the minister have two minutes each.

The reform of July 2008 has altered the system of questions in two ways. First, the remit of oral questions has been extended; article 48 § 5 requires that a session of questions to the Government be organised in both houses during extraordinary sittings. Furthermore, with the allocation of one week a month to the control of the Government, all oral questions, with the exception of the questions to the Government, have been moved to that week.

The Changing Role of Committees

For historical reasons, the 1958 constitution had strongly marginalised committees as an instrument of control. Nowadays, constitutional change and constitutional reform are combining to transform the role of committees in the French Parliament.

Permanent 'Legislative' Committees

Originally, the six permanent committees were meant to confine themselves to legislative work, but research has shown that in reality they have gradually undertaken more activities of control. Committees do not limit themselves to the examination of the legislative text, but they investigate its environment and impact and check on its implementation. Also, in the course of this work, committees need to hear ministers regularly. Consequently, committees ensure that Parliament is informed on matters within their remit. Soon, they came to participate in the control of the Government's activity.

In fact, a law of 14 June 1996 took note of this and strengthened the investigative powers of permanent committees. Since then, permanent committees can call before them anyone they wish; also, they can be granted, for sixth months, powers of investigation equal to those of committees of inquiry. This allows them to conduct specific investigations or fact-finding missions when a topic or public policy is particularly relevant to their remit. The increase of permanent committees from six to eight was indeed meant to help strengthen and deepen their activity of control.

The Constitutional Recognition of Committees of Inquiry

Originally, the 1958 constitution did not include any committee of inquiry. They were introduced by the organic law of 17 November 1958. Committees of inquiry were finally given constitutional recognition in the reform of July 2008. A new article 51-2 specifies that committees of inquiry can be created in either house to collect information with a view to fulfilling the functions of assessment and control of the Parliament.

Committees of inquiry are created by resolution of the house. Proposals for the creation of a committee of inquiry are examined first by the relevant permanent committee. Once a creation is approved, the committee of inquiry will have 30 members in the Assemblée nationale and 21 in the Sénat. The membership reflects the balance of power in the house.

Committees of inquiry are always temporary – created for a maximum period of six months. Nowadays, they benefit from extensive powers of investigation. The reporter of a committee of inquiry can investigate government departments in person and obtain direct access to their records. Anyone called before a committee of inquiry must appear or risk criminal prosecution. Similar penalties apply if access to documents is refused. Committees cannot investigate facts which are the subject of legal proceedings.

In the past, committees of inquiry have met with some criticisms: they were accused of having too few powers, which resulted in incomplete investigations and poor reports. Also, their recommendations were rarely implemented and soon out of date. However, this picture is no longer accurate; in fact, they are resorted to with increasing frequency in both houses.[65]

Parliamentary Delegations, Missions and Offices and the Assessment Committee of Public Policies

The limitation with regard to the number of permanent committees has had an undesirable impact on the structural organisation of each house: beside the temporary and permanent committees other structures have flourished such as delegations, missions, offices or working groups. These may not have any constitutional basis but they establish long-term, albeit flexible, structures to help with the function of control in a specific domain. In fact, when both houses desired in the 1970s to establish a dedicated structure to supervise the work of the European Community, they resorted to creating a parliamentary delegation. The delegations for the European Union were given constitutional recognition in 1992,[66] and they were elevated to the status of parliamentary committees by the reform of July 2008.

With the reform of permanent committees, the number of delegations has diminished noticeably in both houses. At present, both houses have one 'permanent' delegation on women's rights and equal opportunity and two joint delegations: one for the supervision of the secret services and another for the assessment of scientific and technological choices. In May 2009 the Assemblée nationale established a new structure: the committee for assessment and control of public policies. This new committee aims to replace permanent committees when the public policy assessed falls within the remit of two or more permanent committees. In April 2009, the Sénat also chose to set up two new permanent delegations: one on local government and another on policy forecast.

Curtailing the Tools of Extraordinary Control

As explained in chapter three, articles 49 and 50 of the constitution set out the circumstances in which a government is led to resign after a vote of no confidence in the Assemblée nationale. Although these

---

[65] Between 1958 and 1973, only six committees of inquiry had been created in the Assemblée nationale and three in the Sénat. By contrast between 1997 and 2007, 23 committees of inquiry were created in the Assemblée nationale and 13 in the Sénat.

[66] See article 88-4 of the constitution.

provisions have demonstrated their extraordinary character – only one government was ever dismissed by the Assemblée nationale in this way (and in very different political circumstances) – the reform of July 2008 curtailed markedly the use of article 49 § 3 and limited this extraordinary tool of control. This may be seen as way to improve the legislative independence of Parliament, but it does limit this tool of extraordinary control nonetheless.

Resolutions and Political Declarations: Establishing New Lines of Communication

The reform of July 2008 is remarkable in many ways but particularly because it signals an attempt to leave a troubled constitutional past behind. Indeed, the original constitution had felt it necessary to sever most means of communication between the two branches so as to protect the Government and its stability. For this reason, the *Conseil constitutionnel* had always forbidden both houses to pass resolutions other than for internal use.[67] However, in July 2008, article 34-1 was introduced to allow each house to formulate wishes, voice concerns, or draw the attention of the Government to a specific problem, in a word, to communicate its opinion and ideas to the Government. These resolutions cannot bind the Government in any way nor can they trigger a vote of confidence. They simply represent a way for each house of Parliament to engage in a dialogue with the Government.[68]

Again, the new article 50-1 tends to open new lines of communications between Parliament and Government. According to this provision, the Government can come before either house on its own initiative or at the request of a political group and make a declaration on a specific issue. Once the representative of the Government has spoken, the house may be allowed by the Government to debate and even vote on the declaration. The constitution specifies that this vote cannot be regarded as a vote of confidence, showing that this new mechanism pertains to a wider conception of accountability.

Clearly these two provisions aim to open new channels of communication between the legislature and Executive and establish a smoother dialogue than the debate of a motion of censure would be. Interestingly, in both cases, the constitution expressly distances the new mechanisms

---

[67] See C cons no 59-2 DC 17, 18, 24 June 1959 and no 59-3 DC 24, 25 June 1959.

[68] However, the implementation of article 34-1 introduced restrictions which make it more difficult for each house to debate and adopt resolutions. As a result, few resolutions have been adopted by either house so far.

from any possibility of extraordinary control. This is indeed a prerequisite for the growth of the culture of control and assessment mentioned above.

The Rights of the Opposition – article 51-1

The introduction of article 51-1 into the constitution aims to recognise a specific status to opposition parties. In 2006, the Assemblée nationale had attempted to give some rights to opposition parties in its standing orders. However, the Conseil constitutionnel sanctioned the provisions: the difference of treatment between parties of the majority and parties of the opposition was not justified and contrary to article 4 of the constitution.[69] Article 51-1 leaves the content of these rights entirely to the discretion of each house. Both houses have amended their standing orders and go a long way in establishing a real status for the opposition.

In the Assemblée nationale, opposition parties benefit from an increase in the share of parliamentary time: they control the legislative agenda on a number of days, their time allocation during the legislative work has increased markedly and for the functions of control and assessment, the time is shared equally between majority and opposition. This matches more closely the numeric importance of opposition parties. Also, opposition parties ask the first question during parliamentary question time; they chair the committee for financial affairs, and in the other permanent committees, the *bureau* has been enlarged to include members of all political groups. Also, a member of the majority and opposition will lead jointly the missions of assessment and control established by permanent committees. Finally, opposition parties can request the creation of committees of inquiry. In short, the Assemblée nationale has attempted a more equitable working environment for the opposition. Although these powers have not been in force long, the first experience shows a willingness to respect the rights of the opposition.

Similarly, the Sénat has recognised specific rights to the opposition: for instance, majority and opposition share the position of president and reporter in every permanent committee and every mission of assessment and control. Again, the *bureau* of each committee must have a representative of each political group. Also, all parliamentary parties can request the creation of a committee of inquiry every year.

[69] See C cons no 2006-537 DC, 22 June 2006.

The future practice of article 51-1 may well hold the key to the transformation of the French Parliament. Now that the opposition has become a separate community with rights, it may emerge as the champion of the growing culture of control and accountability.

New Powers of Parliamentary Control

The reform of July 2008 has also been innovative and given new powers of scrutiny to the Parliament; these go beyond the traditional power of scrutiny that is usually recognised to the legislative branch.

First, according to article 13 § 4, certain nominations of the President of the Republic are now subject to the approval of the relevant permanent committees in each house.[70] Secondly, the control of the deployment of armed forces has been strengthened. While a declaration of war always rested with the French Parliament, article 35 has been amended to involve the Parliament in the deployment the armed forces abroad. The Government is required to inform the Parliament of a deployment within three days and to state clearly the objectives pursued. After four months, the Parliament must authorise its continuation.[71] The reform of article 35 reflects the reality and evolution of modern warfare: while national armies in Western democracies are only rarely engaged in traditional wars to protect the borders of their countries, they are being deployed abroad with an increasing regularity. The reform of article 35 reflects this evolution and ensures that the French Parliament's control is tailored accordingly.[72]

The Improvement of Financial Control

Although article 14[73] of the Declaration of the Rights of Man gives a clear indication that financial control by individual citizens and elected

---

[70] See chapter 3.

[71] In case of disagreement, the Assemblée nationale has the last word.

[72] On 28 January 2010 Parliament authorised the continued military deployment in Kosovo, Lebanon, Chad, Côte d'Ivoire and the Central African Republic. More recently, on 12 July 2011, Parliament authorised the continued military deployment in Libya.

[73] 'All citizens have the right to ascertain personally or through their representatives, the need for a public tax, to consent to it freely, to watch over its use, and to determine its proportion, basis, collection and duration.'

representatives is essential in a democratic society, the Parliament of the
fifth Republic seemed to eschew in-depth financial control in the early
years. A change of attitude came about in the second half of the 1990s
due to a combination of national and international pressures. First, the
respect of the convergence criteria imposed by the European Union
required that Parliament keep a close eye on public deficit. Secondly, the
steep rise in social security spending forced Parliament to equip itself
with better tools to control and rein in this spending. Nowadays, the
global economic crisis provides yet another reason for the French
Parliament to perform this control strictly.

Consequently, various reforms were adopted in succession to enhance
financial control. The constitutional reform of 1996[74] created a new and
specific legislative procedure for the financing of social security services
and in 2001 a strong cross-party consensus emerged in Parliament to
strengthen the powers of financial control. This led to the introduction
and adoption of a new organic law[75] and to the complete transformation of financial control. More recently, a constitutional reform aiming
to inscribe the 'golden rule' of budgetary equilibrium in the French constitution has stalled: the constitutional bill was passed by both chambers,
but President Sarkozy decided against convening the *Congrès*, as the bill
would not have been supported by the 60 per cent majority.

The Adoption of Financial Legislation

Financial legislation follows a different legislative procedure from ordinary statutes. The procedure is contained in articles 47 and 47-1. There
are three types of ordinary financial legislation: the financial legislation
which contains the annual budget, the annual discharge legislation for
the approval of the implementation of the previous budget and the rec-
tifying financial legislation, which allows for the budget to be adjusted
during the financial year.

The budget is debated and passed in autumn as the financial year in
France follows the calendar year. The procedure followed is strict to
ensure that the financial legislation is in place by 1 January. The authors
of the 1958 constitution wanted to avoid a repetition of the practices of
the third and fourth Republics, which frequently saw the fiscal year

[74] See the constitutional law of 22 February 1996.
[75] See the organic law on State finance of 1 August 2001.

begin with the budget still to be passed by Parliament.[76] Consequently, the legislation containing the annual budget is introduced in the Assemblée nationale on the first Tuesday in October and the Parliament has 70 days to adopt the legislation in full: 40 days are reserved to the Assemblée nationale, while 20 days are reserved to the Sénat (with 10 days for the transfer between the two chambers). Finally, if Parliament fails to adopt the draft legislation within 70 days, the Government can adopt it by ordinance.

In addition, a category of financial legislation was created by the constitutional reform of February 1996. The social security budget had been a controversial topic for a long time in France: not only was social security spending rising fast, but Members of Parliament could not examine it. As social security services are managed jointly by the Government and trade union representatives, the Parliament did not have power to intervene. However, as the deficit grew, the Government's financial liabilities seemed to be spiralling out of control. Parliament demanded more powers to review and possibly curb this spending.[77] The new legislative process for the adoption of the social security budget imposes strict time limits:[78] the Assemblée nationale must adopt the text within 20 days; if it fails to do so it is forwarded to the Sénat, which has 15 days to act. If Parliament fails to adopt the draft legislation within 50 days, the Government can adopt it by *ordonnance*.

---

[76] In fact, during the fourth Republic, only once was the budget adopted before 1 January; see A Archien, 'Article 47' in F Luchaire, G Conac and X Prétot (eds) (n 30) 1151.

[77] At the time, the social security budget amounted to approximately 2 billion francs while the whole budget of the State was marginally less (1.8 billion). It is therefore understandable that Parliament wanted to be involved closely with the adoption of the social security budget.

[78] See article 47-1 of the constitution:

Parliament shall pass Social Security Financing Bills in the manner provided by an Institutional Act.

Should the National Assembly fail to reach a decision on first reading within twenty days of the tabling of a Bill, the Government shall refer the Bill to the Senate, which shall make its decision known within fifteen days. The procedure set out in article 45 shall then apply.

Should Parliament fail to reach a decision within fifty days, the provisions of the Bill may be implemented by Ordinance.

The time limits set by this article shall be suspended when Parliament is not in session and, as regards each House, during the weeks when it has decided not to sit in accordance with the second paragraph of article 28.

The Tightening of Financial Control

The Cour des Comptes or Court of Auditors was created in 1807 by Napoléon Bonaparte to guarantee the legality of the State's finances. Over the centuries, it has come to provide Parliament with information regarding the implementation of the budget. Originally, article 47 § 6 of the constitution simply stated that the Court of Auditors assisted Parliament and Government in controlling the implementation of the financial legislation. However, parliamentary controls remained in the main superficial until the change of attitude of the 1990s. Since then, successive reforms have combined to engineer a change in the control performed by the Court from financial legality to public auditing. This evolution began with the constitutional reform of 1996 as the jurisdiction of the Court of Auditors was extended to assist Parliament and Government with this new type of financial legislation. The organic law of 2001 which exemplifies more fully the evolution noted above came into force on 1st January 2006: it was hailed as a new financial constitution. With this reform, not only does Parliament receive more information on economic and financial matters, but it has gained a new ally in the Court. To this effect, the Court was given new duties and new powers. Since then, the court has been required to produce three documents for Parliament: the first document continues to report on the implementation of financial legislation but since 2006, it has analysed in addition the performance of the various public bodies and State programmes; the second document is a certification of the legality, sincerity and faithfulness of the implementation of the State budget with a description of the checks which were made to ensure this; the third report analyses the financial situation and the plans for the future budget. This is in preparation for the debate over the financial trends and prospects that takes place every year in the spring. The first two reports are attached to the statute of discharge, which is debated and voted in the autumn. The third report is forwarded to the Parliament in the spring jointly with the Government's report on the evolution of the national economy and the prospects for public finances. With regard to the legislation on social security, again the Court of Auditors provides two documents: a report on the implementation and management of the social security budget and a certification of the legality, sincerity and faithfulness of the implementation of this budget. Finally, the organic law has given investigative powers to the presidents of the permanent committees for financial affairs and their reporters: they can request public bodies to provide them with any information and documents of a financial or administrative nature and if necessary they can investigate the matter in situ.

In light of these changes, the constitutional reform of July 2008 introduced a new provision describing more accurately the role of the Court of Auditors and its relation to Parliament, Government and French citizens. The new provision reflects the important advances made since 2001: for instance, article 47-2 specifies that the Court assists Parliament and Government in the assessment of public policy. However, the new provision was also introduced to neutralise a decision of the Conseil constitutionnel.[79] Originally, the 2001 organic law instituted a procedure by which the Court of Auditors submitted its annual work programme in draft to the committees for financial affairs of each house. Each committee could then indicate which specific investigations it wanted pursued. The Conseil constitutionnel annulled this provision in the name of judicial independence. However, in doing so it severed an important link between the Court and Parliament and arguably compromised the new cooperation between the two institutions. The new article 47-2 was drafted so as to provide a constitutional authorisation for this cooperation.

CONCLUSION: FURTHER REFORM?

As analysed above, the Parliament of the fifth Republic has just had a major facelift and it will be some time before one is able to assess the full effects of the reform. Although concerns were expressed with regard (among other things) to the number of the permanent committees (too low), the lack of electoral reform and the concomitant electoral mandates, only future empirical research can determine whether further reform would be beneficial in these domains.[80] A constitutional reform of the importance of the one adopted in July 2008 is unlikely to happen again soon and this may be for the best. Both houses need time to learn the use of their new tools and to create new practices and conventions.

---

[79]　See C cons no 2001-448 DC, 25 July 2001.

[80]　For instance, the recent senatorial elections put a slightly different complexion on the reform of article 24.

However some change to the case law of the Conseil constitutionnel would benefit this process of adaptation: the Conseil gives the concept of 'control' the traditional and extraordinary meaning highlighted above. It would be useful if the Conseil could widen its understanding by recognising different guises and depths to the function of control. For instance, the recognition that information and assessment pertains fully to the function of control would allow a more flexible case law when reviewing the regulations of each house.

FURTHER READING

P Avril, 'Articles 4 & 51-1 – Le statut de l'opposition: un feuilleton inachevé' in J-P Camby, P Fraisseix and J Gicquel (eds), *La révision de 2008: une nouvelle constitution?* (Paris, Librairie générale de droit et de jurisprudence, 2011) 27

J Bell, 'What is the Role of the *Conseil d'Etat* in the Preparation of Legislation' (2000) 49 *ICLQ* 661

A Delcamp, J-L Bergel and A Dupas (eds), *Contrôle parlementaire et évaluation*, no 5012-13 (Paris, *La Documentation française*, 1995)

O Dord, 'Vers un rééquilibre des pouvoirs publics en faveur du Parlement' (2009) *Revue française de droit constitutionnel* 99

P Ducoulombier, 'Rebalancing the Power between the Executive and Parliament' (2010) *Public Law* 688

J Frears, 'The French Electoral System in 1986: PR by Lists and Highest Average' (1986) *Parliamentary Affairs* 489

J Gicquel, 'La reparlementarisation: une perspective d'évolution' (2008) 126 *Pouvoirs* 47

J Hayward, 'Parliament and the French Government's Domination of the Legislative Process' (2004) 10 *Journal of Legal Studies* 79

J-L Pezant, 'Article 48' in F Luchaire, G Conac and X Prétot, *La constitution de la République française*, 3rd edn (Paris, Economica, 2009) 1208

N Questiaux, 'Do the Opinions Expressed by the Conseil d'Etat in its Capacity as Legal Adviser to Government Influence Policy?' (2000) 49 *ICLQ* 672

P Smith, *The Senate of the Fifth Republic* (Basingstoke, Palgrave Macmillan, 2009)

P Türk, *Les commissions parlementaires permanentes et le renouveau du Parlement sous la Ve République* (Paris, Dalloz, 2005)

E Vallet, 'Les commissions d'enquête parlementaires sous la cinquième République' (2008) *Revue française de droit constitutionnel* 247

A Vidal-Nacquet, 'L'institutionnalisation de l'opposition: quel statut pour quelle opposition?' (2009) *Revue française de droit constitutionnel* 153

Relevant websites

Assemblée nationale: www.assemblee-nationale.fr/
Sénat: www.senat.fr/
Cour des comptes: www.ccomptes.fr/fr/CC/Accueil.html

5

The Rise of Judicial Power

———◆◆———

The Search for Judicial Independence – The Rise of the Conseil constitutionnel – Towards a Judicial Power? – Conclusion

T HE TITLE OF this chapter may seem odd to anyone with a little knowledge of the French constitution. There is no mention of judicial power in the constitution: the main judicial institutions are mentioned in the text of the constitution at one point or another but they are not systematically recognised or even organised in a third branch. Also, the independence of these judicial institutions is not systematically safeguarded by the constitution.

In 1958, the authors of the constitution made a number of choices which resulted in the present patchwork of constitutional protection. First, although the judiciary is regulated by Title VIII of the constitution, it only refers to a 'judicial authority' and not a 'judicial power'. The authors of the constitution wanted to underline the inferior status of the judicial branch, thereby reflecting a long tradition of distrust of courts by politicians. Secondly, the judicial authority mentioned in the constitution only refers to the private law courts (*les tribunaux judiciaires*); the administrative courts are not mentioned anywhere in the constitution. Consequently, the independence of the administrative courts is not expressly guaranteed by the text of the constitution. Finally, although the creation of the Conseil constitutionnel represented an audacious break from the past, it was not conceived originally as a constitutional court.

As a result, in 1958, the existence, regulation and protection of a judicial power could not be asserted from the text of the constitution. However, constitutional practice and repeated constitutional amendments have transformed the third branch of the French political system beyond recognition. This chapter will try and map out this evolution, analyse this emerging judicial power and highlight the issues arising from this change.

THE SEARCH FOR JUDICIAL INDEPENDENCE

The French constitution contains three provisions which aim to guarantee judicial independence: articles 64, 65 and 66. Included in Title VIII on judicial authority, these provisions establish the principles and the mechanisms required to secure judicial independence for the private law courts and to protect their legitimacy. This drafting is remarkably concise; in the past, French constitutions often regulated in great detail the independence, recruitment, role, powers, duties and organisation of the judiciary.[1]

A Complex System of Constitutional Values

Even though the three provisions mentioned above are sufficient to establish in outline the constitutional protection for the independence of the private law courts, it is necessary to take a look at the Declaration of the Rights of Man of 1789. Article 16 of the Declaration specifies that a society that does not guarantee rights and freedoms and ensure a separation of powers does not have a constitution. This stark pronouncement is revealing of the links that French constitutional tradition has tended to establish between the protection of rights and freedoms and the principles of separation of powers[2] and independence of the judiciary. Without the protection given by these constitutional principles, fundamental rights and freedoms are at risk.

The close link between fundamental rights and freedoms and independence of the judiciary explains to a large extent the provisions of the 1958 constitution. Interestingly, the principle of independence of

---

[1] On average, French constitutions contained a dozen provisions on the judiciary, with notable exceptions: the constitution of 1791 included 27 articles and that of the *Directoire*, 63 articles.

[2] The Conseil constitutionnel clearly links the principle of independence of the judiciary to the principle of separation of powers; see for example, C cons no 2007-551 DC, 1 March 2007.

the judiciary is only proclaimed implicitly in articles 64 and 66. Indeed, the first paragraph of article 64 states that 'the President of the Republic guarantees the independence of the judicial authority'. In the remaining paragraphs, article 64 introduces mechanisms to make the independence of the judiciary a constitutional reality. There is no grand declaration defining the independence of the judiciary or justifying the need for this principle. Instead, the authors of the constitution embedded this principle in a constitutional structure as described below.

Article 66, however, echoes the link identified above: it states that the judicial authority is the guardian of individual freedom and that no one can be detained arbitrarily. The protection of individual freedom is undeniably determined by the degree of independence guaranteed to the judiciary. Following the constitutional reform of 23 February 2007 the provision prohibiting the death penalty was added to Title VIII in a new article 66-1.

The Mechanisms for the Protection of Judicial Independence

Beyond a statement of principles, Title VIII also contains a number of mechanisms to ensure the reality of this independence.

The Principle of Irremovability

Judicial independence is given a structural expression in article 64 § 4 of the 1958 constitution with the principle of irremovability. This principle signifies that no judge can be dismissed or even moved without his/her agreement. It is important to realise that the principle of irremovability applies to one category of private law judges only: the *juges du siège*.[3] In France, private law judges are divided into two categories: the *juges du siège*, who 'sit' to hear and decide cases, and the *juges du parquet*,[4] who 'stand' and act as prosecutors. The constitution protects mostly the *juges du siège*. They cannot be dismissed at pleasure; they cannot be removed without good cause or due process. As the *juges du siège* are indeed responsible for deciding cases, their independence should be firmly protected. While French law labels the people responsible for prosecuting a

---

[3] It translates as 'judges of the seat'.
[4] It translates as 'judges of the floor'.

case 'judges', they do not fulfil the traditional role identified above. In fact, the *juges du parquet* work largely under the direction of the Ministry of Justice and benefit from a limited protection only. While successive constitutional reforms have tried to strengthen the constitutional position of both categories of judge, the independence of the *juges du parquet* remains mostly aspirational. Indeed, it has been questioned recently by the European Court of Human Rights (ECtHR).[5]

The President of the Republic

The judiciary is given a champion in the guise of the President of the Republic. In accordance with his original role of guarantor of the constitution and of the French State as stated in article 5 of the constitution, the President of the Republic was also given the task of protecting the judiciary and its independence. To this effect, until the revision of July 2008, the President of the Republic also chaired the Conseil supérieur de la magistrature. As the Conseil supérieur de la magistrature acts among other things as a judicial appointments commission, the role of the President of the Republic was always controversial. Nowadays, the President is restricted to issuing opinions on matters relevant to judicial independence. These are received and answered by the Conseil supérieur de la magistrature.

Indeed, successive presidents have intervened publicly to protect the judiciary from attacks (by the press, for instance) or to remonstrate against politicians, the speeches of whom went beyond acceptable political criticism. Still, in view of the evolution of the regime, one wonders whether the President of the Republic should retain such a role.

The Requirement of Organic Legislation

All rules relating to the recruitment, appointment, career, promotions, duties and salaries of private law judges must be stipulated by organic law as required in article 64 § 3. Consequently, the organic law of 22 December 1958 aims to address all aspects of the career for both categories of private law judges. The requirement of an organic law to determine all rules relating to their status and career means that the

---

[5] See *Medvedyev v France* (application no 3394/03, GC, 29 March 2010) and *Moulin v France* (application no 37104/06, 23 November 2010).

legislative procedure contained in article 46 must be followed and that the Conseil constitutionnel must review its constitutionality.

In 2007, the provisions concerning the recruitment, education and accountability of judges were amended by organic law.[6] It aimed to address a number of structural problems with regard to the training and accountability of judges. A number of incidents and scandals showed members of the private law courts and their performance in poor light and Parliament attempted to ensure that all private law judges were fully aware of their responsibilities and that systems were in place to ensure a proper accountability of judges in the performance of their duties.

The Conseil supérieur de la magistrature

The Conseil supérieur de la magistrature is the third mechanism entrusted with the protection of the independence of the judiciary. Article 65 of the constitution describes in detail its functions and powers. Traditionally, the Conseil supérieur de la magistrature is seen as a key institution for the private law courts and their independence: the first Conseil supérieur de la magistrature was introduced in 1883, and soon became a fixture of French constitutional law. With time, the Conseil supérieur de la magistrature has been given more powers and its independence has been strengthened. In fact, the independence of private law judges has been the subject of heated debates all through the fifth Republic. Consequently, the membership and powers of the Conseil supérieur de la magistrature have been questioned and article 65 was amended in 1993[7] and again in 2008[8] to tackle ongoing criticisms.

From the beginning, the Conseil supérieur de la magistrature was created to insulate from the Government decisions that concerned the career of private law judges. Nowadays, the Conseil supérieur de la magistrature is involved in the appointment and disciplinary proceedings of all private law judges, must respond to the opinions issued by the President of the Republic and finally, since the reform of July 2008, hears the grievances that individual citizens choose to bring against individual judges. Still, the membership and the powers of the Conseil supérieur de la magistrature depend largely on the category of judge it is dealing with. The Conseil puts forward names for the highest positions

---

[6] See the organic law of 5 March 2007.
[7] See the constitutional law of 27 July 1993.
[8] See the constitutional law of 23 July 2008.

of the *juges du siège*[9] and makes binding recommendations regarding the appointment of all other *juges du siège*. With regard to the appointment of the *juges du parquet*, the Conseil supérieur de la magistrature only gives an opinion.[10] With regard to disciplinary proceedings, the same distinction exists: the Conseil supérieur de la magistrature is a full disciplinary tribunal for the *juges du siège* but only an advisory body for the *juges du parquet*.

The membership of the Conseil varies according to the role fulfilled and the category of judges. When deciding on appointments for the *juges du siège*, the Conseil is chaired by the first president of the Cour de cassation with the addition of five *juges du siège*, one *juge du parquet*, one judge of the Conseil d'Etat, one barrister and six qualified laymen; the membership changes to the general prosecutor of the Cour de cassation, five *juges du parquet*, one *juge du siège*, one barrister and six qualified laymen when deciding on appointments of the *juges du parquet*. When dealing with disciplinary matters, the membership is increased to include the *juge du siège* or the *juge du parquet* from the other Conseil supérieur de la magistrature depending on the category of the judge brought before the disciplinary body. When responding to the opinions of the President of the Republic, when tackling ethical issues or any questions of judicial administration, the Conseil convenes together in plenary and its membership is made up of the judge of the Conseil d'Etat, the barrister, the six laymen and three of the *juges du siège* and three of the *juges du parquet*. With the exception of disciplinary proceedings, the Minister of Justice can be present at all meetings of the Conseil supérieur de la magistrature but only as observer. While all judicial members of the Conseil supérieur de la magistrature are elected by their peers, the President of the Republic and the presidents of each house of Parliament appoint two qualified laymen each. These appointments are subject to the procedure of parliamentary approval contained in article 13 § 5.

For many years, the independence of the Conseil supérieur de la magistrature itself was doubted. Until 1993, not only did the President of the Republic chair the Conseil supérieur de la magistrature but he

[9] Article 65 § 4 refers to the appointment of the *juges du siège* of the Cour de cassation (the top court), those of the first presidents of the courts of appeal and those of the presidents of the courts of first instance, ie senior judicial appointments.

[10] During the reform of July 2008, an amendment was sponsored by Robert Badinter to give the same powers of appointment to the Conseil supérieur de la magistrature whatever the type of judge, but this was rejected.

nominated all nine members.[11] Also, the Conseil supérieur de la magistrature has jurisdiction over the appointment and discipline of the *juges du siège* only. In 1993 article 65 was amended to adopt for the first time a differentiated college for both categories of judge. Furthermore, while the President of the Republic and the president of each house appointed one layman each, it was decided that all judicial members would be elected by their peers. The reform of 2008 completed the reform of 1993 by removing the President of the Republic entirely from the Conseil and by increasing the number of laymen to six. With this change, private law judges do not have a majority in the Conseil. Although controversial, this solution aimed to address ongoing criticisms of judicial corporatism.

Beyond the Constitution

As explained above, the entire system of administrative courts is excluded from the protection guaranteed by the constitution. However, the requirements of constitutionalism make it impossible for the independence of a whole court system to go unprotected. Furthermore, the Conseil constitutionnel has taken to championing the independence of the judiciary and has intervened on numerous occasions to strengthen it.[12]

The Administrative Courts: The Art of Copying

Although Title VIII of the French constitution does not cater for the administrative courts, a system has been devised to protect their independence. To begin with, a principle akin to the principle of irremovability is proclaimed in article L. 231-3 of the code of administrative justice.[13] According to this provision, judges of the first instance and appeal

[11] The President of the Republic chose each of the judicial appointees from three names proposed by the Cour de cassation for the private law judges and by the Conseil d'Etat for the administrative judge. The President had discretion when appointing the lay members but was always guided by their qualification.

[12] See C cons no 80-119 DC, 22 July 1980; C cons no 86-224 DC, 23 January 1987.

[13] See article L. 231-3: 'When fulfilling the function of judge in an administrative court, the members of the first instance and appeal administrative courts cannot be appointed elsewhere without their agreement, even when promoted.'

administrative courts cannot be removed at pleasure. In addition, the Conseil supérieur de la magistrature acted as a design model for the protection of the independence of the first instance and appeal administrative courts. The law of 6 January 1986 introduced the Conseil Supérieur des Tribunaux Administratifs. It fulfils a similar role to the Conseil supérieur de la magistrature for the first instance and appeal administrative courts: the Conseil Supérieur des Tribunaux Administratifs puts forward all names for appointment to these courts, but makes recommendations only in disciplinary proceedings.

Interestingly, there is a notable gap in the protection of French administrative courts. There is no mechanism (constitutional or otherwise) to protect the independence of the administrative supreme court, the Conseil d'Etat. Although in theory this may be a cause for concern, in practice the Conseil d'Etat is a venerable and formidable institution, the independence of which is strictly respected.

Still, the peculiar structure of the Conseil d'Etat has led to problems with regard to article 6 §1 of the European Convention on Human Rights (ECHR). Indeed, the European Court of Human Rights (ECtHR) has expressed misgivings when it comes to the dual administrative and judicial functions fulfilled by the Conseil d'Etat and similar institutions in other countries.[14] To ensure compliance under the ECHR, the French Conseil d'Etat has had to ensure that both roles are clearly delineated and that structures exist to separate functions and personnel strictly. In the recent decision *Sacilor-Lormines*, the ECtHR seemed to be satisfied with the changes made.[15] Still it is interesting to note that the court chose to concentrate on these aspects but has never questioned the lack of formal protection of the independence of the members of the Conseil d'Etat.

The Requirements of the Conseil constitutionnel

The Conseil constitutionnel has also widened the scope and content of the principle of judicial independence beyond the strict constitutional provisions.

---

[14] See the case *Procola v Luxembourg* (application no 14570/89, 28 September 1995).

[15] In *Sacilor-Lormines v France* (application no 65411/01, 9 November 2006), the ECtHR stated that it did not wish to impose a specific interpretation of separation of powers on the French Conseil d'Etat.

Early on, the Conseil constitutionnel decided that the principle of judicial independence should apply equally to members of the private law courts and members of the administrative courts, even though no reference is made to the latter in the 1958 constitution.[16] Therefore, the independence of all professional judges came to be safeguarded by the case law of the Conseil constitutionnel. It remedied to a large extent the limitations of the constitutional text.

More recently, the Conseil constitutionnel extended further the pool of judicial personnel whose independence needs to be properly guaranteed. By accepting that not all judges are professional and that not all judicial positions are permanent,[17] the Conseil constitutionnel has widened considerably the protection of the 1958 constitution. Basically, it is fair to say that according to the Conseil constitutionnel, so long as someone participates directly in judicial decision making, his/her independence must be protected. This increases the personnel whose independence is constitutionally guaranteed and widens markedly the scope of the constitution.

Finally, the Conseil constitutionnel has also had to specify how strict it intends to be with regard to interferences by other branches of government. There, the Conseil constitutionnel does not allow any interference with judicial decision making itself, whether by the Executive, the Parliament, an independent authority or the public. The Conseil constitutionnel has implemented a strict separation of powers and shields judges from all interferences. For instance, the Conseil constitutionnel struck down a provision allowing the Ombudsman to trigger disciplinary proceedings against a member of the judiciary on the request of a member of the public. Even though the Ombudsman was only a trigger with no other involvement in the proceedings, the Conseil constitutionnel decided that the mechanism infringed the independence of the judiciary.[18] This strict interpretation has led the Cour de cassation to declare that judicial decisions can only be challenged via standard procedures such as appeal.[19]

Also, the Conseil constitutionnel has controlled strictly the possibility of retroactive parliamentary validations of administrative actions. For various reasons (legal certainty, public interest etc) it is sometimes

---

[16] See C cons no 80-199 DC, 22 July 1980.
[17] See C cons no 94-355 DC, 10 January 1995.
[18] See C cons no 2007-551 DC, 1 March 2007.
[19] See C cass no 83-90963, 9 March 1983.

necessary to validate administrative decisions after their illegality has been declared by the courts. With time, the Conseil constitutionnel has increased its control and multiplied the conditions allowing Parliament to validate administrative decisions retroactively.[20]

Still, all these changes are marginal when compared to the evolution of the Conseil constitutionnel itself.

THE RISE OF THE CONSEIL CONSTITUTIONNEL

While the creation of the Conseil constitutionnel was audacious, it might not have been the break from constitutional tradition that is often portrayed. Historically the idea of control of constitutionality was clearly part of the institutional arsenal known to constitutional lawyers as early as the eighteenth century.[21] In the past, this control was never granted to a court: in 1799 and in 1852 the two imperial regimes bestowed the control of constitutionality on the Sénat; and in 1946 not only was the new constitutional committee staffed with elected representatives (namely the President of the Republic and Members of Parliament) but the control of constitutionality consisted in forcing the constitution to align itself with a contravening statute. Clearly, the implications of constitutionalism were not fully understood: the statute (rather than the constitution) was seemingly regarded as a true expression of the will of the Nation.

To a large extent, the Conseil constitutionnel followed this tradition; only its subsequent evolution represents a break from it. The membership, organisation and original mechanisms for control all seemed to indicate a quasi-political entity.

The Changing Role of the Conseil constitutionnel

The Conseil constitutionnel was meant to keep the Parliament of the fifth Republic in check. The Parliament of the previous Republic had repeatedly breached the constitution and it was felt necessary to avoid a repetition. Also, the Conseil was meant to look after the constitution in

---

[20]   See C cons no 2004-509 DC, 13 January 2005.
[21]   See M Troper, 'Sieyès et le jury constitutionnaire' in *Mélanges Pierre Avril* (Paris, Montchrestien, 2001) 265.

difficult times. In fact, the Conseil was conceived as 'a weapon against the deviations of the parliamentary regime'.

Still, the drafters had not wished to endow the new institution with a power of constitutional review. Unlike the American or German models, the Conseil constitutionnel was not allowed to control the constitutionality of laws against substantive rights and freedoms. Originally, the Conseil was to regulate the jurisdictional divide between Parliament (article 34) and Government (article 37). Experience had proved that Parliament could not be trusted to respect the prerogatives of the Executive: an institution was necessary to enforce these new arrangements if they were to prevail.

In fact, proposals to give a full control of constitutionality to the Conseil constitutionnel on reference from either supreme courts, Members of Parliament or citizens were systematically rejected during the adoption of the 1958 constitution.[22] Furthermore, a provision requiring that statutes respect the rights and freedoms proclaimed by the Preamble of the constitution was also rejected. When discussed, it was stated that the Preamble of the constitution which cites both the Declaration of the Rights of Man of 1789 and the Preamble of the 1946 constitution had no legal value.

A Regulation of Parliament

According to the constitution, the Conseil controls Parliament in two ways: it oversees the legislative procedure and checks the constitutionality of new laws. It was therefore possible to imagine that the Conseil may evolve beyond the role of guard dog of the Executive. With time, this control has been transformed beyond recognition.

Protecting the Integrity of the Legislative Procedure

As explained in chapter three, the 1958 constitution limited the legislative jurisdiction of Parliament. In addition, the constitution gave the Conseil constitutionnel the duty to protect this jurisdictional delineation. Even though this revolution has never really happened, articles 37 § 2 and 41 combined to establish a formidable protection of these separate domains. With article 37 § 2, the Government is allowed to amend acts of Parliament

---

[22] See *Documents pour servir à l'histoire de l'élaboration la Constitution du 4 octobre 1958*, vol 1 (Paris, *La Documentation française*, 1988) 382.

taken in the Government's jurisdiction after consultation of the Conseil d'Etat if these were adopted prior to the entry into force of the present constitution. If the statutes were adopted after the entry into force of the present constitution, the Conseil constitutionnel decides on their jurisdictional attribution. Similarly, in the event that a bill or amendment appears to breach the jurisdictional divide, the Government or the President of the relevant house can oppose it. In the event of a disagreement, the Conseil constitutionnel settles the dispute.

Finally, according to article 39 § 2, in the event that the Government and a president of a house of Parliament disagree on an alleged breach of the organic law regulating the legislative procedure, the Conseil rules on the issue.

Ensuring the Respect of the Constitution By-laws

Many changes have taken place since 1958 with regard to the control of the constitutionality of laws by the Conseil constitutionnel. Constitutional reforms and political practices have combined to establish the sophisticated system of control that exists today.

The constitution does not require that the Conseil constitutionnel controls systematically all texts passed by Parliament. At the time of drafting, it must have been thought unnecessary and much too onerous. Only key texts are checked automatically by the Conseil; still, the others are controlled in an increasing number of ways.

The Compulsory Controls

According to article 61 § 1, two categories of text trigger a systematic control by the Conseil constitutionnel: the regulations of the houses of Parliament and the organic laws. These create a high risk of unconstitutionality as both types of text interpret and implement directly the provisions of the constitution.

In addition to these two controls, the reform of July 2008 has given the new task to the Conseil of controlling the constitutionality of referendums requested by popular initiatives. The Conseil constitutionnel reviews the constitutionality of the text itself and enforces the constitutional conditions for such referendums. According to article 11 § 3, this new control concerns only referendums resulting from a popular initiative. Referendums sponsored by the President of the Republic are not controlled automatically by the Conseil. This difference of treatment is surprising. When one considers the use of article 11 by de Gaulle in

1962 and in 1969, one may be excused for believing that a compulsory control of all draft referendums would not be superfluous.

The Optional Controls

First as the controls presented here are all optional, it is important to determine when they are triggered: until the reform of July 2008, all controls were a priori, ie the legislation was referred to the Conseil constitutionnel before promulgation by the President of the Republic.[23] This allowed for a legal fiction to survive into the fifth Republic: the Conseil constitutionnel controlled bills only; it was less of an attack on the sovereignty of legislation. However, this has changed with the constitutional reform of July 2008.

• The Control A Priori

Originally, ordinary statutes (article 61 § 2) and international treaties (article 54) could be referred to the Conseil before promulgation or ratification by four individuals only: the President of the Republic, the Prime Minister and the presidents of each house. This system accentuated further the political nature of French constitutional review. Only a small number of texts were ever reviewed this way: the four office holders did not make frequent references.[24] If this had not changed, the case law of the Conseil would not have grown much and the institution in all likelihood would not have the importance it has today.

Following the evolution triggered by the Conseil's decision in 1971,[25] President Giscard d'Estaing sponsored an amendment of the constitution which unlocked the potential of the institution.[26] Since then, 60 *députés* or 60 *sénateurs* can refer collectively ordinary bills to the Conseil. In effect, the opposition always masters enough members to refer a text in this way. Indeed, this is often regarded as the last obstacle that the opposition can put across the path of a bill. While the 1974 reform concerned ordinary legislation only, this possibility was extended to international treaties by the constitutional reform of 25 June 1992.[27]

---

[23] In fact, the President of the Republic is informed that a reference to the Conseil constitutionnel is imminent. Thus, a constitutional convention requires that the President waits to promulgate the new legislation to allow potential challenges.

[24] Most years, the Conseil decided only three or four cases.

[25] C cons no 71-44 DC, 16 July 1971, Freedom of association.

[26] See the constitutional law of 29 October 1974.

[27] See chapter 7.

According to article 54, international treaties and agreements can be controlled by the Conseil constitutionnel before ratification. If the Conseil finds that a treaty is contrary to the constitution, the constitution must be amended prior to ratification. This avoids unauthorised transfers of sovereignty and ensures that treaties respect the constitution.

Still, the bulk of the Conseil constitutionnel's work consists in reviewing the constitutionality of ordinary bills referred to it by Members of Parliament. This control had allowed the Conseil to build up a large case law and to recognise many constitutional principles, rights and freedoms – so much so that members of Parliament have been sometimes reluctant to make a reference to the Conseil. By choosing selectively the bills they forwarded for control, Members of Parliament hoped to rein in the creativity of the Conseil and avoid the adoption of permanent constraints on the legislative branch.[28] However, with the introduction of a control a posteriori, this self-limitation has become largely inoperative.

• The New Control A Posteriori

Many had argued that the control of the Conseil constitutionnel needed to be extended to check the constitutionality of legislative provisions already in force. It was felt that a control a priori was insufficient since many bills were not referred to the Conseil. In view of the institution's evolution, it was opportune to transform the Conseil into a body resembling a constitutional court. Two attempts were made in 1990 and in 1993 to amend the constitution accordingly. Both failed.

Finally, the reform of July 2008 gave ordinary citizens the possibility to trigger this control in the new article 61-1 of the constitution. Called preliminary ruling on an issue of constitutionality, the new provision of the constitution was conceived as a means to strengthen the rights of French citizens.

Article 61-1 was implemented by the organic law of 9 December 2009, which created the necessary mechanisms for the new control. In the organic law, only claimants (and not the courts) can trigger this preliminary ruling. Furthermore, the control is not automatic: a number of conditions must be fulfilled. When the reference is made by a first instance or appeal court, the supreme court (ie the Conseil d'Etat or the Cour de cassation) has two months to issue a reasoned opinion allowing

---

[28] See D Schnapper, *Une sociologue au Conseil constitutionnel* (Paris, Gallimard, 2010) 111.

or rejecting the challenge. It checks that the following conditions are met: first, the provision the constitutionality of which is challenged must be applicable in the case; secondly, the provision must breach a constitutional right or freedom; thirdly, the question must be serious. Finally, this review is limited to legislative provisions which have not been controlled previously by the Conseil constitutionnel – with one notable exception: the Conseil can intervene anew if 'a change in the circumstances' has occurred. The Conseil has begun to elaborate on what constitutes such a change in the circumstances: for instance, it can be a change in the factual background[29] or in the legal context.[30] On receiving the challenge, the Conseil constitutionnel has three months to decide. If it annuls a legislative provision, the Conseil can give directions for its implementation and can delay the effects of an annulment.

By November 2011, the Conseil had already handed down 164 decisions on the basis of article 61-1. References have been forwarded from the Conseil d'Etat and the Cour de cassation. The Conseil has annulled legislative provisions in a large number of cases and many of these decisions have attracted the attention of the media.[31] Furthermore, the Conseil made use of its powers to determine the effects of one annulment early on. As the Conseil declared unconstitutional the provisions aiming to grant equal pension rights to civil servants and military personnel regardless of residence or nationality, the annulment would have had serious and adverse effects for the people involved. Consequently, the Conseil directed that Parliament introduce new legislation by 1 January 2011 and that all relevant judicial proceedings be suspended until then.[32]

---

[29] For instance, in a decision concerning police custody, the Conseil constitutionnel noted that the number of persons brought into police custody had grown to 790,000 in 2009. This did constitute a change of circumstances, see C cons no 2010-14/22 QPC, 30 July 2010.

[30] For instance, in a decision concerned with taxation, the Conseil d'Etat argued that the numerous legislative reforms in this domain did constitute a change in the circumstances, see CE 9 July 2010, *Mathieu* no 339081. This reasoning was impliedly accepted by the Conseil constitutionnel in its decision C cons no 2010-44 QPC, 29 September 2010.

[31] See, for instance, the decision that annulled several key provisions of the criminal procedure code dealing with police custody, C cons no 2010-14/22 QPC, 30 July 2010.

[32] C cons no 2010-1 QPC, 28 May 2010.

A Protection of the Constitution in Difficult Times

The Conseil constitutionnel intervenes also during elections and in periods of exceptional circumstances.

The Control of Elections

Elections are traditionally difficult times for any political system. The electoral challenge can so easily degenerate into violent struggle before, during and after the elections. Also, politicians have been known to resort to questionable practices to secure their election. Consequently, constitutions tend to regulate both electoral campaigns and elections closely. Unsurprisingly, in the French constitution, the Conseil constitutionnel was given the task from the outset of overseeing to varying degrees the elections of the President of the Republic (art 58) and Members of Parliament (art 59) and the adoption of referendums (art 60).

Presidential Election

The control of the election of the President of the Republic concerns the organisation of the election and the election itself. First, the Conseil constitutionnel helps establish the list of candidates. Presidential candidates must fulfil a number of conditions before becoming official candidates: not only must they be at least 23 years old and have paid a deposit, but they need to have the support (and signature) of 500 elected representatives. Failure to obtain these signatures, bars anyone from running for the presidency.

Also, the Conseil constitutionnel controls the organisation of the electoral campaign. Article 7 § 3C of the constitution specifies that presidential elections must take place between the 35th and the 20th day before the end of the current presidential mandate; the Conseil ensures that this time frame is respected. In case of resignation or death in office, the Conseil declares the position vacant and triggers the electoral campaign. The Conseil constitutionnel is also responsible for deciding on the vacancy of the office in case of illness, accident or disappearance of the President of the Republic. This last provision has never been used; although Pompidou and Mitterrand suffered from cancer while in office it was felt that their intellectual abilities had not been impaired by illness.

Also, the Conseil oversees the official electoral campaign, which lasts a month altogether. The Conseil controls the publicity used by candidates: commercial publicity is strictly prohibited, and appearance on State television is limited to two hours for each candidate.

During the elections, the Conseil constitutionnel often sends delegates into individual polling stations to oversee the electoral process itself. These delegates are chosen from the judiciary. They are not entitled to act in the place of the authorities responsible for the organisation of the elections, but they can make suggestions and give advice on specific practices or points of law. They report in writing to the Conseil.

After the elections, voters, State representatives, candidates (or their representatives) have 48 hours to contest the result of the elections before the Conseil.[33] Once all the cases have been investigated, the Conseil proclaims the results. This is done for both rounds of elections.

Finally, the Conseil controls the electoral accounts of each candidate as a law of 15 January 1990 created an upper limit for electoral expenses; at present, it amounts to 16.851 million euros for the first round and 22.509 million euros for the second. All candidates must provide their accounts for the Conseil to check. If the Conseil accepts the accounts, the candidates who received at least 5 per cent of the votes are reimbursed 25 per cent of their expenses by the State, while the candidates who scored less than 5 per cent receive only 20 per cent. If the Conseil rejects the accounts, the candidate can only be reimbursed if the breach was neither intentional nor serious.

Parliamentary Elections

Historically, the control of parliamentary elections was given to the Conseil constitutionnel to avoid the abuses which had taken place during the fourth Republic.[34]

When it comes to the elections of Members of Parliament, the Conseil intervenes mostly with regard to irregularities during the elections themselves. When the results of an election are contested, the Conseil annuls an election but does not alter the results.

The Conseil only invalidates the election of a Member of Parliament if serious illegalities have been committed – such as 800 electoral mandates illegally drawn up or the presence of three ballot boxes in a polling station when only one was required – and only when the candidate was

---

[33] As far as voters and the representatives of candidates are concerned, they must have registered their complaint at the polling station first.

[34] In 1956, the elections of 11 *députés* were annulled by their chamber as they belonged to an anti-parliamentary party.

elected by a narrow majority. It is often argued that the Conseil constitutionnel is not strict enough when performing this control:[35] even
serious irregularities do not trigger a systematic annulment.[36] In fact,
few elections are annulled each time.

Finally, only the candidates and the voters registered in the constituency can challenge the election results of that constituency.

Referendums

With regard to referendums, the attitude of the Conseil was driven by
political circumstances: it has been ambiguous and controversial from the
beginning. In 1962, when de Gaulle used article 11 to amend the constitution, the president of the Sénat referred the referendum for constitutional
control after the vote had taken place. Unsurprisingly, the Conseil constitutionnel refused to intervene, arguing that its jurisdiction, defined in article 61 of the constitution, was strictly limited to organic and ordinary
laws. Interestingly, it also specified in the last sentence of the decision that
neither the constitution nor any organic law gave the Conseil constitutionnel the power to control a bill adopted by the French people in a referendum.[37] Here, the Conseil is clearly mindful of the legitimacy of popular
sovereignty. The French people had spoken; it would have been prepos-
terous on the part of the Conseil to annul the referendum, especially in
view of its own legitimacy at the time. This case law has been confirmed
since: the Conseil refused to control the constitutionality of the referendum which approved the Maastricht Treaty.[38]

Still, with time, the Conseil has accepted some control over the
organisation of referendums. According to article 16 of the organic law
of 7 November 1958, the Conseil is consulted by the Government on
all the provisions and texts required to organise the referendum. At first,
the Conseil refused to intervene, arguing the consultative nature of its

[35] See D Rousseau, *Droit du contentieux constitutionnel*, 7th edn (Paris, Montchrestien,
2006) 388 and J Robert, *La garde de la République* (Paris, Plon, 2000) 154.
[36] The most extreme and controversial example of this took place during the
elections for the Assemblée nationale in 1997. Although 7,228 voters had been registered fraudulently on the electoral roll of the 5th district of Paris, the Conseil constitutionnel did not annul the election of the *député*, Jean Tiberi (even though town
halls are responsible for maintaining electoral rolls and Jean Tiberi had been the
mayor of this district until 1995).
[37] See C cons no 62-20 DC, 6 November 1962, Referendum.
[38] See C cons no 92-313 DC, 23 September 1992, Ratification of the Treaty on
the European Union.

jurisdiction, but since, the Conseil constitutionnel has accepted control-ling the legality of the preparatory texts.[39] Also, the Conseil was granted the power to control the conditions for submitting a popular initiative to a referendum by the constitutional reform of July 2008.[40]

Finally, on the day, the Conseil oversees the process by using observ-ers and delegates. After the referendum, the Conseil has three duties: it receives the results, investigates complaints and proclaims the results.

The Regulation of Article 16

Arguably, article 16 of the constitution, which concentrates all constitu-tional power in the hands of the President of the Republic in times of national emergency, is a form of constitutional dictatorship. De Gaulle had insisted on this provision at the time of drafting in memory of the events of July 1940. Unsurprisingly, controls exist to frame the applica-tion of this provision.

The Prime Minister, the presidents of both houses and the Conseil con-stitutionnel are all consulted on the use of Article 16. They give their opin-ion on the exceptional character of the circumstances and judge whether article 16 ought to be triggered. The reasoned opinion of the Conseil is published in the Official Journal. Also, the Conseil is consulted by the President of the Republic on any subsequent measures taken on the basis of this provision. Finally, Parliament must sit when article 16 is in use.

Last but not least, the question of the duration of article 16 has been hotly debated since the controversial use of this provision in 1961.[41] While consultations are necessary prior to using article 16, there was no equivalent requirement to end it. As many believed that de Gaulle had used this power well after the exceptional circumstances had ceased, a remedy was needed. The reform of July 2008 put new mechanisms in place: after 30 days, the president of either house or 60 *députés* or 60 *sénateurs* can request that the Conseil constitutionnel checks whether the circumstances still justify the use of article 16. The opinion of the Conseil is published in the Official Journal. Also, at any time after 60 days, the Conseil has the power to review the circumstances and decide whether the use of article 16 is still justified. Article 16 may be framed more tightly, but there is a limit to the legal controls that can be imposed successfully over this type of power.

[39] See C cons 25 July 2000, Hauchemaille I.
[40] See article 11 § 3 and § 4.
[41] See chapter 3.

A Dynamic Protection of Constitutional Rights

To understand the rise of the Conseil constitutionnel, it is necessary to present its protection of rights and freedoms. As it is impossible to present coherently in the limited space available the whole case law of the Conseil constitutionnel, only a small selection of rights and freedoms will be presented in outline. These will exemplify the creativity of the Conseil in this domain.

The Range of Constitutional Rights and Freedoms

The Conseil constitutionnel has granted constitutional status to a wide range of rights and freedoms. In fact, a close study of the case law reveals that not only have all provisions of the Declaration of 1789 and the Preamble of 1946 been enforced by the Conseil constitutionnel, but so have the majority of those proclaimed by the Charter on the Environment.[42] Also, the Conseil found it necessary to supplement these texts from the outset; in addition to the Declaration of 1789, the Preamble of 1946 and the Charter of 2004, it relies on the 'Fundamental Principles recognized in the legislation of the Republic',[43] which it unearths when required.

Consequently, the Conseil protects all the standard freedoms and human rights: individual freedom,[44] right to human dignity,[45] freedom of movement,[46] freedom from arbitrary arrest,[47] freedom of conscience and religion,[48] freedom of expression, right to respect for private life,[49] right to property,[50] equality[51] etc. Still, now and then, the Conseil proclaims the existence of a right or a freedom which surprises. For

---

[42] In the decision C cons no 2008-564 DC, 19 June 2008, the Conseil declared the constitutional value of the whole Charter: it is only a matter of time before all provisions are enforced.

[43] See chapter 2 for a presentation of this category of principles.

[44] See C cons no 74-54 DC, 15 January 1975.

[45] See C Cons no 99-419 DC, 9 November 1999.

[46] See C cons no 80-127 DC, 20 January 1980.

[47] See C cons no 2004-492 DC, 2 March 2004.

[48] See C cons no 76-67 DC, 15 July 1976.

[49] See C cons no 94-352 DC, 18 January 1995.

[50] See C cons no 81-132 DC, 16 January 1982.

[51] See C cons no 73-51 DC, 27 December 1973.

instance, in 1984, the Conseil constitutionnel recognised a new funda-mental principle of independence of university professors.[52]

In addition to these first-generation rights, the Conseil has recognised many social and economic rights. The Conseil constitutionnel has relied heavily on the Preamble of 1946 to protect many second generation rights early on: right to work,[53] right to strike,[54] right to healthcare,[55] right to social security[56] etc.

However, the Conseil constitutionnel has needed some encourage-ment to move beyond first- and second generation rights. The adoption of the Charter has helped the recognition of environmental rights such as the principle of sustainable development,[57] but the Conseil has resisted giving constitutional status to other third-generation rights.[58] The Conseil may feel that the definition and scope of these rights is still debated, that a consensus is yet to emerge, and that elected representa-tives are better equipped than judges to decide on these issues.[59]

To exemplify the dynamism and creativity of the Conseil con-stitutionnel, the interpretation of three constitutional rights will be presented and analysed below: the right to property, the right to human dignity and the right to rest.

The Right to Property: A Legitimacy Crisis

In a decision of January 1982,[60] the Conseil constitutionnel recognised for the first time the constitutional character of the right to property alongside a freedom of enterprise. Not only would the recognition of such rights be controversial at the best of times, but the context of the 1982 decision was particularly sensitive. For the first time since the

---

[52] See C cons no 83-165 DC, 20 January 1984, Freedom of university professors.

[53] See C cons no 99-423 DC, 13 January 2000. The Conseil does not assert that every citizen is entitled to be in gainful employment. It is only an objective for Parliament to try and secure full employment in France.

[54] See C cons no 75-105 DC, 25 July 1979.

[55] See C cons no 80-117 DC, 22 July 1980.

[56] See C cons no 86-225 DC, 23 January 1987.

[57] See C cons no 2005-514 DC, 28 April 2005.

[58] See bio-ethics, S Hennette-Vauchez, 'Bioéthique et constitution' in B Mathieu (ed) *Cinquantième anniversaire de la constitution française* (Paris, Dalloz, 2008) 505.

[59] The Conseil has repeatedly stated that it does not have a general power of deci-sion comparable to that of Parliament; see, for instance, C cons no 74-54 DC, 15 January 1975, Abortion.

[60] See C cons no 81-132 DC, 16 January 1982 and C cons no 82-139 DC, 11 February 1982.

beginning of the fifth Republic, a socialist President and a left-wing majority had been elected to the Presidency and the Assemblée nationale respectively. As a result of party manifesto promises, the Government was seeking to put in place a vast programme of nationalisations. Accordingly, left-wing politicians, concerned that the bill may be stopped by the Conseil constitutionnel, were responsible for a preemptive attack on the institution,[61] while the opposition put pressure on the Conseil to declare the bill unconstitutional.

Against this background, the decision of the Conseil constitutionnel may appear courageous. First the recognition of a constitutional right to property may flow easily from article 17 of the Declaration of 1789, but may appear provocative when purporting to control the constitutionality of nationalisations; especially since the Conseil did not simply recognise the constitutional nature of this right, but specified that its conservation is an aim of the political system. This was clearly meant to serve as a constitutional limit to curb the extent of the nationalisations. Secondly, the Conseil proclaimed the constitutional character of another freedom – the freedom of enterprise – which is not mentioned in any constitutional texts. The Conseil justified it simply by reference to the general freedom provision contained in article 4 of the Declaration of 1789. Indeed, one may regard the freedom of enterprise as a collective expression of the individual right to property. Thirdly, the complex constitutional framework established by the Conseil to control these nationalisations is far from straightforward. The Conseil may have erected a complex system of constitutional justifications to legitimise its interpretation, but it contains a few constitutional leaps: to begin with, the Conseil imposed a certain reading of constitutional history to deduce the importance of the right to property in the present time. The Conseil mentioned the rejection by referendum of the first draft constitution in May 1946 to explain France's attachment to a traditional right to property; in doing so, it referred impliedly to the opinion of some commentators that the new declaration of rights, which was attached to the draft constitution and which aimed to replace the Declaration of 1789 and its values, was partly responsible for the failure of the referendum. Furthermore, the Conseil specified that although there had been some

---

[61] For instance, in 1982, the president of the Assemblée nationale attacked viciously the president of the Conseil constitutionnel while presiding over the debates in the house. The content of the speech was such that President Mitterrand intervened publicly.

changes over time with regard to both the extent and the limits of the right to property since 1789, it remains to this day an essential and core right. With the importance of the right to property established, all the Conseil needed were constitutional rules and principles to frame the process of nationalisation: there, the Conseil chose to extend article 17 of the Declaration of 1789, which regulates compulsory purchase to the control of nationalisations. According to this provision, the State cannot compulsorily purchase a property in the absence of public interest and must pay fair and prior compensation. In the 1982 decision, the Conseil found that the compensation was neither fair nor timely and declared the bill unconstitutional. Parliament amended the relevant provisions and the legislation was subsequently cleared by the Conseil constitutionnel. On reading the decision, it appears that the Conseil made a few questionable choices. For instance, the reading of constitutional history given by the Conseil was criticised: many felt that constitutional history was being manipulated considerably to legitimise the decision. Furthermore, the ruling of the Conseil dissatisfied politicians of both majority and opposition: While the majority was incensed that the bill had been struck down, the opposition was equally unhappy that nationalisations received a constitutional seal of approval. It is not surprising, therefore, that the legitimacy of the Conseil constitutionnel was strongly contested at the time. In reality, the decision achieved a balance and allowed a great degree of economic freedom to the Government. Indeed, the same provisions would serve a few years later to approve the privatisations of a newly elected right-wing majority.[62]

Furthermore, when presenting the right to property in the case law of the Conseil constitutionnel, another creation of the Conseil should be mentioned alongside: the right to decent housing. This constitutional objective, which first appeared in 1995,[63] aims to give effect to the pronouncements included in paragraphs 10 and 11 of the Preamble of the 1946 constitution that 'the Nation ensures to all individuals and their family the conditions necessary to their development'. Indeed, the Conseil constitutionnel accepted explicitly that this constitutional objective of decent housing could limit the right to property so long as the limitations did not compromise the overall nature and integrity of this right.[64]

---

[62] See C cons no 86-207 DC, 25–26 June 1986, Privatisations.
[63] See C cons no 94-359 DC, 19 January 1995.
[64] See C cons no 98-403 DC, 29 July 1998.

The Right to Human Dignity: A Late Recognition

The late recognition of the right to human dignity by the Conseil constitutionnel may seem at odds with the dynamism of its case law. Still, the existence of this right was proclaimed only in July 1994:[65] the Conseil had needed this right to strengthen its control over two bills on bioethics. At the time, the French Parliament had adopted three bills: one on data protection of information with regard to health research, a second on the respect for the human body and a third on donation and use of parts and by-products of the human body and medically assisted reproduction. Even though the bills had been drafted after a long pre-legislative process and reflection,[66] the progress in Parliament had been particularly slow. The Conseil was forwarded only the last two bills for control by the president of the Assemblée nationale and 68 *députés*. The *députés* were particularly concerned with the ethical dimension of many provisions and wanted the Conseil to recognise new constitutional principles or increase the scope of existing rights and freedoms: for instance, while the Conseil was asked to recognise a new principle of integrity and respect of the human body, it was also requested to extend to embryos the right to life and equality. In view of the arguments put to the Conseil constitutionnel, the resulting recognition of a right to human dignity may have paled in comparison.[67] It is clear from the decision that the Conseil did not feel the need for a whole array of new constitutional tools. Indeed, the recognition of the right to human dignity came only in the penultimate paragraph of the decision and was not used to invalidate a specific provision but to underline the importance of the principle in this context and possibly infuse the interpretation of the two bills with these considerations.

Still, the recognition of the right to human dignity and its study reveals some interesting dynamics with regard to the creativity of the Conseil constitutionnel: first, as the right to human dignity is not expressly protected by the 1958 constitution, the Conseil had to resort to a rather loose interpretation of the Preamble of the 1946 constitution. In its opening paragraph, the 1946 Preamble reminds that 'after

---

[65]   See C cons no 343-344, DC 27 July 1994, Bio-ethics.

[66]   Two separate reports were produced on these issues: one by the Conseil d'Etat, *Science and Life*, in 1988 and one by a committee chaired by Noëlle Lenoir, *To the Borders of Life*, in 1991.

[67]   In fact, many commentators thought that the Conseil's decision fell well short; see B Edelman, 'Le Conseil constitutionnel et l'embryon' (1995) I *Dalloz*, 205.

the victory of the free peoples over those regimes that attempted . . . to degrade human beings, the French people proclaim anew that all human beings . . . have inalienable and sacred rights'. From this statement, the Conseil deduced the existence of a right to human dignity in the French constitution. Although the link to the constitutional text is tenuous, the recognition aimed to meet the concerns expressed by Members of Parliament (and the wider public); consequently, the legitimacy of this new tool was not contested. This exemplifies the complex relationship that exists between the Conseil constitutionnel, the Parliament and public opinion. It sheds some light on the process of recognition of rights and freedoms and the legitimacy of doing so. It would have been difficult to contest the recognition of such a right; in fact, for many, the Conseil did not go far enough.

Subsequent use of this right may seem controversial though. For instance, when controlling the legislation on civil partnerships or PACS, the Conseil decided that the right to break the PACS unilaterally by one of the partners was not a breach of human dignity as his/her liability was open to challenge in the private law courts.

Finally, the Balladur committee contemplated the incorporation of this right into the constitution. However, the committee did not recommend further constitutional recognition and noted that its content was already well defined by case law.[68]

The Right to Rest

The rights and freedoms that have been presented above are those that many constitutions recognise and protect. However, to some, the decision to grant full constitutional protection to people's days off or holiday entitlement may appear somewhat disproportionate. However, there is an explicit mention of the need to guarantee rest in paragraph 11 of the Preamble of the 1946 constitution.[69] It may have seemed a simple statement of intention, but given the right circumstances, the Conseil constitutionnel would be justified in declaring its constitutional status. Indeed in 2000,[70] the Conseil chose to specify in its ruling on the bill reducing the working week to 35 hours, that the provisions aimed

---

[68] See the Balladur report, p 86 http://www.ladocumentationfrancaise.fr/var/ storage/rapports-publics/074000697/0000.pdf.

[69] See Paragraph 11: '[The Nation] guarantees to all – in particular children, mothers and old workers – health protection, material security, rest and leisure . . .'

[70] See C cons no 99-423 DC, 13 January 2000.

to give effect to paragraphs 5 (right to work) and 11 of the 1946 Preamble.

More recently, the Conseil constitutionnel clarified the content of this right.[71] The bill submitted to the Conseil amended the system of derogations from the principle of the Sunday rest, ie the principle that all workers benefit from a day off on Sunday. Parliament wished to widen the existing derogations to take account of the growing impact of tourism. However, the right to a weekly rest (generally on Sunday) has been recognised in the statute of 13 July 1906 and is regarded as one of the great advances of labour law. At present, it is firmly ensconced in article L3132-1 of the labour code. The Members of Parliament who challenged the constitutionality of the bill argued that the Sunday rest is guaranteed by reference to paragraph 11 of the 1946 Preamble and that the new system of derogations infringed this right. Although the Conseil decided that the constitutional provision had not been breached in this instance, it indicated that the principle of a Sunday rest came under paragraph 11 of the 1946 Preamble.

This demonstrates that the case law of the Conseil is rather all embracing and that few areas have escaped its attention. Indeed this creative activity has had a definite and lasting impact on French constitutional law.

The Revenge of French Constitutional Law and the Triumph of Legal Constitutionalism

The evolution of the Conseil constitutionnel's role has had other unexpected but concomitant effects: French constitutional law has been transformed in three different ways. As explained in chapter one, the effectiveness of many past constitutions was often compromised. Prior to the fifth Republic, the constitution may have been a legal document but it was not easily enforceable: neither the Conseil d'Etat[72] nor the Cour de cassation[73] accepted jurisdiction to review the constitutionality of primary legislation. Consequently, political behaviour took place outside, and sometimes in breach of, the constitutional document. By ensuring that the constitution is finally guaranteed through law, the Conseil constitutionnel has encouraged the rise of legal constitutionalism. The

---

[71] See C cons no 2009-588 DC, 6 August 2009.
[72] See CE 1936 *Arrighi*.
[73] See C. cass. 1833 *Paulin*.

fifth Republic has witnessed the normative awakening of the French constitution.

The control of the Conseil constitutionnel has also changed the very content of French constitutional law. Traditionally, constitutional law concentrated on the description and analysis of the political institutions, their respective powers and their interrelationships. Considering the failure of many past constitutions to regulate the political system and to submit political behaviour to the law, this focus of constitutional law was to be expected. However, the case law of the Conseil constitutionnel has altered this understanding of constitutional law: with the recognition of many rights and freedoms, substantive constitutional law has acquired a normative dimension previously unknown.[74] The revolutionary ideal encapsulated in article 16 of the 1789 Declaration that a constitution must contain and impose both institutional and substantive limitations, has become a constitutional reality.

Finally, the creativity of the Conseil constitutionnel has had far greater impact than may appear at first: as the normative content of the constitution grows, so does the influence of constitutional law over the entire legal system. Nowadays, few areas of law are impermeable to constitutional law: labour law, contract law, medical law, criminal procedure, administrative law and property law, to name but a few, all have strong constitutional elements. Indeed, some commentators have argued that this was a long-awaited 'revenge' of constitutional law: the reach of constitutional law is now so great that many areas of law have an incontrovertible constitutional core. From being peripheral, constitutional law has moved and settled at the centre of the legal system, displacing more traditional subjects such as property, contract or administrative law. In doing so, both constitutional law and constitutionalism have leaped forward. In turn, this transformation has served to legitimise the Conseil constitutionnel.

The Need for Further Change

One issue would need to be addressed still to strengthen the Conseil constitutionnel in its role of constitutional court: its membership. Also,

---

[74] However, the case law of the Conseil d'Etat guaranteed a number of constitutional rights and freedoms when reviewing secondary legislation.

in the short term, the three supreme courts need to improve their relationship.

The Membership of the Conseil constitutionnel

When analysing the mode of recruitment to the Conseil constitutionnel, it is necessary to remember that it was never meant to undertake a full constitutional review. Article 56 of the 1958 constitution states that the Conseil constitutionnel is staffed with nine members appointed for a single term of nine years; membership is renewable by a third every three years. The President of the Republic, the president of the Assemblée nationale and the president of the Sénat appoint three members each. These appointments are subject to the procedure of parliamentary approval contained in article 13 § 5 of the constitution.[75] Furthermore, the President of the Republic appoints the president of the Conseil constitutionnel. This last appointment is crucial as the president casts the deciding vote if the Conseil is equally divided on a decision. Also, the president of the Conseil constitutionnel plays a key institutional role: he appoints the General Secretary,[76] designates the *rapporteur* in each case,[77] chairs the debates, and represents the institution to the outside world. One wonders whether he/ she would not be better chosen by the members of the Conseil themselves. It would certainly increase the independence of the institution. In addition to the nine ordinary members, former Presidents of the Republic are automatically members of the Conseil for life.

This system of appointment reflects the ambiguity of the institution highlighted before. The Conseil may be a court but it has a strong political flavour. First, there is no requirement that the appointees have any

[75] Claire Bazy-Malaurie was the first member of the Conseil to be heard formally according to this procedure in August 2010. However, the previous three appointees had been subjected to informal hearings. Overall, the experiences were not fully convincing.

[76] The General Secretary heads the administrative services of the Conseil constitutionnel and he is a key figure.

[77] For each decision, a member of the Conseil is chosen to act as *rapporteur* or reporter. He/she will be in charge of researching the case in depth, analysing the case law of the Conseil itself and of any other relevant courts (eg ECJ or ECtHR) and preparing a draft decision for discussion by the Conseil constitutionnel. The president of the Conseil looks to an individual member's qualifications and experiences when choosing him/her to act as *rapporteur* on a given case.

legal qualifications or training. Secondly, the 'political past' of many members of the Conseil constitutionnel indicates the reality of a 'political bias' with regard to the recruitment process. It is not surprising, therefore, that a number of appointments have been criticised in the past[78] and that some have even threatened the legitimacy of the institution.[79] Surprisingly, although the Conseil constitutionnel has been transformed by successive constitutional reforms, little has been done to strengthen the recruitment and membership of the Conseil; the 2008 reform may have required that appointments to the Conseil be confirmed by the new procedure for parliamentary approval, but this is not enough. Recruitment and membership need to be reformed further.[80]

An Analysis of the Appointees of the Conseil constitutionnel

81 members of the Conseil constitutionnel have been appointed to this day and a number of conclusions can be drawn from the analysis of these appointments.[81] First, a majority pursued a legal career: 11 professors of law, 15 members of the Conseil d'Etat, 16 barristers, four judges of the Cour de cassation, two members of the Court of Auditors, one solicitor, one head of the legal service of a public corporation etc. When it comes to legal qualifications, 50.6 per cent have a law degree and 30 per cent have a doctorate in law. Furthermore, of those without legal education or career, a number had highly relevant prior experience: Robert Fabre may have been a pharmacist by training but he had been the Ombudsman prior to his appointment to the Conseil constitutionnel; similarly, Daniel Mayer may have been a journalist and politician but his work for the protection of human rights and his presidency of the Ligue des droits de l'Homme made him a desirable appointee; and Edmond Michelet may have been a salesman originally, but he was Minister of Justice prior to his appointment to the Conseil. Also, for an

---

[78] The appointment of Badinter as president of the Conseil constitutionnel by President Mitterrand was rightly criticised. Badinter was minister for justice at the time and the party in power was about to lose the election. It is widely believed that this decision was taken in view of the predicted losses for the socialist party in the upcoming election.

[79] Notable crises of legitimacy were experienced in 1993 and 2000; see D Schnapper (n 27) 100.

[80] See D Rousseau 'Article 56, une procédure de nomination toujours discutable' in J-P Camby, P Fraisseix and J Gicquel (eds), *La révision de 2008: une nouvelle constitution?* (Paris, Librairie générale de droit et de jurisdiction, 2011) 315.

[81] Life members were excluded from this analysis.

institution which reviews the constitutionality of all primary legislation, the membership gains from being varied: other the years, the input of a chemist, a pharmacist, a sociologist, a diplomat, an engineer and journalists can only have been beneficial. In practice, the Conseil is staffed with a similar proportion of lawyers as other constitutional courts. Still, as there is no legal requirement of prior legal education or judicial training, the present balance may be altered at any time.

Secondly, many members of the Conseil constitutionnel have strong political affiliations, if not a previous political career. Among the 81 members, 22 have been ministers at some point during their career. In fact, a few members of the Conseil constitutionnel were ministers at the time of their appointment (see Robert Badinter, Gaston Palewski) and others became ministers after their tenure (see Edmond Michelet, Pierre Legatte, Noelle Lenoir) or on resigning (Georges Pompidou who became Prime Minister and later President of the Republic). The career of many members of the Conseil constitutionnel is clearly political: 56 per cent of all appointees have had a political career. Interestingly, this strong link with politics has never damaged the legitimacy of the institution. Also, the appointees are often political sympathisers or friends of the person whose duty it is to make the appointment. René Cassin was a friend of de Gaulle. However, as a brilliant lawyer and Nobel peace prize winner nobody could object. Similarly, Mitterrand appointed his Minister of Justice, Robert Badinter, and later his Minister for Foreign Affairs, Roland Dumas. But again, both were renowned lawyers prior to their ministerial appointments. Robert Badinter had also campaigned tirelessly for the abolition of the death penalty. Indeed, the appointment of renowned lawyers has helped establish the credibility of the institution.[82] Although, one commentator has remarked that the number of politicians appointed to the Conseil has diminished in recent years and has warned against this trend,[83] the recent appointments have seen the nomination of two senators, a past European Commissioner (February 2010) and a president of chamber of the court of auditors and top civil servant (August 2010). For many, this combination of legal and political experience is essential to the success of the Conseil constitutionnel; still,

[82] For instance, Badinter is credited with the transformation of the institution into a credible court.

[83] See G Carcassonne, 'Les membres du Conseil constitutionnel: 1958–2008', Colloque du cinquantenaire du Conseil constitutionnel, 3 November 2008, Conseil constitutionnel.

in view of the recent reform, one may worry about the legitimacy of the institution.

The Former Presidents of the Republic

According to article 56 of the constitution, former Presidents of the Republic are members of the Conseil for life. This provision was meant to recognise the crucial role that both Presidents of the fourth Republic had played in the return of de Gaulle to political life. Furthermore, the choice was understandable in view of the role that the President of the Republic was originally meant to fulfil. The President was conceived as a constitutional referee, above party politics and responsible for the proper functioning of the political system. In this context, it made sense to make past Presidents members of the Conseil constitutionnel automatically and for life; it was a continuation of their previous role. However, the presidential interpretation of the constitution undermines the rationale for this membership and strengthens further the political outlook of the institution.

Furthermore, the attitude of former Presidents with regard to their appointment has given rise to criticisms. Although the appointment is automatic, the practice of past presidents has varied greatly: de Gaulle refused to sit altogether while René Coty took up his appointment. Vincent Auriol decided to leave the institution after disagreeing strongly with de Gaulle's interpretations of the constitution but returned in 1962 to support the challenge by the president of the Sénat of the use of article 11 to amend the constitution. Similarly, Giscard d'Estaing announced on losing the elections in 1981 that he would only sit when the legislation before the Conseil threatened the institutions or the unity of the Republic. In reality, he was only able to sit from March 2004 as he held electoral mandates prior to that. Among other things, he chaired the Convention on the Future of Europe, responsible for drafting the new constitutional treaty. For this reason, he took an active part in the campaign for the referendum on the European constitution in May 2005 while all the time an official member of the Conseil constitutionnel. More recently, Jacques Chirac announced that he would not sit as a member of the Conseil for the duration of the criminal trial in which he was involved.[84] These practices do not help with the legitimacy of the institution.

---

[84] See Jean-Louis Debré, 'M. Chirac ne siégera pas durant la durée de son procès', *Le Monde*, 6 March 2011.

Finally, with the mandate of the President of the Republic reduced to five years, the number of past Presidents in the Conseil constitutionnel is likely to increase rapidly. By 2012, Sarkozy could be joining Giscard d'Estaing and Chirac. In an institution which numbers only nine appointees, three ex-Presidents may cause a serious imbalance. All in all, it would be much better if past Presidents were no longer members of the Conseil by right. Indeed, it is a pity that the amendment to this effect debated in the Sénat during the 2008 constitutional reform was not adopted.

A Difficult Judicial Cooperation

The reform has had a difficult beginning. As explained above, the new preliminary ruling requires a degree of cooperation between the three supreme courts: Conseil constitutionnel, Conseil d'Etat and Cour de cassation. However, the relationship between them has been fraught, particularly when it comes to the Cour de cassation.

Although the Cour de cassation and Conseil d'Etat declared a willingness to cooperate when the reform was adopted, one year on, the assessment is not so favourable. The Cour de cassation rebelled against the new procedure from the outset; it began the hostilities early with a decision of 16 April 2010, which referred to the Court of Justice the organic law of 10 December 2009 implementing article 61-1. It wished to engineer a confrontation between the preliminary reference of the European Union and the new procedure for a preliminary ruling on an issue of constitutionality. The Cour de cassation argued that once legislation is validated by the Conseil constitutionnel, it could no longer be the subject of a reference under article 267 of the Treaty on the Functioning of the European Union (TFEU). The Cour de cassation was trying to involve the Court of Justice in an internal struggle between supreme courts. The Court of Justice rose to the challenge:[85] it endorsed the new procedure but specified that all courts should always be free to make a reference under article 267 TFEU. Back in Paris, the Cour de cassation aggravated the Conseil constitutionnel further by deciding the entire case on the basis of European law without ever investigating whether the conditions for a preliminary ruling on an issue of constitutionality were met.

---

[85] See ECJ C-188 and 189/10, 22 June 2010, *Melki and Abdeli.*

The rebellion of the Cour de cassation led to further skirmishes all through 2010 and continued into 2011. In fact, the attitude of the Cour de cassation has made an enemy of the Conseil constitutionnel and of the French Parliament. This rebellion has even revealed disagreements between the various chambers of the Cour de cassation. In October 2010 the criminal chamber of the Cour de cassation decided that the rules relating to police custody were not compatible with article 6 § 1 of the ECHR but that in the interests of the administration of justice, these rulings could not take immediate effect, thereby giving effect to the earlier ruling of the Conseil constitutionnel on this question, albeit indirectly. However, the plenary of the Cour de cassation decided in four rulings on 15 April 2011 that the provisions on police custody breached article 6 § 1 of the ECHR and that this pronouncement had immediate effect. Not only did this violate the authority of the decisions of the Conseil constitutionnel (by altering the deadline), but it aggravated Parliament too. The Cour de cassation handed down its decision one day after Parliament had successfully adopted the new legislation on police custody. The decisions of the Cour de cassation gave immediate effect to the right of access to legal representation and to the warning of the right to silence during police custody.

By contrast, the Conseil d'Etat had always indicated its wish to enter into loyal cooperation with the Conseil constitutionnel. In practice, relationships may be a little tense but open rebellion is not on the agenda. Still, the Conseil d'Etat refused to forward a preliminary ruling on an issue of constitutionality which questioned the constitutionality of the internal organisation and dual functions of the Conseil d'Etat: court and advisors of the Government.[86]

Reasonable cooperation between the three supreme courts will have to be established sooner or later. In the meantime, the serenity of judicial proceedings is being compromised.

TOWARDS A JUDICIAL POWER?

Although the French judiciary is not labelled a power by the 1958 constitution, it has been transformed beyond recognition. Indeed, the recent reform of the Conseil constitutionnel has helped complete this constitutional transformation.

---

[86] See CE 16 April 2010 no 320667, *Association Alcaly*.

The Institutional Transformations

Although it was possible to conceptualise the French judiciary as a judicial power prior to the constitutional reform of July 2008, the changes made then have greatly clarified the constitutional position. The creation of the new preliminary ruling on an issue of constitutionality has endowed the Conseil constitutionnel with the status of a quasi-constitutional court; it is no longer the ambiguous and reluctant guardian of the Executive. The evolution that began in 1971 has been brought to a successful conclusion: the Conseil ensures that fundamental rights and freedoms are placed at the top of the hierarchy of norms.

Also, the new procedure requires that both supreme courts play a pivotal role in its exercise. In doing so, the reform has associated both supreme courts with the control of constitutionality: with the Conseil constitutionnel they establish a tight network of constitutional review. Their activity in this domain has certainly transformed their constitutional status. In fact, were the means of the Conseil with regard to judicial and administrative staff not increased to match the success of the institution in the future, the Conseil constitutionnel may have to rely on the supreme courts to keep the case load manageable. Interestingly, the Conseil constitutionnel was keen to avoid a strict hierarchy between the three courts; it indicated that it would not review the manner in which either court applied the conditions triggering the preliminary procedure.[87] This new and complex judicial structure of constitutional control contributes greatly to the recognition of the third constitutional power. Again, the oddity and limitations of Title VIII of the 1958 constitution have been transcended by a combination of constitutional reform and constitutional change.

The Changing Role of the French Judiciary

Many structural changes to the French judiciary were dictated by a sharp rise in the demand for justice. This demand found its expression in the exponential growth of the case load of all French courts: be they civil, criminal or administrative.[88] Year on year, the number of cases increased

---

[87]   See C cons no 2010-1 QPC, 28 May 2010, Consorts L.

[88]   See J Royer, J-P Jean, B Durand, N Derasse and B Dubois, *Histoire de la justice en France*, 4th edn (Paris, Presses universitaires de France, 2010) 1124.

substantially for most courts: for instance, the number of civil cases doubled during the period 1982–91. As a consequence, more courts or more chambers within each court were created and more judges were appointed. Although the number of new cases seems to have levelled for both the private and administrative courts, the system is stretched and cases are often heard after long delays. Indeed, the ECtHR has condemned France repeatedly on this ground.[89] Many commentators have argued (and deplored the fact) that this demand for justice has 'judicialised' all aspects of society. Judges are required to intervene with regard to most societal issues and they pass judgment on an ever-widening range of questions: moral, economic, political, ethical, scientific etc. Since the 1970s, a number of court cases have triggered fundamental debates in society and even heralded major legislative reforms: for instance, the prosecution for unlawful abortion of Marie-Claire X, despite the fact that she was barely sixteen and a rape victim, undermined the legitimacy of the ban. Not only was she freed but abortion was legalised soon after. Similarly, two criminal cases militated in the 1970s for the abolition of the death penalty. In 1971, Bontemps and Buffet led a prison revolt which ended with the killing of two hostages; they hoped that their death sentence would serve to abolish the death penalty. Later, the likely miscarriage of justice which led to the condemnation and execution of Christian Ranucci finally decided left-wing parties to endorse the abolition of the death penalty. This was done by the newly elected Socialist majority in October 1981.[90]

Also, courts have increasingly turned their attention to the political system and its accountability. Until recently, the French Parliament had neither the tools nor the political will to control closely the activity of the Executive. Consequently, an accountability gap had opened during the first part of the fifth Republic. Courts perceived and tried to fill it. For instance, during the 1990s, in an effort to 'clean up politics', the private law courts tackled a number of political scandals in relation to the illegal funding of political parties or the illegal use of public money. These criminal prosecutions often involved members of Government (past or present) and their aides. However, the inevitable media coverage disturbed many politicians and divided public opinion: for instance, the

---

[89] See *Cretello v France*, 23 January 2007. Mr Cretello was remanded in custody for 5 years before his case came before the court.

[90] See the statute of 9 October 1981.

investigation led by Eva Joly and Laurence Vivichievsky into the commissions paid by the directors of Elf to foreign governments appeared repeatedly on the front pages of newspapers. Roland Dumas, previously Minister for Foreign Affairs, was charged while president of the Conseil constitutionnel and he had to resign. Later, the court issued a verdict of 'not proven.'

Also, efforts have concentrated on improving the criminal liability of members of the Executive: while the constitutional reform of 1993 clarified the criminal liability of members of Government, the constitutional reform of 2007 specified the extent of the presidential immunity.

Finally, the Conseil constitutionnel itself has been conceptualised as a true judicial counter-power and the recent constitutional reform will only serve to strengthen this interpretation further.

Not surprisingly, the public has begun to demand more accountability for a judiciary frequently involved in deciding society's major choices and in regulating many aspects of social and political life. The French judiciary may be asked to be omnipresent but increasingly it is required to be accountable for it.

A Difficult Accountability

As explained above, the French courts have become key participants in many of the debates that shape French society and have endorsed a role of social regulator. It is not surprising, therefore, that demands are made for a better organisation of their accountability. However, the accountability of independent courts is challenging for most constitutional orders. In France, this question is complicated further by choices which impact the system of accountability.

A System of Collective Accountability

In France, judicial decision making is traditionally a collective process: ideally decisions are not taken by single judges but by judicial panels.[91] Furthermore, agreement on a ruling is achieved by negotiation between the panel members. Finally, the judicial drafting style, which is both concise and abstract, obliterates any individual opinions. In this context, the influence of individual judges is limited and mechanisms for individual

---

[91] Although the number of decisions taken by single judges has increased markedly in the last decades.

accountability have been largely overlooked. Indeed, the search for accountability has focused on collective processes. Procedures for appeal and review by higher courts correct erroneous legal interpretation of lower courts, but do not identify the judge(s) responsible. Also, the annual reports produced by the top courts detailing their workload, analysing the case law and proposing legislative reform do not report on the activity of individual judges. Similarly, the financial control performed by the Cour des comptes checks the overall cost and efficiency of the public service but does not investigate the actions of individual judges either. Even when a mistake or a failure of the public service can be attributed to one judge, the State is held liable in their stead, and many doubt that individual promotions and career prospects are really affected by such findings. Consequently, this emphasis on collective accountability in contrast to individual responsibility has been denounced time and again.

In fact, the Outreau affair revealed clear dysfunctions and obvious limitations of the system of judicial accountability. Several people were prosecuted and condemned for belonging to a paedophile ring but were found several years later to have been completely innocent.[92] On remand from the beginning, the accused and their families had had their lives ruined by this miscarriage of justice. This scandal shocked the Nation and the President of the Republic apologised officially to the families concerned in an attempt to own up to the facts. Unsurprisingly, a search for the 'culprit(s)' began. A scapegoat was found in the person of Francis Burgaud, the investigating magistrate, even though the parliamentary inquiry revealed serious dysfunctions and a poor culture of accountability in the judicial institutions concerned. In reality, a miscarriage of justice of this gravity could only have been the result of a catastrophic and systemic failure of the system of administration of justice. Still, not only was Burgaud the object of disciplinary proceedings (which culminated in a decision of the Conseil supérieur de la magistrature), but he was also heard at length during an unprecedented parliamentary inquiry into the event. Soon after, a reform attempted to increase individual accountability of the judiciary: the organic law of 5 March 2007 introduced a new disciplinary offence[93] and created a

---

[92] After a long investigation, 17 persons were prosecuted for belonging to a network of paedophiles. Seven were acquitted and 10 were condemned by the assizes court. On appeal, six persons more were acquitted. One man died while in custody.

[93] With the new offence, judges can be disciplined for 'a serious and deliberate breach of an essential procedural guarantee'.

procedure for complaints against individual judges before the *Médiateur*. However, these provisions were deemed to breach the principle of judicial independence by the Conseil constitutionnel. Again collective accountability had prevailed. However, in the wake of the reform of July 2008, the organic law[94] was amended to organise the new right to complain and trigger disciplinary proceedings before the Conseil supérieur de la magistrature as authorised by the new article 65 § 10 of the constitution.

The Issue of Corporatism

The accountability of the French judiciary is often said to be compromised by the corporatism (or *esprit de corps*) of its members. The recruitment, training and career structure of judges tend to strengthen this latent corporatism. Although not all judges are recruited from a *Grande Ecole*, a large contingent (if not a majority) will have passed through the *Ecole Nationale de la Magistrature* (ENM) for the private law judges or the *Ecole Nationale d'Administration* (ENA) for the administrative law judges. For many, the corporate identity begins in the 'school'. Also, a communality of ideas is derived from the values and principles that imbue the French public service (eg equality, neutrality, continuity, general interest etc); not only are these values internalised by judges early on but in all likelihood, they influence individual judges' outlook on many issues. Finally, judges in both the administrative and private law courts are represented by trade unions that relay their demands effectively, play a major role in professional bodies and have a direct influence over individual careers. They are often regarded as major contributors to this judicial corporatism.

   This separate corporate identity is said to influence the attitudes and societal choices of judges. For some, it may even compromise their understanding of society. Also, detractors regard corporatism as a threat to judicial accountability: latent corporatism may distort the processes of internal accountability and may compromise those ensuring external accountability. For this reason, attempts have been made to diversify judicial recruitment and since the constitutional reform of July 2008, private law judges are in a minority in the Conseil supérieur de la magistrature.[95] Still criticisms have not been quelled yet.

[94] See the organic law of 22 July 2010.
[95] See article 65 of the constitution.

CONCLUSION

The French judiciary seems to be emerging from the successive constitutional reforms as a renewed judicial power. Indeed, the recent reform of the Conseil constitutionnel has confirmed this evolution. However, the balance between the independence and the accountability of the judiciary is fragile and regularly comes under fire. It may be that both the independence and accountability of all French courts should be conceptualised and organised as a whole under the same driving principles. However, such a reform may be a long way off.

In any event, as the Conseil constitutionnel continues to grow in importance, the appointment and membership of this institution ought to be altered. Otherwise, the fragile balance described above runs the risk of being destabilised yet again. Also, a loss of legitimacy in constitutional review would adversely impact the Cour de cassation and the Conseil d'Etat as their new involvement increases greatly their exposure. The legitimacy of the whole judicial system may be at stake.

FURTHER READING

J Bell, *French Legal Cultures* (Cambridge, Cambridge University Press, 2001) chapter 6

S Boyron, 'The Independence of the Judiciary: A Question of Identity!' in G Canivet, M Andenas and D Fairgrieve, *Independence, Accountability and the Judiciary* (London, British Institute of International and Comparative Law, 2006) 77

C Guarnieri, 'Appointment and Career of Judges in Continental Europe: The Rise of Judicial Self-Government' (2004) *Legal Studies* 169–87

D Ludet, 'Conseil supérieur de la magistrature, une liberté . . . surveillée?' Les Petites Affiches, 19 December 2008, no 254, 111

La question prioritaire de constitutionnalité (2011) 137 *Pouvoirs*

C Maugüé and J-H Stahl, *La question prioritaire de constitutionnalité* (Paris, Dalloz, 2011)

F-X Millet, 'Le dialogue des juges à l'épreuve de la QPC' (2010) *Revue de droit public* 1729

A Roblot-Troizier, 'La QPC devant les juridictions ordinaires, entre méfiance et prudence' (2010) *Actualité juridique: droit administratif* 80

D Rouseau, *Droit du contentieux constitutionnel*, 9th edn (Paris, Montchrestien, 2010)

V Roussel, *Affaires de juges – Les magistrats dans les scandales politiques en France* (Paris, La Découverte, 2002)

H Roussillon and P Esplugas, *Le Conseil constitutionnel*, 7th edn (Paris, Dalloz, 2011)

A Stone, *The Birth of Judicial Politics in France: the Constitutional Council in Comparative Perspective* (Oxford, Oxford University Press, 1992)

Relevant websites

Conseil constitutionnel: www.conseil-constitutionnel.fr/
Conseil d'Etat: www.conseil-etat.fr/
Cour de cassation: www.courdecassation.fr/
Conseil supérieur de la magistrature: www.conseil-superieur-magistrature. fr/

6

The Constitution and its People

———◦———

The French People and the Constitution – The Sovereign Expression of the French People – A Culture of Rights Protection – Conclusion: A 'New' Citizen?

A FTER THE THREE branches of government, the people of the French political system need to be presented, especially as the concept holds a key position in the constitutional order: together French people form the sovereign. Indeed, the most important principle of French constitutional law is mentioned in the very first paragraph of article 3 of the 1958 constitution: 'National sovereignty belongs to the people who exercise it through their representatives and by means of referendum.' The constitution in this regard is clear and devoid of ambiguity: sovereignty is first and foremost located in the French people. Not only do the people serve to legitimise the regime, the institutions and the decision making, but they have and are the last word. The political system only serves to organise the expression of this sovereignty whether directly or indirectly. Indeed, many rules exist to channel the expression of the sovereign people and to ensure its accuracy.

Although the concept of popular sovereignty has a long historical lineage in France, the emphasis on a direct expression of this sovereignty is a more recent trend. In an attempt to get disaffected citizens interested in politics, a number of constitutional amendments were adopted in the last decade to bolster the status of citizens, involve them in rights protection and increase the tools of direct democracy.

In order to understand the growing place of the people in the French constitutional order, this chapter will first review the various constitutional incarnations of the sovereign people. It will then analyse the tools at the disposal of the people to express their sovereignty and guarantee their rights.

THE FRENCH PEOPLE AND THE CONSTITUTION

To assess the position of the people in the 1958 constitution, it is necessary to begin with the concept of national sovereignty mentioned in article 3 of the constitution. It will make it easier to understand the people in all its other constitutional guises.

National Sovereignty

Title I of the 1958 constitution on sovereignty contains three articles: while article 2 identifies among other things[1] the guiding principle of the French Republic as 'the Government of the people, by the people, for the people' and article 4 gives constitutional recognition to political parties, article 3 places sovereignty firmly in the French people and sets out key rules framing its expression.

For many commentators,[2] article 3 makes an ambiguous reference to two competing theories of sovereignty: national and popular sovereignty. These two understandings of sovereignty are rooted in diverging political theories. Popular sovereignty is based on the ideas of Rousseau, who states that only the actual French people can exercise sovereignty; this should be done preferably directly by referendum but also via elected officers who are deputised to the Parliament with a binding electoral mandate. These officers are not representatives of the people as the will of the people can never be represented. On the contrary, national sovereignty finds its expression through representative democracy and was inspired by Montesquieu. This theory places sovereignty in the Nation, which is an abstract and historical extrapolation of the French people, past, present and future. In this context, the Nation expresses itself via its elected representatives; these representatives are inherently free of any mandate. Although these theories are reconciled

---

[1] For an analysis of the characters, symbols, motto and guiding principle of the French Republic, see chapter 2.

[2] See G Drago, 'Article 3' in F Luchaire, G Conac and X Prétot (eds), *La constitution de la République française*, 3rd edn (Paris, Economica, 2008) 179.

with difficulty, the 1958 constitution seems to combine (and neutralise) both conceptions successfully: not only does it state that national sovereignty belongs to the people (and not to the Nation) but it organises a direct expression of sovereignty (popular sovereignty) alongside the standard institutions of representative democracy (national sovereignty). Also, in article 27 of the constitution, the logic of national sovereignty and representative democracy prevails again: the provision specifies that binding mandates are void and that the right to vote of Members of Parliament is personal.

The 1958 constitution may have reconciled creatively two conceptions of sovereignty, but arguably the originality with regard to sovereignty in the constitutional order is now elsewhere. First, with the constitutional reform of 1962, arguably the President of the Republic became an elected representative himself, a role which belonged exclusively to Members of Parliament prior to that.[3] Secondly, recent constitutional reforms have bolstered the tools of direct democracy and promoted a more active participation of the people in the constitutional order.

Citizenship: An Under-developed Concept?

The French people, whose expression participates in the exercise of national sovereignty, are made up of individual citizens. However, the term 'citizen' is only briefly mentioned in the 1958 constitution: article 1 states that [the Republic] 'ensures equality before the law of all citizens without any distinction of origins, race or religion'. In addition, article 6 of the Declaration of the Rights of Man and of the Citizen of 1789 states that 'the law is the expression of the general will' and that 'all citizens have the right to participate personally or via their representatives in its creation'. There, the constitution defines 'citizens' by their sovereign rights.

In fact, commentators argue that the concept of citizen or citizenship is still underdeveloped or imprecise[4] and is in need of restatement[5] in

---

[3] The Conseil constitutionnel states that all those elected by the French people participate in the exercise of sovereignty; see C cons no 76-71 DC, 29–30 December 1976, Election of the European Parliament.

[4] See D Lochak, 'La citoyenneté, un concept juridique flou' in D Colas, C Emeri and J Zylberberg (eds), *Nationalité et citoyenneté. Perspectives en France et au Québec* (Paris, Presses universitaires de Frances, 1991) 180.

[5] See A-S Michon-Traversac, *La citoyenneté en droit public français*, coll Thèses (Paris, Librairie générale de droit et de jurisprudence, 2009) 7.

France. In reality, studies investigating this concept abound but reflect differing views and opinions as to its content and import.[6] Paradoxically, many note that the term citizen or citizenship is very much used and abused in France: for instance, the existence of 'an administrative citizenship' has been put forward and the expression 'citizen car'[7] has been officially registered. After two hundred years in constant use, it would seem that the meaning of citizen needs to be restated.

In 1789 there was a clear tendency to assimilate the rights of citizens to those of men in general. This can be explained by the universality of the declaration of 1789: the rights of citizens contained therein should be those of all humans. This rather philosophical attitude does not reflect the legal reality then or now. To this day, not every human on French soil is a French citizen. In 1789, less than half the population could aspire to be a citizen as neither women nor domestic servants had the right to vote. Furthermore, citizens were either active or passive: for a long while, the right to vote was not open to all men but subject to the payment of a tax. Those citizens who did not pay a certain amount in tax were 'passive citizens' only. Although the content of citizenship may not be easily extrapolated from the provisions of the constitution, the right to political participation remains its main component: citizens need the political rights necessary to voice the will of the sovereign. Not only is this conveyed by article 6 of the 1789 Declaration but the Conseil constitutionnel seems to agree with this interpretation: in a decision of 18 October 1982, it specified that the status of citizen triggers the right to vote and to be elected.[8]

The Electorate

Beyond the principle of national sovereignty, article 3 contains key rules framing the expression of this sovereignty. It states that the suffrage is always universal. This is relatively recent progress: universal suffrage for men may have been constant since 1848, but women were only given the right to vote in 1944.[9] In fact, the authors of the constitution did not

---

[6] See B Hérisson, *L'évolution de la citoyenneté en droit public français*, unpublished thesis, Paris I, 1995 and Michon-Traversac (n 5).
[7] See www.voiturecitoyenne.fr.
[8] See C cons no 82-146 DC, 18 November 1982, Quotas I.
[9] See the ordinance of 21 April 1944.

leave the composition of the electorate to the discretion of the legislator: article 3 states in paragraph 4 that 'all French nationals of both sexes who have reached the age of majority are electors, so long as they benefit from civil and political rights'.

There, French nationality conditions citizenship. Consequently, the concepts of citizenship and nationality have developed a symbiotic relationship.[10] In fact, since the law of 8 December 1983, once nationality has been granted by naturalisation, the person obtains immediately the right to vote and to be elected. Therefore, all French nationals of 18 years or over have the right to vote barring two exceptions. According to the electoral code, a judge may remove the right to vote from an adult whom he has made a ward of court.[11] Also, a citizen may be deprived of the right to vote on receiving a criminal sentence. While some crimes carry a systematic loss of political rights for five years,[12] for others, the court will make an individual decision whether or not to deprive the person of his/her political rights.[13]

Nationality has therefore become the main criterion when determining someone's voting rights. However, the evolution of the recognition and attribution of nationality in France has been relatively complex and has had no linear history. The two conceptions of *jus soli* (place of birth) and *jus sanguinis* (parentage) have alternated through time: for instance, while the legislation resulting from the 1789 Revolution granted French nationality to those born in France, the civil code of 1804 did so on the basis of parentage. Still, later legislation adapted the principle of *jus sanguinis* to allow for naturalisation.[14] Again, an important wave of naturalisation was necessary after World War I and culminated in the law of 10 August 1927. This was stopped in the run-up to World War II, and during the Vichy regime the rights of naturalised citizens were restricted. After 1945, the circumstances changed again and the code of nationality was born.

During the mid 1980s the debates intensified between the two conceptions as the broad consensus of the past began to wane; immigration

---

[10] See F Borella, 'Nationalité et citoyenneté' in D Colas, C Emeri and J Zylberberg (eds) (n 4) 209.
[11] See article L. 5 of the electoral code. A stay in psychiatric hospital (forced or not) does not deprive the patient of his/her voting rights, see articles L. 3211-2 and 3211-3 of the code for public health.
[12] See article L. 7 of the electoral code.
[13] See article L. 6 of the electoral code.
[14] See the law of 29 January–7 February 1851.

was adding another layer of complexity to the question of nationality.[15] Important changes were made in 1993,[16] when the code of nationality was replaced by the code on asylum rights and on entry and stay of foreigners. Since then, the debate on immigration has driven the debate on nationality.[17] In fact, it has also coloured the question of voting rights: the possibility of granting some voting rights to permanent residents is proposed with increasing regularity.[18]

At present, the concepts of citizenship and nationality seem to be moving further apart.[19] At supranational level, EU citizenship conditions voting rights in local elections for all EU permanent residents. This is recognised in article 88-3 of the French constitution. Also, at subnational level, the Noumea agreements have resulted in a distinct New-Caledonian citizenship separate from the French one. In turn, it led to the recognition of a separate electorate.[20]

French People or French Peoples of the Republic?

Still, this latest evolution at subnational level is restricted: article 3 states in its second paragraph that 'no section of the people and no individual can usurp for itself, or himself the exercise [of national sovereignty]'. It is not surprising that the unity of the French people is proclaimed so starkly in this provision: the very integrity of the sovereign is at stake. Any subgroup of the French people can never aspire to sovereignty.

The principle of unity of the French people is also required by the principle of equality: each French citizen is equal in his/her exercise of

[15] See Commission de nationalité, *Etre français aujourd'hui et demain*, which proposed that children born of foreign parents should no longer be granted French nationality systematically.
[16] See the law of 22 July 1993.
[17] In recent legislation, the questions of immigration and nationality are regulated together, see the laws of 24 July 2006 and of 16 June 2011.
[18] J-M Denquin, 'Citoyenneté' in D Alland and S Rials (eds), *Dictionnaire de la culture juridique* (Paris, Lamy-PUF, 2003) 198. For instance, a constitutional reform that aimed to grant voting rights in local elections to all permanent residents on French soil has been revitalised by the Sénat recently.
[19] See Sophie Duchesne, 'Citoyenneté, nationalité et vote' in (2007) 120 *Voter–Pouvoirs* 71.
[20] Article 77 § 4 was added by constitutional reform of February 2007. This aimed to neutralise a decision of the Conseil constitutionnel which favoured a softer New-Caledonian citizenship.

national sovereignty (ie one voter, one vote). This political equality may not reflect economic or social reality, but it has a strong legal and symbolic content in France.

For these reasons, the Conseil constitutionnel is particularly careful to protect the indivisibility of the French people. In the decision concerning the territorial entity of Corsica,[21] the Conseil listed the references to the French people in the constitution. It also recalled that the expression 'French people' has been used in many constitutional documents during the last two hundred years. It could only conclude that the principle has constitutional value. Furthermore, the Conseil specified that not only the concept of 'French people' is constitutional, but so too is the 'principle of unity of the French people'. Consequently, in the 'Corsica' decision, the Conseil constitutionnel specified that the Corsican people could not be recognised as a distinct entity and could not be granted a separate Corsican identity. Even though the legislation stated that 'the Corsican people' were a component of 'the French people', and that the rights of conservation of their cultural identity and of protection of their specific economic and social interests were exercised in respect of national unity, the Conseil constitutionnnel declared the provision to be unconstitutional. It must have felt justified in adopting a strict interpretation in view of the implications for national sovereignty. In fact, this statement was followed with further declarations of unconstitutionality: the Conseil annulled the provisions organising the electoral representation of the Corsican territorial entity. Among other things, it rejected the electoral system chosen specifically for the island.

Similarly, when controlling the European Charter for Regional or Minority Languages,[22] the Conseil constitutionnel debated the recognition of these languages. It specified that articles 1 and 3 of the constitution prohibit strictly the recognition of collective rights to any group on the basis of origins, culture, language or faith. As the charter tackled possible administrative obstacles to the use (spoken and written) of regional and minority languages and encouraged the creation of separate institutions to protect and promote these languages, the Conseil reached the conclusion that the Charter was granting specific rights to the speakers of these languages and that this recognition was clearly prohibited by the constitution.

[21] See C cons no 91-290 DC, 9 May 1991, Corsica.
[22] See C cons no 99-1412 DC, 15 June 1999, European Charter for Regional or Minority Languages.

THE SOVEREIGN EXPRESSION OF THE FRENCH PEOPLE

Now that 'the French people' have been analysed in their various constitutional guises, the mechanisms used by the sovereign people to express their views will be presented and examined.

Also, the constitution may contain provisions indicative of direct or representative democracy, but in practice, French people have been known to make themselves heard in other ways, ways which are not devoid of constitutional roots.

The Indirect Expression of the French People

As identified in article 3 of the constitution, the election of representatives contributes to the indirect expression of the sovereign people. In fact, French citizens elect the President of the Republic and both houses of Parliament. Only the Prime Minister escapes this electoral endorsement.

From the beginning, the constitution has tried to frame the electoral process, albeit with a relative degree of abstraction. Increasingly, the constitution and Parliament have had to intervene to regulate the elections, the electoral process and its various participants.

The Elections

The constitution protects the electors when they exercise their right to vote, but arguably it is less particular with the accuracy of their representation.

The Right to Vote: Some Constitutional Protection

In paragraph 3, article 3 states that the suffrage is not only universal, but it is also equal and secret. Secrecy is indeed essential for the freedom of political expression. In practice, this is translated by the provision of polling booths in all polling stations and the strict obligation for all citizens to make use of them.[23]

---

[23] See article L. 62 of the electoral code.

The requirement of equality of suffrage is an application of the general principle of equality proclaimed in article 1 of the constitution.[24] However, in this particular instance, it has given rise to some difficulties and controversies. In practice, the principle of equal suffrage means that each elector can cast one vote only, thereby ensuring that the vote of each citizen has equal value. The Conseil constitutionnel has always taken this requirement very seriously. For instance, it has declared plural voting to be prohibited by the constitution.[25] Furthermore, this requirement of equality has important implications when determining constituency boundaries.[26] The Conseil has stated repeatedly that equal suffrage requires that a (roughly) equal part of the French population elects each representative; otherwise, the ballot of some electors has more weight than the ballot of others. Consequently, the Conseil has stressed on numerous occasions that the boundaries of constituencies must be drawn by reference to demographic data and that they should be reviewed at regular intervals.[27] However, by the time the Balladur committee met, the boundaries had not been reviewed since 1986 and at least 40 constituencies were in breach of the Conseil constitutionnel's directions. Consequently, the Balladur committee recommended that constituency boundaries be reviewed automatically every 10 years and that this be supervised by an independent boundary commission.[28] Consequently, a boundary commission was introduced in article 25 § 3 of the constitution by the reform of July 2008. The commission was set up in April 2009 and new boundaries were approved by a law of 23 February 2010.[29]

Finally, the Conseil constitutionnel's strict interpretation of the requirement for equal suffrage has created consternation and controversy among politicians. For a better representation of the people, many felt it necessary to increase the number of women in Parliament. To do so, legislation was passed in 1982 to impose a minimum quota of female

---

[24] See chapter 2.

[25] See C cons no 78-101 DC, 17 January 1979.

[26] See P Avril, 'Un homme, une voix?' in *Voter–Pouvoirs* (n 19) 123.

[27] See C cons no 85-196 DC, 8 August 1985, *New Caledonia I*, and also its observations published on 7 July 2005 for the upcoming elections.

[28] See the report of the Balladur committee, p 71.

[29] Commentators have criticised the consultative role of the commission, see C Benelbaz, 'Le redécoupage électoral sous la Vè République' (2010) *Revue du droit public* 1661.

candidates sponsored by political parties. However, the Conseil declared unconstitutional all attempts at positive discrimination.[30] In doing so, the Conseil asserted that the principle of equality was not restricted to the right to vote but also applied to eligibility. A constitutional reform was adopted in July 1999[31] to neutralise the case law of the Conseil. In article 1 of the constitution, a new paragraph 3 states that laws shall promote equal access of men and women to electoral mandates and elected offices. Since the constitutional reform of July 2008, this obligation has extended to leadership positions in private companies, charities and trade unions.

The search for better representation

The regime of the fifth Republic requires of electors to vote more frequently than ever before. With presidential, parliamentary, municipal, departmental and regional elections (not counting a referendum now and then), some have argued that this over-representation results in a certain electoral fatigue.[32]

Surprisingly, the constitution is quite laconic when it comes to elections. As explained above, article 3 states general principles only. Further information can be found elsewhere in the constitution: for instance, articles 6 and 7 of the constitution set out in relative detail the process for the election of the President of the Republic. By comparison, article 24 contains little information with regard to the elections for both houses of Parliament. It does not even cite the relevant electoral systems.

However, the Balladur committee noted the need for better representation of the French people by Parliament. In fact, ways to improve representation have been debated repeatedly, especially in the last two decades. Arguably, the reform of the electoral system for the Assemblée nationale in 1986 aimed to do just that. However, proportional representation in the long term would have compromised the majority phenomenon and undermined the political stability of the regime; it was soon abandoned. Similarly, the failed reform of the electoral college of the Sénat in 2000[33] left that question unsolved. Unsurprisingly, the

---

[30] See C cons no 82-146 DC, 18 November 1982, Quotas I.

[31] See the constitutional law of 8 July 1999. It added a paragraph to article 1 of the constitution.

[32] Between 1958 and 2005 there have been only 10 years without any elections (national or local).

[33] See chapter 4.

Balladur committee identified four pressing issues with regard to representation: the electoral system of the Assemblée nationale, the determination of the constituency boundaries, the composition of the electoral college of the Sénat and the representation of French citizens abroad.[34] The committee made proposals on all these. However, the constitutional reform of July 2008 made no change to the elections of either house of Parliament.

Still, following an amendment of article 24 § 5 of the constitution, French citizens abroad will be now represented in both the Sénat (as was the case before) and the Assemblée nationale.[35] One cannot help thinking that representation was only improved marginally by the reform of July 2008.

Limiting the Electoral Mandates

Politicians of all parties share a practice which is at variance with the practice of their counterparts in other Western democracies: in France, 80 per cent of Members of Parliament also hold a local electoral mandate. This accumulation of national and local mandates has been regarded as a serious problem for a long time as it leads to a high level of absenteeism in both houses of Parliament.[36] Consequently, successive reforms have limited this practice. Since the law of 30 December 1985, Members of Parliament are limited to one other electoral mandate.

The Regulation of Political Competition

Elections do not take place in a vacuum: representative democracy needs political parties to channel citizens' demands and organise political debate. In addition, for political parties to thrive and compete, they must evolve in a carefully regulated democratic space.

The Constitutional Status of Political Parties: Article 4

The 1958 constitution contains a recognition of political parties for the first time in French constitutional history. Arguably, the constitution aimed to control the activity of political parties as these were responsible

[34] See the report of the Balladur committee (n 28) p 69.
[35] Eleven new constituencies were created to cover all regions of the globe: see the ordinance of 29 July 2009.
[36] French Members of Parliament with multiple mandates often favour their local mandate over their parliamentary one.

for so many dysfunctions in the previous republic. Still, article 4 § 1 of the constitution establishes a status for political parties in outline only: it proclaims their freedom by ensuring that they are created and exercise their activities freely.[37] At the same time, article 4 § 1 imposes obligations: political parties must 'respect the principles of national sovereignty and democracy'.[38] This requirement is enforced by checking the aims and activities[39] of each of the political parties. If a party's aims or activities contravene either of these principles, it can be dissolved on the basis of the law of 10 January 1936 on combat groups and militia.[40] In addition, article 4 § 2 requires that political parties promote and apply the constitutional principle of parity as stated in article 1 of the constitution. The constitutional reforms of 1999 and 2008 aimed to increase the participation of women in public life and have forced political parties to choose male and female candidates in equal number. In practice, political parties are penalised financially if they do not respect parity: deductions are made from their share of State financing.[41]

Article 4 § 1 describes also the role assumed by political parties, albeit rather narrowly: political parties 'participate in the expression of suffrage'. There, they are conceived in the electoral context only. Not only is this description silent on the key aims of political parties – to assume and exercise political power – but it does not reflect their pivotal role in the political system. Among other things, political parties structure public opinion, participate in civic education, control and participate in the activity of government, facilitate the emergence of political elites, and put forward ideas and programmes etc. Still, the constitution may not mention these functions, but it leaves political parties free to perform them.

Finally, article 4 also indicates that Parliament needs to take appropriate measures to safeguard the plurality of opinions and the equal participation of political parties in the democratic life of the Nation. As a result,

---

[37] Prior to 1988, political parties were regulated for a large part by the law on associations of 1901. With the law of 11 March 1988 on financial transparency of political life, political parties have been granted a distinct legal status.

[38] See article 4 § 1.

[39] This does extend to the control of the internal organisation of political parties.

[40] See the dissolution of the extreme Right party 'Unité radicale' in 2002, after one of its members, Christian Brunerie, tried to assassinate the President of the Republic during the parade of 14 July 2002.

[41] See J-C Colliard, 'L'action de la constitution sur les partis politiques' in B Mathieu (ed), *Cinquantième anniversaire de la constitution française* (Paris, Dalloz, 2008) 573.

article 4 makes Parliament responsible for protecting this plurality and for ensuring the equal participation of all political parties. In practical terms, this provision gives a constitutional basis for the financing of political parties and for the regulation of access of political parties to the media, particularly during electoral campaigns.

The Financing of Political Life

The regulation of financing of political parties and electoral campaigns has been gradually strengthened by legislation since a law of 11 March 1988. The recurrence of politico-financial scandals linked to the financing of political parties and electoral campaigns made such regulation necessary. Originally, donations by private companies were regulated so strictly that political parties unable to rely exclusively on membership fees turned to 'alternative' ways of financing their expenses, such as fictitious employment, fake invoicing, overcharging for public procurement contracts and so on.

The law of 11 March 1988 introduced the State financing of political parties but limited it to parties represented in Parliament. It also imposed a limit on campaign expenses for the elections of the President of the Republic and the Assemblée nationale. The law of 15 January 1990 strengthens the 1988 legislation: State financing was extended to political parties not represented in Parliament[42] and campaign expenses were limited for all elections. Also, an independent authority was created to audit expenses accounts and finances of political parties.[43] Interestingly, the law allowed political parties to receive financial donations from private companies or persons. Finally, the law of 19 January 1995 prohibited all financial donations from legal persons and raised the level of State financing to 50 per cent of campaign expenses.

At present, political parties must appoint an agent or form an association to receive all donations and keep the accounts required by law: the campaign accounts for each election and an annual party account. These are submitted to the authority for approval.

Although the legislation has been tightened considerably since 1988, politico-financial scandals still occur with astonishing regularity: for instance, it was alleged in the Karachi scandal, that Edouard Balladur,

---

[42] Since the law of 11 April 2003 political parties need to have received 1% of the votes in 50 constituencies to benefit from State financing.

[43] This authority is called the Commission nationale des comptes de campagne et des financements politiques.

then Prime Minister, had benefited from retro-commissions from the sale of military submarines to Pakistan. The commissions are said to have funded in part his presidential campaign of spring 1995.

A Democratic and Constitutional Space

The Conseil constitutionnel was the first to recognise that beyond voting rights and the regulation of political parties, a democracy depends on the existence of a constitutional and democratic space. This space finds its constitutional basis in the highest constitutional principles: national sovereignty and democracy. For the sovereign to express its opinion in democratic elections or referendums, it needs to be able to form an opinion first. Public opinion is informed in part only by the activity of political parties. Nowadays, the media plays a key role in shaping public opinion by either relaying the ideas and manifestos of politicians and their parties, or by adopting a political stance of its own. Citizens' decisions are strongly influenced by the media, be it newspapers, radio, television or the internet. Consequently, the Conseil constitutionnel took great care when developing its case law on freedom of expression to create a democratic and constitutional space where political parties and the media could express themselves without endangering the foundations of democracy itself.

To do so, the Conseil constitutionnel realised that it needed to strengthen its theoretical analysis of freedom of expression: it needed to go beyond the protection of individual citizens and acquire a wider remit. Since 1984 the Conseil has protected the freedom of modern media through the freedom of communication. This freedom encompasses all new media and little by little the Conseil has created a rather impressive protection: with regard to the press, their freedom forbids the introduction of a licensing system;[44] with regard to radio and television, a system of licensing is unavoidable and must be used to safeguard a healthy competition and pluralism in the industry;[45] finally, with regard to the Internet, the Conseil recognised a right of access to the Internet and described it as a component of democracy.[46]

Also, in the course of these decisions, the Conseil noted that transparency and pluralism are necessary to protect freedom of communication further: while transparency is conceived as a means to achieve

[44] See C cons no 84-181 DC, 10–11 October 1984, Freedom of the press.
[45] See C cons no 86-217 DC, 18 September 1886, Freedom of communication.
[46] See C cons no DC, 10 June 2009, HADOPI.

pluralism, the preservation of pluralism is elevated to the status of constitutional objective. This objective is crucial to safeguard the democratic and constitutional space: it ensures the freedom of choice of readers (with regard to the press) and allows the circulation of a wide range of ideas and opinions through other media. Ultimately, this contributes directly to the information, education and opinion of the sovereign people.

This objective of pluralism has also been used to regulate political parties more closely; for instance, the Conseil stipulated that the provisions for the State financing of political parties must not contravene pluralism and impair the expression of new trends of ideas and opinions.[47] Interestingly, the Conseil d'Etat has also began to police this democratic and constitutional space: in its *Hollande* decision, it decided to take account of the political radio and television appearances of the President of the Republic (and his advisors) to give equal access to the parties in opposition.[48]

Finally, in view of the growing importance of pluralism, the Balladur committee had recommended the creation of a new council on pluralism; this new independent authority was to merge and replace all independent authorities that protected freedom of communication and pluralism.[49] Although the constitutional reform of July 2008 did not create such a council, it recognised the constitutional objective of pluralism in article 4 § 3 of the constitution. This strengthens the case law of the Conseil constitutionnel and lends legitimacy to its protection of the democratic and constitutional space.

The Direct Expression of the French People

The tools of direct democracy have been part of constitutional law for millennia. In France, they were used in the period following the 1789 Revolution and during the first and second empires. However, the misuse of referendums in both imperial regimes turned many politicians

---

[47] See C cons no 89-271 DC, 11 January 1990; in this decision, the Conseil specified that a minimum threshold of 5% of votes in 75 constituencies before receiving State financing was too high and would compromise the emergence of new parties.

[48] See CE 8 April 2009, *Hollande* (2009) *Revue française de droit administratif* 351 concl Catherine de Salins.

[49] See the Balladur report (n 28) p 94.

against them. The fifth Republic, in an attempt to break from a parliamentary past, returned to a more popular interpretation of sovereignty. In fact, the position of French citizens in the constitutional landscape has continued to grow in importance: the 'sovereign people' have an increasing number of tools at their disposal to voice opinions and policy choices.

Furthermore, there is a long and established tradition of the French people expressing political discontent by demonstrations and direct action. Indeed, the 'street' has been responsible for many regime changes in constitutional history. With good cause, politicians of the fifth Republic continue to be wary of the people taking to the street.

Referendums

From the beginning, the 1958 constitution resorted to referendum in a rather innovative way: not only could 'the people' approve a constitutional reform,[50] but they could also pass legislation concerned with State powers or authorise the ratification of a treaty impacting the institutions. Since the reform of March 2003 referendums and consultations can be organised at local level also.

Evolution and Reform of Article 11

Until 1995 a referendum could be organised in two circumstances only: to approve primary legislation concerned with the organisation of the State powers or to authorise a treaty impacting the institutions. Initially, de Gaulle had wanted to give article 11 a wider scope: in an early draft, it allowed the President of the Republic on proposal of the Prime Minister to submit to referendum any legislation opposed by Parliament or any issue key to the life of the nation. However, many politicians did not share de Gaulle's enthusiasm for referendums and in the final text the scope of the provision was narrowed considerably. Also, de Gaulle made an extensive and somewhat controversial use of article 11.[51] Since then, referendums have been used sparingly: only four times in 40 years.

In view of this practice, the wish to increase the scope of article 11 may appear paradoxical. Still, the limitations of article 11 have come under repeated attacks and several attempts have been made to widen

---

[50] See chapter 8.
[51] See chapters 3 and 8.

the scope of this provision. In 1993, the Vedel committee recommended that the provision be used to approve legislation on constitutional rights and freedoms and to ratify treaties concerned with fundamental rights and international organisation. However, the reform of August 1995 simply extended article 11 to include economic and social reforms and those concerned with public services. The scope of the provision was further extended by the reform of July 2008: it has added reforms concerned with the environment to this list. Although article 11 has been amended twice and debated actively, its scope is still narrow and at variance with the idea in the 1958 constitution that the people are the ultimate sovereign.

In view of the previous use of article 11 and the ambiguity of its drafting, a procedural safeguard may be welcome. The Vedel committee recommended that the opinion of the Conseil constitutionnel be sought on all projects of referendum. Although such control has been introduced for the new popular legislative initiative, it is yet to be extended to referendums.

Finally, it is important to note that the text of the constitution does not really match political practice: article 11 § 1 may specify that the initiative of a referendum belongs to the Prime Minister and to the houses of Parliament jointly, but in reality the President of the Republic has always been in control of this process: in practice, both the initiative and the decision of its organisation rests with the President. Still, the introduction of the popular initiative may change this.

Popular Legislative Initiative

Although the 1958 constitution has recognised a more prominent place to referendums than previous regimes, it was felt that more should be done to strengthen participation of the people. In 1993, the Vedel committee had recommended that a right of legislative initiative be granted to citizens. Unfortunately, this proposal was not included in the August 1995 reform. In July 2008 article 11 was finally amended to grant citizens, in conjunction with Members of Parliament, the possibility of triggering a referendum. Although commentators qualify this amendment as a spectacular innovation, they also express concerns about the restrictions that the new procedure imposes.[52]

---

[52] See S Diemert, 'Le référendum législative d'initiative minoritaire dans l'article 11, révisé de la Constitution' (2009) 77 *Revue française de droit constitutionnel* 55.

The referendum triggered by popular initiative has the same narrow scope as an ordinary referendum. Moreover, further temporary restrictions exist: first, it is not possible to repeal by popular initiative a law which was adopted in the last year; and secondly, if a legislative proposal has been rejected by referendum, it is not possible to organise a referendum on the same topic for another two years. Furthermore, the decision to call a referendum requires the support of a 'large minority' of the electorate: it needs to be endorsed by 10 per cent of the citizens on the electoral roll (ie 4.4 million electors). Also, the decision is not left entirely to citizens: it must be endorsed by 20 per cent of Members of Parliament (ie 182 members). These conditions have been denounced by commentators as unrealistically high; it will be a struggle to fulfil them. However, once the Conseil constitutionnel has verified that these conditions have been met, a referendum will be organised. Interestingly, if Parliament does not examine the popular initiative put forward by the electors within two years of receiving it, the President of the Republic must organise the referendum automatically.

The new provision may be a step in the right direction but one wonders whether it will receive much application.

Local Referendums, Consultations and Petitions

The reform of March 2003 aimed to strengthen local democracy and introduced a number of mechanisms to enhance it. To this effect, article 72-1 of the constitution gave local electors ways to voice their opinions: consultations, referendums and petitions. Both consultations and referendums can only be organised on subject-matters within the jurisdiction of the relevant territorial entity. This means that issues impacting the territorial entity (eg large infrastructure projects) but outside its jurisdiction can never give rise to either mechanism. Also, in the case of consultation, the result is not binding on local politicians. Finally, local electors have a right of petition: they can ask that a specific issue be tabled for the next meeting of the elected assembly.

In practice, the use of these mechanisms has been somewhat disappointing and has not heralded the emergence of a thriving participative democracy at local level.[53]

---

[53] See P Sadran, 'La démocratie locale: réalités et prespectives' in *Les collectivités territoriales: trente ans de décentralisation*, Cahiers français no 362 (*La Documention française*, 2011) 65.

Finally, referendums play a different role in overseas territories as these benefit from self-determination: a referendum is organised systematically prior to any change of their status or organisation.[54]

The Right of Petition and the Social, Economic and Environmental Council

The social, economic and environmental council, which aims to regroup within the same institution various social, economic and environmental actors of the country, is composed of representatives chosen mostly by trade unions and associations and of qualified personalities appointed by the Government. As a result the council is quite representative of French civil society. It has a consultative role only,[55] and since the reform of July 2008, it can be consulted by Parliament as well as the Government on any economic, social or environmental issue or bill. Also, it is possible for a member of the council to be heard by Parliament to explain the reasons behind its opinion. Despite its activity, commentators agree that the economic, social and environmental council is still little known or understood by ordinary citizens.

However, this may change with the new power of petition[56] given to citizens by the reform of July 2008. Citizens are now allowed to petition the economic, social and environmental council on any issue within its remit. After investigation, the council makes recommendations as to the outcome of the petition. This new power may help raise the profile of the institution and may even lead to a transformation of its role in the political system. Only time will tell.

The 'Street' Demonstrations and Strikes

The French people have a reputation for expressing their discontent forcibly by way of strikes and demonstrations. In the past, 'the street' as it is familiarly called, has been responsible for regime change and is known to force government to drop policies or do legislative u-turns. There is certainly a deeply imbedded culture of direct political action in France. Interestingly, this cultural trend is reflected in the constitution itself: article 2 of the Declaration of 1789 specifies that the aim of any political system is the protection of the natural rights of man and ranks

---

[54] See articles 72-4 and 73 § 6 of the constitution.
[55] See article 70 of the constitution.
[56] See article 69 § 3 of the constitution.

among those rights the principle of resistance to oppression alongside
the principles of liberty, property and security.[57]

Furthermore, one may find another proof of this cultural imprint in
the public law principles regulating demonstration, assembly and, to
some extent, strike action. Overall, the rules are liberal and emphasise
these as freedoms and rights. For instance, public meetings or proces-
sions on the public highway will be banned only when a clear danger to
public order exists. This will be controlled strictly by the administrative
courts, which always choose to emphasise freedom over prohibition.
Public law may thus demonstrate a wish to capture a practice of direct
action by law, but it also undeniably facilitates it. Still, the marked
increase in direct democracy tools and rights protection may make it less
compelling to take to the streets than in the past.

A CULTURE OF RIGHTS PROTECTION

Since its inception, the 1958 constitution has increased drastically its
protection of rights, thereby improving substantially the status of
French citizens. While the people may not have been at the heart of the
early constitution, unexpected constitutional change has engineered a
transformation of the constitutional document. Nowadays, not only
have people's rights and their guarantees increased notably but citizens
are involved directly in their protection, thereby creating a strong culture
of rights protection.

Constitutional Rights: A Near Perfect List?

The fifth Republic may have started with a weak protection of constitutional rights but this state of affairs was reversed swiftly. The quiet revolution of the Conseil constitutionnel, which in 1971 incorporated two
sources of constitutional rights into the formal constitution, marked an
important beginning: primary legislation was to respect the Declaration
of the Rights of Man of 1789 and the Preamble of the 1946 constitution for the first time in history. This judicial activism has been so successful that the list of protected rights was regarded to be sufficient

---

[57] The Declaration of Rights of 1793 even defined 'oppression' in article 34.

until recently. Only in the last decade has the incorporation of new rights been discussed. The debates have concentrated on two main questions: the recognition of third-generation rights and the modernisation of rights already protected to take account of new concerns (eg diversity).

With regard to third-generation rights, the charter for the environment adopted in 2004 was successfully annexed to the constitution in March 2005[58] and while legislation on bio-ethics is under constant review, there is a consensus that they should not be part of the constitutional settlement yet. Furthermore, the recent review by the Veil committee found that the rights already protected in the constitution did not need modernising; Parliament and courts simply needed to change their policies, case law and attitudes on these matters.

Finally, the constitution has been amended to increase the protection of citizens in three other areas: the abolition of the death penalty, the recognition of the principle of parity and the recognition of a principle of pluralism of opinions. While the incorporation of new rights into the constitution has been modest, it has been achieved when necessary.

The Role of Independent Administrative Agencies

Independent administrative authorities have been part of French public law since the 1970s: the *Médiateur*[59] or Ombudsman was the first to appear in 1973 and it was soon followed by the national commission on electronic data and freedom[60] and then by the administrative commission for access to administrative documents.[61] The numbers of independent authorities have increased dramatically since then. The parliamentary office for the evaluation of legislation identified 39 such independent authorities in 2006.

The expression 'independent administrative authority' was coined for the first time in 1978 by the law establishing the national committee on electronic data and freedom,[62] and was used in 1984 by the Conseil

---

[58] See the constitutional law of 1 March 2005.
[59] See the law of 3 January 1973.
[60] See the law of 6 January 1978.
[61] See the law of 17 July 1978.
[62] See article 6 of the statute of 6 January 1978.

constitutionnel to label the high authority of audiovisual communication.[63] The diversity of these independent authorities makes it difficult to craft a definition which would fit them all. However, both the Conseil d'Etat[64] and the parliamentary office for the evaluation of legislation[65] believe that these authorities have three common characteristics: all have real authority (whether legal or moral), are administrative in nature and are independent from the Executive. There might be other characteristics shared by a large number of independent authorities but not by all.

Although independent authorities are all quite distinctive and singular, commentators often divide them into two categories: some authorities are created to ensure the effectiveness of constitutional rights while others aim to regulate the economy or a sector of it. By and large, the former category is the one more directly relevant to our present analysis. Indeed, the Ombudsman was the first independent authority and it aimed to protect the rights and liberties of citizens against public bodies through another medium than the courts. Similarly, the national committee on electronic data and freedom was put in place to oversee the use of electronic data by public bodies and to ensure that the rights and privacy of individuals would not be breached. In another context, the high council for the audiovisual[66] was created to regulate the media independently of the Executive and to ensure (among other things) the respect of pluralism and transparency. Moreover, all these authorities require an active participation of citizens to ensure fully the protection of their rights; depending on the authority, citizens can make complaints or representation and can sometimes even participate in the regulatory process. In doing so, independent administrative authorities play an important role in strengthening further the culture of rights protection in France.

In fact, one worry of commentators and politicians with regard to independent authorities is their proliferation. They argue that too many independent authorities may only serve to confuse citizens as to which authority to consult. In turn, this may become an obstacle to the protection of people's rights. It is not surprising, therefore, that the consti-

---

[63] See C cons no 84-173, 26 July 1984.
[64] See Conseil d'Etat, *Rapport public 2001*, 290.
[65] See its report of 25 June 2006 on 'the independent administrative authorities'.
[66] See the law of 17 January 1989.

tutional reform of July 2008 regrouped and consolidated a number of independent authorities into one: the new defender of rights.[67]

The Reform of July 2008: A Leap For Rights Protection?

As seen above, the status of citizens has improved markedly with the reform of July 2008. The procedural guarantees given to French citizens to protect their rights have increased considerably. This will strengthen further the culture of rights protection described above.

Better Access to the Courts

As explained in the previous chapter, citizens were not able to challenge the constitutionality of primary legislation before a court prior to March 2010. Indeed, this was regarded as a major gap in the protection of constitutional rights in France. However, with the introduction of the preliminary ruling on an issue of constitutionality, people are better able to protect their rights; in view of the activity of the Conseil constitutionnel, it is fair to say that this guarantee has already proved most effective.

Furthermore, citizens have been granted access to the Conseil supérieur de la magistrature to bring complaints against private law judges.[68] It is difficult to predict the future impact of this procedure, but some commentators feel that it may help in bringing proceedings against a few judges who otherwise may not have been disciplined.[69]

The 'New' Defender of Rights

As explained above, an ombudsman was introduced in France by legislation in 1973. It was the first independent administrative authority to be created. Although it had few formal powers, the success of this institution grew steadily over the years. The Balladur committee decided that it was time for this authority to be given constitutional status and recommended the creation of a defender of rights inspired by the Spanish *Defensor del Pueblo*. The transformation of the institution aimed to reflect

---

[67] See article 61-1 of the constitution.
[68] See article 65 § 10 of the constitution and the organic law of 22 July 2010.
[69] See G Carcassonne, 'Article 65' in *La constitution*, 10th edn (Paris, Seuil, 2011) 315.

the growing attention given to the protection of citizens' rights and to add yet another weapon to the growing arsenal at the public's disposal.

Furthermore, in an attempt to rationalise the constitutional landscape, the Balladur committee suggested that the defender of rights regroup all the independent authorities working in the field of rights protection. However, the drafting of new article 71-1 on the defender of rights was so vague that it was impossible to infer much from this text; only the mission of the defender of rights was clearly stated in the new provision.[70] Great uncertainty prevailed with regard to the powers, the organisation and the scope of the new institution; these have been partly dispelled with the adoption of the law and organic law of 29 March 2011.

The legislation passed in March 2011 states that the new institution combines the mission and jurisdiction of four independent authorities: the ombudsman, the defender of children, the security committee and the equality commission. Moreover, the new institution was granted the same powers as those vested in the four institutions. For instance, the defender has powers now to enter and search premises for information, powers that the Ombudsman never benefited from. Also, the obligation to refer a complaint via a Member of Parliament has been relaxed: while it is still possible to do so, it is no longer compulsory. Although the future success of the institution depends largely on the way the four authorities manage to work together, it has the potential for becoming a powerful 'defender of rights' indeed.

CONCLUSION: A 'NEW' CITIZEN?

An analysis of the powers granted to citizens in the present constitution shows a marked evolution since 1958; a 'new' citizen seems to be emerging from the amended constitution. However, on closer examination, the all-encompassing concept of citizen may no longer be appropriate to describe the various powers and their attributes to different categories of people: for instance, EU nationals can vote in local elections and can make a complaint to the defender of rights. However, they cannot vote in parliamentary or presidential elections or support a popular legislative

---

[70] See the first paragraph: 'The defender of rights ensures the respect of rights and freedoms by Government departments, territorial entities, public bodies, any body fulfilling a public service and any body designated by organic law.'

initiative. In order to acquire a deeper understanding of the position of the people in the 1958 constitution, it may be necessary to identify and analyse the various groups of citizens or constitutional participants on the basis of their constitutional rights and duties. This, however, runs counter to the logic of French constitutional law and in the medium term this constitutional tradition may compromise the conceptual development of this renewed citizenship. To meet this challenge, French constitutional lawyers may need to concentrate more of their efforts to the study of the 'peoples' in the French constitutional order.

FURTHER READING

F Aumond, 'Le Défenseur des droits: une peinture en clair-obscur' (2011) *Revue française de droit administratif* 913

M de Cazals, 'La saisine du Conseil économique par voie de pétition citoyenne: une Ve République "plus démocratique"' (2010) *Revue française de droit constitutionnel* 289

M Gentot, *Les autorités administratives indépendantes*, coll clefs (Paris, Montchrestien, 1994) 199

R Ghevotian, 'Les systèmes électoraux' in B Mathieu (ed), *Cinquantième anniversaire de la constitution française* (Paris, Dalloz, 2008) 599

La Rue – *Pouvoirs* (2006) 116

N Lenoir, 'The Representation of Women in Politics: From Quotas to Parity in Elections' (2001) *ICLQ* 217

S Marcilloux-Giummarra, 'Le financement des partis politiques' (2011) *Revue française de droit constitutionnel* 163

D Schnapper, *Qu'est-ce que la citoyenneté?* (Paris, Gallimard, 2000)

M Verpeaux, 'Référendum local, consultations locales et constitution' (2003) *Actualité juridique: droit administratif* 540

Voter – *Pouvoirs* (2007) 120

Relevant websites

Le défenseur des droits: http://defenseurdesdroits.fr/

Le Conseil économique, social et environnemental: www.conseil-economique-et-social.fr/

La commission nationale des comptes de campagne et des financements politiques: www.cnccfp.fr/

7

From Centralised Unity to Multilevel Constitutionalism

───※◆※───

The Rise of Territorial Government – Keeping a Check on the European Union – Conclusion

W HEN THE 1958 constitution proclaims in its first article that 'France is indivisible', the statement reflects centuries of constitutional tradition. The principles of unity and indivisibility of the French territory had already been proclaimed by the monarchy before being enthusiastically reasserted in the aftermath of the 1789 Revolution. Moreover, the indivisibility of the French republic has been stated in many constitutions since then.[1]

Since 1958 the constitution has had to evolve considerably in this respect: while the ideas of unity and indivisibility have long been understood to imply a centralised organisation of government, the repeated demands at both local and supranational levels have forced a transformation of the original constitutional conceptions. The French constitution has had to resolve tensions caused by the competing demands for more freedom at local and regional levels and for more integration at European and even international levels. It is not surprising, therefore, that the need for repeated amendments of the constitution has been felt: the French constitution is attempting to reflect and frame these evolutions. In fact, it might be argued that in this respect at least, the text of the constitution has been amended to match relatively closely a

---

[1] The principle can be found in the first constitution of 3 September 1791, the first Republic of 24 June 1793, the *Directoire* of 22 August 1795, the *Consulat* of 13 December 1799, the second Republic of 4 November 1848, and finally the fourth Republic of 27 October 1946.

rapidly changing political reality and an emerging consensus. Indeed, if in many respects the text of the constitution has lagged behind and has not captured nor reflected political reality and practices, this cannot be said of territorial organisation and European integration.

Consequently, this chapter will first demonstrate the slow emergence of a new principle of territorial freedom, its incorporation into the constitution and the vagaries of its evolution. It will then analyse the various constitutional reforms and the creative responses of the Conseil constitutionnel made necessary by the growing pace of European integration. The chapter will thereby attempt to capture the rise of multi-level constitutionalism that these changes have triggered.

THE RISE OF TERRITORIAL GOVERNMENT

In a unitary organisation of government, not only do the institutions of central government make up for a large part the constitutional system, but they tend to have a monopoly over normative production. In France, the rise of territorial government implied a move away from this model and required an exercise in multilevel constitutionalism: the addition of other levels of government demanded constitutional originality with regard to both distribution of power and institutional design.

Territorial Government and the Indivisibility of the Republic

As mentioned earlier, article 1 of the French constitution proclaims unequivocally the territorial indivisibility of the republic. This complemented the unitary character of the State and reflected the conceptual indivisibility of national sovereignty.[2] However, this understanding of indivisibility does not sit well with the recent search for autonomy and self-government of territorial entities. Not only is federalism incompatible with these fundamental traits of French public law, but so would be an extreme form of decentralisation.[3]

---

[2] See D Roux, 'Une République une et diverse?' in B Mathieu (ed), *Cinquantième anniversaire de la constitution française* (Paris, Dalloz, 2008).

[3] See M Verpeaux, *Les collectivités territoriales en France*, 3rd edn (Paris, Dalloz, 2011) at 2: 'Decentralisation can be defined as the recognition, next to the State, of territorial entities with administrative powers. These entities benefit from a relative freedom or autonomy of decision and management.'

The Organisation of Territorial Government and the 1958 Constitution

The territorial organisation that was originally devised by the 1958 constitution hankered after the past. Soon after the Revolution, the old *provinces* were abolished and the French territory was divided into *départements*;[4] many of them still respect today the boundaries adopted then.[5] Remarkably, by 1958, French territorial organisation had not changed considerably since the end of the eighteenth century. At the end of the nineteenth century, the duties and powers of the *communes*[6] and *départements* were adapted to match the democratic ideals of the third Republic.[7] Only in the 1946 constitution were territorial government entities granted their first constitutional recognition.

From the beginning, title XII of the 1958 constitution aimed to set up and regulate territorial government. Article 72 listed the territorial entities and declared that they administered themselves freely by elected assemblies. It also specified that the central government appointed an agent to protect national interests, trigger administrative controls and ensure the respect of laws. Although the constitution tried to strike a balance between the respective powers of central and territorial governments, in 1958, central government was clearly favoured.

Already, articles 73 and 74 brought some flexibility for overseas territories: for the *départements d'outre-mer* (overseas *départements*), article 73 specified that both the legislative framework and the administrative structure could be adapted to meet specific needs and for the *territoires d'outre-mer* (overseas territories), article 74 proclaimed that these overseas territories benefited from a special organisation to respect their specific interests. Still, originally, the 1958 constitution resolved the tension between the principles of unity and indivisibility and territorial government freedom in favour of the former.

The Slow Emergence of a Territorial Government Freedom

The regime of the fifth Republic had not been long established before the territorial government's structure and organisation was accused of

---

[4] This is the second level of French territorial government.

[5] The *départements* were created by dividing the *provinces* of pre-Revolutionary France.

[6] This is the first level of French territorial government: it administers towns and villages.

[7] See the statute of 5 April 1884.

being obsolete. While the existence of neither *communes* nor *départements* was contested, it was felt that new and larger *régions*[8] would be beneficial to the economy. The territorial exiguity of *départements* was believed to compromise the development of both national and local economies. However, the first attempt by de Gaulle to establish *régions* as territorial entities in 1969 failed to gain popular support.[9]

Beside the tentative appearance of the *régions* as administrative entities, few reforms took place until the law of 2 March 1982. This reform aimed to establish the *régions* as full territorial entities, to grant the presiding officer of both the *départements* and the *régions* full executive powers,[10] and last but not least to abolish the control over the merit of decisions of all territorial entities. Since the reform, the central government representative can only challenge the legality of these decisions before the administrative courts. The reform of 1982 had truly decentralised French territorial organisation. Between 1982 and 2003, a number of laws were passed, mostly to clarify and support further this movement in favour of local democracy.

In 2003, it was felt necessary to reform the constitution itself to continue this trend. The constitutional amendment of 28 March 2003 inscribed the decentralised organisation of the French territory in the constitution and softened accordingly the principle of indivisibility of the republic.[11] The constitution was also altered to regulate more clearly the transfer of powers from the State to territorial entities.[12] Finally, an attempt was made to guarantee financially the autonomy of territorial entities through taxation.

The reform of 2003 may have been implemented, but the perennial problems of the organisation of territorial government in France

---

[8] This is the third level of French territorial government.

[9] The French people were concerned with the reform to the *Sénat* and rejected the referendum.

[10] Mayors already held executive powers for the *communes*.

[11] The principle of indivisibility was considered to be a real obstacle to further decentralisation; see J-B Auby, J-F Auby and R Noguellou, *Droit des collectivités locales*, 3rd edn (Paris, Presses universitaires de France, 2004) 20.

[12] Two innovations were introduced in article 72: first, a principle akin to subsidiarity states that the competences bestowed on each level of territorial government must be those best exercised to enhance effective decision making and secondly, a power of experimentation allowed territorial entities to alter temporarily statutory provisions within the exercise of their powers. Still, this experimentation cannot affect a fundamental right.

remained. Consequently, a new statute that purports to reorganise territorial government was adopted on 16 December 2010. However, the new reform seems to compromise the constitutional principles proclaimed in 2003.[13]

The Structures of Territorial Government

Article 72 of the constitution lists all territorial entities, namely: *communes*, *départements*, *régions*, territorial entities with specific status and overseas territorial entities. Also, it adds that Parliament can create new ones. To determine whether a specific structure is a territorial entity, one needs to look to its organisation and power. The constitution specifies in article 72 that all territorial entities must be granted specific competences; they must be administered freely[14] by an elected body;[15] and they must have the necessary regulatory powers to fulfil their given competences. Accordingly, if an entity is missing one of these characteristics, it is not a territorial entity.

The Ordinary Territorial Entities

There are three ordinary territorial entities in mainland France.

The Communes

Communes form the first level of territorial government in France and administer towns and villages. They were an early innovation of the regime following on from the 1789 Revolution. France is unusual among

---

[13]   See J-F Brisson, 'La loi du 16 décembre 2010 portant réforme territoriale ou le droit des collectivités territoriales en miettes' (2011) *Juris-Classeur périodique (administratif)* 8.

[14]   The principle of free administration has limits: it cannot lead to a disparity in the level of rights protection; it cannot authorise the usurpation of the competences of another territorial entity; and finally, it can never undermine the exercise of national sovereignty.

[15]   The constitution requires election by universal, but not direct, suffrage. Still, direct universal suffrage has been used to elect the municipal council of *communes* and the general council of *départements* under all republican regimes since their inception and some commentators have even argued that direct universal suffrage constitutes a 'fundamental principle recognised by the laws of the Republic'.

its European neighbours in that it possesses a considerable number of them: there are 36,779 *communes* in mainland France.[16]

This provides an administrative unit close to citizens and establishes the foundations for a tight network of local democracy. The *communes* are run by a municipal council elected for six years with a mayor presiding.[17] The mayor and his deputies, who are selected by absolute majority of the council, make up the executive branch. In addition to these executive functions, the mayor is an agent of the State. As such he is responsible for the publication and the implementation of primary and secondary legislation, for the adoption of public security measures and for any functions granted to him by statutes.

Because of their proximity to citizens, *communes* have jurisdiction for the type of services that have a direct and daily impact: nursery and primary education, urban development, urban transport, some aspects of cultural policy (libraries, concert halls, museums and festivals). If one adds to these the central government functions fulfilled by the mayor, the *communes* are responsible for many aspects of people's daily life. Not surprisingly French citizens are strongly attached to this level of territorial government.

However, the large number and small size of *communes* have attracted considerable criticisms. Commentators note that France is clearly an exception among its European partners. While this is not an issue in itself, these arrangements have serious and adverse financial implications: this extreme fragmentation does not favour an economy of scale and many *communes* are limited with regard to the services they can provide. Consequently, considerable efforts have been made to encourage *communes* to join forces. As will be explained below, the reform of 16 December 2010 emphasises this solution.

The Départements

The *départements* were created in 1789 by dividing the old *provinces*. The *département* needed to be of a size which allowed easy access to its capital.

---

[16] This figure has been relatively stable throughout history as there were approximately 40,000 *communes* during the first Empire of Napoléon I (1804–1815). Of these 36,779 *communes*, 35,827 have a population of less than 10,000 inhabitants and 3,907 of less than 100.

[17] The number of members elected to the municipal council varies with the population: from nine members for fewer than 100 inhabitants to 69 for more than 300,000 inhabitants.

There are 96 *départements* in mainland France. At present, each *département* is administered by an elected general council with a chairman presiding.

Presently, *départements* are in charge of social services: they are responsible for vulnerable members of the community, ie children (adoption, protection), families in financial difficulties, the handicapped (special housing and integration) and the aged (sheltered housing, home help etc). In fact, the largest share of the departmental budget goes to the delivery of these services. *Départements* are also responsible for some aspects of the education and culture policies (eg the lower tier of secondary education). Finally, *départements* also renew and maintain the large network of departmental roads.

The Régions

In 1982, the *régions* became territorial entities to foster economic growth but not to meet a demand for regional recognition and autonomy.[18] There are 26 *régions* in mainland France. At present, they are administered by an elected regional council with a chairman presiding.

Régions have been granted powers to nurture economic development in their area: they are responsible for economic planning and the creation of the necessary infrastructures. The organisation of regional transport, particularly regional train networks, is their responsibility. *Régions* also participate in the financing of new high speed train networks (*TGV*) as these are key to the development of economic activity. In addition, *régions* develop and manage both ports and airports.[19] Finally, the organisation of the upper tier of secondary education, adult education and professional training is the responsibility of the *régions*, which thereby aim to educate the workforce to meet the needs of employers. More recently, *régions* were given new powers for the protection of the environment.

Still, research has demonstrated that *régions* have not been used to their full potential and that wider and more coherent regions are needed for a better economic impact.[20]

---

[18] In fact, the boundaries of many *régions* are contested and some clearly straddle regional identities.

[19] These powers were only handed over by legislation in 2002 and 2004 and these transfers are only experimental. A review at the end of the experimental period will decide the final allocation.

[20] See R Savy, 'Vingt ans après: ou les régions françaises au milieu du gué' in *Mélanges Jean-François Lachaume* (Paris, Dalloz, 2007) 961.

Territorial Entities with Derogative Status

Derogative status is resorted to largely for overseas territories. No longer a colonial power, France retains a few overseas territories. For some, the issue of political autonomy, self-determination and independence is a live issue. In fact, the Conseil constitutionnel considers that 'the constitution distinguishes the French people from overseas peoples to whom is recognised a right to self-determination'.[21]

Generally, the question of striking the right balance between the respect of rules and statutes in force in mainland France (the principle of legislative identity) and the respect of the cultural, economic and social specificities of each overseas territory (the principle of adaptation) dominates the debate and drives the derogative status and institutional design of these territories. Consequently, the constitution has recognised a number of different categories of overseas territories.

The Départements *and* Régions d'outre-mer *(DROM): A changing conception*

The *départements d'outre-mer* (overseas *départements*) were created in 1946 and reflected a political wish to bestow an organisation similar to that of mainland France on the four oldest colonies: Guadeloupe, French Guiana, Martinique and Réunion. For these territories, the principle of integration and assimilation had always been the guiding principle.[22] When the *régions* were introduced, each overseas *département* was also designated an overseas *région*, with both territorial governments simply superimposed (thereby becoming a DROM). Mayotte joined this category on 31 March 2011, a change driven by a strong demand of the population.[23]

However, this organisation is complex in the extreme and proposals for rationalisation were soon put forward. As a result of a decision by the Conseil constitutionnel,[24] article 73 was amended by the constitutional reform of March 2003 to authorise a single assembly for these territories. Since then, the populations of both French Guiana and

---

[21] See C cons no 91-290 DC, 9 May 1991, Status of Corsica.

[22] This choice was explained by a long and common history: Guadeloupe, Guyane, Martinique and Réunion became part of the kingdom of France during the seventeenth century.

[23] This was supported by 95.2% of the electors on 29 March 2009.

[24] In the decision C cons no 82-147 DC, 2 December 1982, the Conseil stated that the circumstances did not justify the creation of a single assembly to administer both territorial entities together.

Martinique have approved the move to a single assembly.[25] As Mayotte retained a single assembly, only Guadeloupe and Réunion are still administered by the dual institutional structure.

Finally, the policy of assimilation had been increasingly questioned since the 1980s. Consequently, the constitutional reforms of March 2003 and July 2008 maintained the principle of legislative identity but tempered it with wide exceptions.

The Collectivités territoriales d'outre-mer – *COM (Overseas Territorial Entities)*

In 2003 the constitutional reform abolished the former category of overseas territories, which had lost its original usefulness, and introduced the new category of *collectivités territoriales d'outre-mer* in article 74 of the constitution. At present, the category includes the following territories: Saint-Barthélemy, Saint-Martin, Saint-Pierre-et-Miquelon, Wallis and Futuna, and French Polynesia. Each is granted an individualised status to protect its specific interests within the French Republic.

New Caledonia – The Search for Independence

The struggle between the indigenous and non-indigenous populations of New Caledonia led to the Noumea agreements in 1998. These agreements recognised the existence of a separate and indigenous Kanak identity and have paved the way for the future independence of New Caledonia. Consequently, the status of New Caledonia could not come within any of the existing constitutional categories. A new title XIII was added to the constitution by the reform of 20 July 1998. It laid the foundations for a new institutional framework and set up a system of self-government and shared sovereignty for New Caledonia. Furthermore, accession to full independence is foreseen; in view of this, a New Caledonian citizenship separate from French citizenship was organised.

Territories with Special Status

This category was created to meet the specific needs of overseas territories. Presently, there is only one such territory left: Corsica. The adoption of a special status for Corsica was and is still controversial. The strong demand for autonomy had driven Parliament to grant the territory of

---

[25] The law and organic law of 27 July 2011 gave effect to this decision.

Corsica special status in 1991.[26] Prior to that, Corsica had always been treated as if part of mainland France. A reformed special status with deep institutional changes was adopted in 2003 but rejected by the Corsican population in a referendum.

French Territorial Government: Problems and Cures?

After the 1789 Revolution, successive regimes may have rationalised successfully the organisation of the French territory, but with the passage of time, many benefits of the early model have been lost. It had become widely accepted that French territorial government, although having undergone a series of rapid reforms, was still in need of major reform.[27] Consequently, President Sarkozy planned to tackle the organisation of territorial government after the constitutional reform of July 2008. Accordingly, Balladur was appointed to chair yet another expert committee to make proposals for the modernisation of French territorial government. As the title of the report indicates, many felt that it was high 'time to decide' on these reforms.[28]

The report highlights the (perennial) failures of the system and proposed a number of options to address them. First, the territory is covered by too many territorial government entities for them to be efficient. The institutional landscape needed to be simplified, especially since the policy of cooperation between territorial entities has increased greatly this institutional complexity. Secondly, the distribution of competences between central and territorial government and between territorial entities is not clear. Again, rationalisation and simplification is needed there. Thirdly, the present spread of territorial entities no longer reflects the demographic realities of the French territory. While the majority of urban populations are underrepresented, depleted rural populations are captured by numerous territorial entities. Finally, the system of local taxation is outdated and impacts adversely both the territorial and national economies; it also compromises the financial

---

[26] Law of 13 May 1991.

[27] See P Warsmann, 'Pour un big-bang territorial: dix principes pour clarifier l'organisation territoriale française' rapport d'information, Assembleé nationale no 1153, 2008.

[28] See Rapport du comité pour la réforme des collectivités locales, 'Il est temps de décider', 5 March 2009.

autonomy of territorial government at all levels. In view of these failures, the new legislation tried to find some answers. While the budget for 2010 tackled the issue of revenue and taxation for territorial entities,[29] the law of 16 December 2010 reformed French territorial government in four ways: the cooperation of the *communes* is strengthened, the *départements* and the *régions* are coupled together, new territorial entities are created and competences for each level of territorial government are transformed.

Enforced Cooperation between the Communes

Unlike the policies pursued by other European states,[30] France has never reduced the number of its territorial entities. This could have been achieved by replacing the *départements* with the *régions* and by grouping *communes* together. Interestingly, the reform of December 2010 does not attempt this policy either. Consequently, the sheer number of territorial entities and their size, especially at the level of *communes*, has required the promotion of an active policy of cooperation. This policy has allowed coordinated actions and the pooling of resources by communities that are geographically and/or culturally close.

Cooperation between *communes* was encouraged as early as the nineteenth century,[31] but remained unsatisfactory for most of the twentieth century. It improved with the adoption of yet another law in 1992,[32] but triggered increased institutional complexity. In 1999, Parliament promoted a new format of cooperation between *communes*.[33] Not only were the structures extremely flexible, but the legislation addressed the question of cooperation in its totality and created a complete framework of rules, principles and structures. The law was successful and cooperation between *communes*, also known as 'intercommunality' increased markedly.

With the law of 16 December 2010, this intercommunality will become systematic and rationalised. It will be driven not so much by the *communes* themselves as by the decisions of the representative of central govern-

---

[29] See the financial law of 30 December 2009.
[30] Between 1950 and 2007, while Germany and the UK reduced the number of territorial government entities by 41% and 79% respectively, France only reduced the number by 5%.
[31] See the syndicates of *communes* of the law of 22 March 1890.
[32] See the law of 6 February 1992.
[33] See the law of 12 July 1999.

ment who has been given wide powers in this matter. Intercommunality may be necessary, but the freedom of *communes* is not enhanced by the reform. Furthermore, with policies increasingly made in the structures of intercommunality, the transparency and legitimacy of decision making may soon be questioned.

The New Coupling of Départements *and* Régions

Beyond the complex network of schemes that promoted horizontal cooperation, structures also existed to encourage a vertical and functional cooperation between *départements* and *régions*.

However, the law of 16 December 2010 goes further and creates an institutional link between the *région* and the *départements* of that *région*. From 2014 both levels of territorial government will be managed by the same elected councillors. The new territorial councillors will replace both the regional and general councillors and will sit in both the regional council and the general council. This will reduce the number of elected councillors (but not the number of assemblies) and should transform the relationship between the two levels of territorial government. Although no one really knows what this institutional engineering will deliver, it aims to achieve a better coordination of policies between the two levels of territorial government. Whether this represents the first step of a merger has not been fully articulated.

The Creation of New Structures

Although the law of 16 December 2010 wished to simplify the institutional landscape, it introduces new structures, notably the new *commune* and the *métropole*. The new *commune* provides a framework to allow a number of ordinary *communes* to merge together and form a single new one.

The new *métropole* tries to address the institutional needs of large urban areas. This scheme is reserved for towns with a population in excess of 500,000 inhabitants. In this new organisation, not only does the *métropole* benefit from the transfer of all competences from the *communes* and some competences from the *départements*, but it can also receive transfers of competences from the *région* and arguably from the central government.

This proliferation of new structures has a marked drawback: it increases further the complexity of the institutional landscape, which the reform was meant to simplify. Also, these new structures appear unnecessarily complex and often at variance with past practices of territorial cooperation. Considering these limitations, one wonders whether they will have much success.

A New Distribution of Competences?

Finally, the distribution of competences is another perennial problem of territorial government in France. Ideally, each level of government should be granted exclusive competence in clearly identified areas.

Indeed, the law of 16 December 2010 introduced a speciality and exclusivity provision whereby competences transferred to a territorial entity are exclusive to this entity. However, on close inspection, changes appear mostly cosmetic; some areas of competences continue to be shared between various levels of territorial government and overall the distribution of competences does not appear to have been simplified much (if at all).

The evolution of institutional designs and constitutional principles guiding the organisation of territorial government in France highlights the difficulties when engaging in multilevel constitutionalism. Constitutional principles may have emerged to inform the institutional design, but this has not ensured a successful evolution. The system of territorial government needs to be overhauled still; difficult decisions are yet to be made. The present reform may have tried to transform the system without having to take such decisions, but it is unlikely to deliver on its promises. Parliament hopes that the institutional engineering described above will develop its own dynamic and achieve the legislative aims, but it is far from certain. It is clear, however, that the reform has marginalised the framework and principles resulting from the constitutional reform of March 2003 and shifted the balance in favour of central government.

The possible failure of the present reform raises another issue: the transformation of regions is also rendered necessary by the European Union. Many EU policies are implemented and delivered at regional levels. To participate effectively in these, French regions would need to play a more important role. Paradoxically, the European Union has fuelled demands for stronger regional government too. Many European citizens are left feeling alienated by the process of European integration; consequently, proximity of decision making and regionalism has acquired an increasing normative and institutional appeal. This was recognised by the

European legal order through the principle of subsidiarity and the Committee of the Regions. Complex trends of multilevel constitutional-ism seem to be emerging indeed.

This trend is strengthened further by the French response to European integration. Successive constitutional reforms have struggled to protect the integrity of the 1958 constitution in the face of the European Union's transformation. Consequently, multilevel constitu-tionalism has impacted the French constitutional landscape further.

KEEPING A CHECK ON THE EUROPEAN UNION

As explained in chapter two, article 55 of the constitution gives prece-dence to international treaties and agreements over primary and second-ary legislation once they have been ratified or approved and published. In this monist system, European regulations or directives as a species of international law always took precedence over national legislation; there was no need to amend the constitution. This may explain why for a long time, there was no reference to the European Union in the French con-stitution.

The Conseil constitutionnel ensures the constitutionality of interna-tional treaties and agreements in two ways: a treaty can be referred to the Conseil under article 54[34] of the constitution, and the bill ratifying the treaty in Parliament can be referred to the Conseil under article 61 § 2 of the constitution.[35] The Conseil constitutionnel duly censures any breach of the constitution. When this happens, the constitution must be amended before the treaty can be ratified or approved. Over time, the Conseil con-stitutionnel sharpened its case law to ensure a more adequate constitu-tional control and a better protection of the French constitution.

As the process of European integration gathered momentum, resist-ance to the European project grew. The Single European Act was the

[34] See Article 54 of the constitution: 'If the Constitutional Council, on a reference from the President of the Republic, from the Prime Minister, from the President of one or the other assembly, or from sixty deputies or sixty senators, has declared that an international treaty or agreement contains a clause contrary to the Constitution, authorization to ratify or approve the international treaty or agreement in question may be given only after amendment of the Constitution.'

[35] For instance, the Maastricht Treaty was referred to the Conseil constitutionnel twice: the President of the Republic forwarded the Treaty under article 54 and sixty *députés* forwarded the bill authorising the ratification under article 61 § 2.

last European treaty to be ratified by the French Parliament with little fuss. The mood changed radically with the Maastricht Treaty in 1992. This led to the emergence of a multilayered constitutional protection: the constitution was amended to authorise the process of European integration and to strengthen the French Parliament's control over the activities of the European Union.

The Conseil constitutionnel and the European Union

At first, the Conseil elaborated principles which applied equally to all international treaties and agreements. In practice, the Conseil was referred mostly European treaties[36] and the case law has always been informed by the European experience. More recently, the Conseil adapted its case law to address specifically the European Union and to protect more effectively French national sovereignty in this context.

A Complex Framework of Control

To ensure that no international treaty breached the constitution or encroached on national sovereignty, the Conseil identified the incompatibilities that would require an amendment of the constitution before ratification or approval. This control has evolved over time. With the advent of the European Union, the Conseil constitutionnel added a preliminary enquiry: it checked that participation in the European Union was authorised by the French constitution.

The First Rampart – the Exercise of National Sovereignty

As early as 1970,[37] the Conseil constitutionnel specified that any compromise of the 'essential conditions of the exercise of national sovereignty' would infringe the French constitution and require a constitutional amendment. The interpretation of this principle and the manner in which it triggers a declaration of unconstitutionality has fluctuated over the years.

At times, the Conseil distinguished between limitations of sovereignty, which were acceptable, and transfers of sovereignty, which were

---

[36] So far, the Conseil constitutionnel has controlled 11 treaties on the basis of article 54 and only three were not concerned with the European Community/Union.

[37] C cons no 70-39 DC, 19 June 1970, Treaty of Luxembourg.

not. The 1946 Preamble refers only to limitations of sovereignty and the Conseil deduced that transfers of sovereignty (in part or in whole) were prohibited. This dichotomy was used in the decision of 29–30 December 1976[38] to determine the constitutionality of direct suffrage for the election of MEPs, but appears to have been abandoned. Although it may have been possible to distinguish conceptually between limitations and transfers of sovereignty, in practice it was difficult: limitations imposed on a State are often the result of transfers to an international organisation. It was therefore a challenge to decide what was authorised or prohibited under the French Constitution.

In the Maastricht Treaty decision,[39] the Conseil constitutionnel returned to its early case law and concentrated on determining what constitutes a breach of the 'essential conditions of the exercise of national sovereignty'. This expression, which cannot be found anywhere in the constitution, has become a key tool for the control of the constitutionality of treaties. The Conseil indicates that limitations or transfers of competences are not in themselves forbidden by the constitution, but they must not compromise 'the essential conditions of the exercise of national sovereignty'. If they do, a revision of the constitution is necessary.

As it is difficult to determine in the abstract a breach of national sovereignty, the Conseil constitutionnel may have resorted to this test to make its control as concrete as possible. First, to determine whether the essential conditions of the exercise of national sovereignty have been compromised, the Conseil constitutionnel looks at the subject matter under review. Over the years, the Conseil has identified a number of key areas which are particularly important for the exercise of national sovereignty: justice, taxation, monetary policy, border control, defence, national security. A transfer/limitation of competences in these areas is more likely to compromise an 'essential condition of the exercise of national sovereignty'. Secondly, the Conseil will also assess the extent of the transfer: the wider the powers, the more likely that the essential conditions of the exercise of national sovereignty will be violated. Finally, the Conseil determines whether there are institutional safeguards to protect the exercise of sovereignty: for instance, a decision-making process requiring unanimity of all Member States would be deemed to

---

[38] C cons no 76-71 DC, 29–30 December 1976, Election of the European Parliament.

[39] C cons no 92-308 DC, 9 April 1992, Maastricht Treaty.

protect national sovereignty by guaranteeing France's freedom of choice. The transfer is then more acceptable to the Conseil. The test of 'the essential conditions of the exercise of national sovereignty' has therefore two aspects: a substantive one – whether the subject matter of the transfer compromises national sovereignty – and an institutional one – whether the institutional design guarantees the exercise of sovereignty still. This two-stage reasoning helps the Conseil identify the concrete implications of transfers or limitations of competences and avoid vague and theoretical pronouncements. Also, it builds considerable flexibility in the case law.

The Second Rampart: The Constitution and the Rights and Freedoms

Since the decision on the Constitution for Europe,[40] the Conseil constitutionnel has made clear that the constitution needs to be amended if a treaty breaches a provision of the constitution or violates a constitutional right or freedom. In the circumstances, the new ground of constitutional review was not altogether a surprise. It coincided with the transformation of the European treaties into a Constitution for Europe, a constitution to which the Charter of Fundamental Rights was attached.

For the first time, the Conseil acknowledged that the rights and freedoms of the French constitution (as construed by the Conseil constitutionnel) may not be reconciled easily with those of the Charter of Fundamental Rights. In the event of a conflict arising between the rights contained in the two documents, the constitution would need to be amended prior to the treaty being ratified. In the 2004 decision, the Conseil did not limit itself to theoretical and abstract findings, but identified three areas of conflict (freedom of religion, right of minorities and right to a fair trial) and engineered a confrontation of the rights and freedoms protected by the two legal orders. The Conseil created real controversy by the way it solved many of the constitutional conundrums it had purposely created.

Membership of the European Union: A Sophisticated Authorisation

Beyond the identification of the grounds for the constitutional review of all international treaties, the Conseil constitutionnel combined and contrasted a number of constitutional provisions to establish a constitutional basis for France's participation in the European Union.

---

[40] C cons no 2004-505, DC, 19 November 2004, The Constitution for Europe.

The Conseil constitutionnel began by identifying the principle of national sovereignty as the key obstacle to France's participation in the European Union. The Conseil then listed the provisions which could authorise such membership. The Preamble of the 1946 constitution contains two paragraphs on international law: while paragraph 14 rules that 'France shall comply with the rules of international public law', paragraph 15 states that 'Subject to reciprocity, France shall consent to those limitations of sovereignty necessary for the organisation and defence of peace'. The Conseil also noted that article 53 of the constitution recognised the existence of legally ratified international treaties relating to international organisation. Finally, in 1997,[41] the Conseil added article 88-1, which contains a constitutional recognition of the European Union, to the list of provisions providing a constitutional basis for the membership of the European Union. In short, the Conseil relied on the provisions cited above to neutralise the potential prohibition derived from national sovereignty.

Finally, to keep a tight control over this constitutional authorisation, the Conseil described the main characteristics of the European Union as a permanent organisation with legal personality and decision-making power by virtue of transfers of competences from Members States. These characteristics condition the constitutional authorisation; any significant transformation of the European Union in the future would invalidate it.

An Ethno-Centric Order of the Constitutional Space

The Conseil constitutionnel did not simply adapt its methods of control to review the constitutionality of European treaties. It redesigned the constitutional space in an attempt to define the exact relationship between the two legal orders. In doing so, it imposed its vision of the nature and characteristics of the French and European legal orders respectively.

Supremacy of European Law and the French Constitutional Exception

Until 2004 the Conseil constitutionnel had ignored the principle of supremacy of European law. Unlike the German constitutional court, the Conseil had never indicated its position in the event of a Community act conflicting with a provision of the French constitution. However, in

---

[41] See C cons no 97-234 DC, 31 December 1997, Amsterdam Treaty.

the decision of 10 June 2004,[42] with a European constitution waiting in the wings, the Conseil prepared the ground for the recognition of primacy of European law and made pronouncements similar to those of the German constitutional court.[43]

The Conseil was asked to check the constitutionality of a bill which purported to implement the Directive on electronic commerce. There, the Conseil wondered whether it should review the constitutionality of the directive at all. First, the Conseil proclaimed a new constitutional duty of implementation of directives arising from Article 88-1 of the constitution. In doing so, the Conseil was indicating that Article 88-1 aimed to introduce into the French legal order the fundamental doctrines of European law, such as supremacy. As a result of this incorporation, the Conseil acknowledged the case law of the Court of Justice with regard to the control of Community acts. Then, it proceeded to draw the implications for its own control: the Conseil ruled that in the future it would refrain from examining the constitutionality of a statute implementing a directive as this would otherwise amount to an indirect control over the legality of a Community act – a control that national courts have been strongly dissuaded from performing since the *Foto-frost* ruling.[44]

Although the Conseil seemed to be making a deliberate show of accepting the Court of Justice's pronouncements on supremacy, it made two important caveats. It expressly regretted that it was unable to avail itself of Article 267 TFEU and refer cases to the Court of Justice: the short time limit for its decisions did not allow it. More importantly, the Conseil indicated that, exceptionally, it would decide on the constitutionality of a directive in the event that its provisions conflicted directly with a rule or principle defining French constitutional identity. After reading these pronouncements, the link with the decision of November 2004 on the constitutionality of the Constitution for Europe is clear for all to see. The Conseil had paved the way for the pronouncement that the principle of primacy codified in the Constitution for Europe did not contravene the French constitution.

Since then, the Conseil d'Etat has had to rule on similar issues. In the *Arcelor* case,[45] the legality of a French regulation implementing the direc-

---

[42]   C cons no 2004-496, DC 10 June 2004, Confidence in the digital economy.
[43]   See *Brunner v The European Union Treaty* [1994] 1 CMLR 57.
[44]   See C-314/85 *Foto-frost v Hauptzollamt Lübeck-Ost* [1987] ECR I-4199.
[45]   CE Ass 8 February 2007 (2007) Revue française de droit administratif, 384 concl Guyomar.

tive on exchange of quotas for carbon emission was challenged. The parties argued that the French regulation was illegal because the directive it purported to implement was itself illegal. According to Arcelor, the directive had set up a system of exchange of quotas for carbon emission which breached the principle of equality: both the aluminium and plastic industries were excluded from the scheme for no apparent reason. The Conseil d'Etat followed quite closely the reasoning of the Conseil constitutionnel but diverged slightly: the Conseil d'Etat would only check the constitutionality of a directive if the French principle contravened had no equivalent in European law. In this instance, the Conseil d'Etat suspected a breach of the European principle of equality and made a reference to the Court of Justice. The Conseil d'Etat chose to emphasise the complementary nature of the control by subjecting its intervention to the existence of a gap in rights protection. Still, both courts may appear to have accepted the case law of the Court of Justice on supremacy 'lock, stock and barrel', but in fact, they have clearly rejected the supremacy of European law over the French constitution and have braved the censure of the Court of Justice by introducing a constitutional exception.

The Recognition of the European Union: A Sub-System of the French Constitution

In its early decisions, the Conseil constitutionnel regarded the European Union as a standard international organisation. It ignored the pronouncements of the Court of Justice in this matter and rejected for a long while the specificity of the European legal order. In the Maastricht Treaty decision, the Conseil abandoned its earlier pronouncements and noted that the European Union is a permanent international organisation, albeit one with legal personality and decision-making powers by virtue of transfers of competences from Member States. In fact, the statement returns as a leitmotiv in later decisions. In the Constitution for Europe decision, the Conseil constitutionnel cited Article 88-1 and accepted the specificity of the European legal order as distinct from the international legal order. Still, it reasserted that the new Constitution for Europe was simply an international treaty in view of its mode of adoption, amendment and denunciation. Although it sharpened its description of international organisation, it continued to adhere to the three characteristics mentioned in its earlier cases: legal personality, permanence and decision-making powers. The nature of the European

Union seems fixed, whatever the changes made by successive treaty reforms. This description is very formal and does not attempt to capture the content of the treaties nor the political reality. Furthermore, the Conseil constitutionnel engineered a reconstruction of the constitutional space so as to dictate the relationship between the respective legal orders and ensure the precedence of the French constitution. In fact, the Conseil constitutionnel used the recognition contained in article 88-1 to transform the legal order of the European Union into a subsystem of the French constitution.

The Conseil constitutionnel and Multilevel Constitutionalism

As a result of its early case law, the Conseil constitutionnel contrived to stand clear from all international treaties for a long while.[46] It had only begun to grapple with the implications of a multilevel protection of fundamental rights when the preliminary reference on an issue of constitutionality completely redefined the context in which this court evolves.

Dictating Loudly

In addition to supremacy, many expected that fundamental rights would present an insurmountable obstacle to the ratification of the Constitution for Europe. The Charter of Fundamental Rights was seen to reflect different choices, especially with regard to freedom of religion and minority rights and the decision to incorporate fundamental values at variance with those of the constitution was questioned. For many, the rejection of most minority rights and the interpretation of freedom of religion within the confines of a secular state expressed deep cultural and societal choices that the 1958 constitution mirrors. Any other interpretation would contravene the constitution and open deep conflicts within French society. The Conseil could have declared the treaty unconstitutional on these grounds but the resulting constitutional reform was doomed to fail. If the Constitution for Europe was going to be ratified, a different approach was required. Instead, the Conseil constitutionnel adopted a rather unexpected strategy of multilevel judicial interpretations when reviewing the content of the Charter. It began by identifying the possible incompatibilities with the French constitution: the right to fair trial, freedom of religion and the

---

[46] In the decision C cons no 74-54 DC, 15 January 1975, Abortion, the Conseil constitutionnel refused to control the conformity of bills with international treaties and directed ordinary courts to perform it.

rights of minorities. Then it noted that it was the interpretation that these rights and freedoms would receive once the Charter was in force that was in issue.

Consequently, the Conseil constitutionnel found ways of influencing the case law of the Union courts for the future. An analysis of the Conseil's adventurous reasoning with regard to freedom of religion will exemplify the method used. Article 10 of the Charter recognises a right to manifest one's religious belief publicly. However, the French choice of strict secularism in the public sphere may at times curtail the right to manifest one's religious beliefs in public. Consequently, the Conseil looked to the explanations of the Praesidium to secure an interpretation which would be compatible with the French constitution. There, it was indicated that the freedom guaranteed by Article 10 of the Charter had the same content and ambit as the freedom contained in Article 9 of the European Convention on Human Rights (ECHR). The Conseil then argued that the European Court of Human Rights (ECtHR) recognised the idea of secularism and allowed a wide margin of appreciation to those States wishing to conciliate freedom of religion with a principle of secularism as required by their constitutional traditions. To strengthen its reasoning, the Conseil referred to the case law of the ECtHR and cited the decision in *Leyla Sahin v Turkey*. However, the choice of case could hardly be more controversial: not only was the decision not final at the time, but its solution has been criticised by many commentators since.[47] The ruling of the Conseil constitutionnel was also questionable as it appeared to come dangerously close to judicial blackmail: France can ratify the treaty and the Charter so long as (1) Union courts adhere to the case law and judicial policy of the ECtHR on freedom of religion; and (2) the ECtHR does not alter its case law on this matter. In one stroke, the Conseil found a 'legitimate' way to control the case law of both European courts. Some may argue that the Conseil engaged in a 'judicial dialogue', but its method is more consistent with an idea of forced cooperation. Whether the Conseil tried to assert its authority or sound a warning, the ruling was certainly part of a complex pre-emptive strategy: after the constitutional exception, came the reserves of interpretation. The Conseil was indeed placing itself at the centre (and summit) of the constitutional space.

---

[47] See T Lewis, 'What Not to Wear: Religious Rights, the European Court and the Margin of Appreciation' (2007) 56 *ICLQ* 395.

A Difficult Judicial Dialogue

The new preliminary ruling on an issue of constitutionality has created considerable tensions between the French supreme courts. Indeed, the Cour de cassation attempted to play the European Court of Justice against the Conseil constitutionnel to undermine the new procedure.[48] This judicial incident is indicative of an important change to the working environment of the Conseil constitutionnel. In the context of the new procedure, the Conseil deals with 'real cases', and the law applicable in these must comply with the ECHR and EU law. Since March 2010, the Conseil constitutionnel has evolved in a landscape where the European Court of Justice and the ECtHR play an important part. As a result, the Conseil has been forced to enter into a judicial dialogue of sorts.

The question raised by the Cour de cassation concerning the priority of the two procedures (preliminary ruling on an issue of constitutionality or preliminary reference under article 267 of the Treaty on the Functioning of the European Union (TFEU)) has led the Conseil to declare its lack of jurisdiction over a preliminary ruling on an issue of constitutionality concerning the implementing legislation of a directive. It stated that, with the exception of rights or freedoms relevant to French national identity, the respect of fundamental rights is ensured exclusively by the European Court of Justice via the preliminary reference procedure.[49] This conciliatory attitude of the Conseil constitutionnel aimed to diffuse the situation and avoid 'a war of the judges' to establish a strict priority between the two procedures.

With regard to the ECHR and its court, the attitude of the Conseil is more complex: the new procedure allowed the Conseil constitutionnel to declare unconstitutional provisions of the criminal procedure code on police custody.[50] Not only had the constitutionality of these provisions been in doubt for a long time, but they contravened the case law of the ECtHR. However, the potential for conflicts remains: the new legislation amending the criminal procedure code on police custody was adopted on 14 April 2011 and it has been referred already through the preliminary procedure. In its decision,[51] the Conseil indicated that a suspect could be

---

[48]   See chapter 5.
[49]   C cons no 2010-79 QPC, 17 December 2010, Mr Kamel D.
[50]   See C cons no 14/22-2010 QPC, 30 July 2010, Police custody.
[51]   See C cons no 2011-191/194/195/196/197 QPC, 18 November 2011, Police custody II.

interviewed without a lawyer present if he/she consents to it freely, thereby disregarding the pronouncements of the ECtHR on this point.[52]

It is clear that the Conseil's practice of multilevel constitutionalism has been transformed by the new procedure: the Conseil no longer dictates the term of the debate but is engaged in rather a difficult dialogue.

Increasing the Constitutional Controls

In 1992, after the Maastricht Treaty had been signed, the President of the Republic referred the Maastricht Treaty to the Conseil constitutionnel. The Conseil found that the treaty violated the constitution: the single currency, the determination of visa requirements for third-country nationals and the right for EU citizens to participate in municipal elections all breached the constitution.[53] To ratify the treaty, the constitution needed to be amended first. The resulting constitutional reform introduced into the constitution a separate title concerning the European Union.

The Authorisation by the Constitution: A Step by Step Approach

Before 1992, some may have thought that the addition of one or two provisions providing a blanket authorisation of membership of the European Community would be sufficient. However, with the creation of the European Union, it became clear that the authorisation of all transfers, present and future, once and for all, would not be opportune.

Consequently, in 1992 the constitutional bill introduced a new title XV into the constitution with two provisions only: one authorised the transfer of competences for the single currency and the determination of visa requirements for third-country nationals and the other granted EU citizens the right to participate in municipal elections. Sovereignty and its exercise were to be surrendered step by step. With the exception of the Nice Treaty, all European treaties negotiated since then have required an amendment of the constitution.

At the moment, Articles 88-2 and 88-3 of title XV contain a list of narrowly defined constitutional authorisations in relation to freedom of

---

[52] See aff 7377/03 *Dayanan v Turkey*, 13 October 2009.
[53] C cons no 92-308 DC, 9 April 1992, Maastricht I.

movement, the European arrest warrant and the right for EU citizens to participate in municipal elections. All of these powers and transfers of competences were found to be incompatible with the French constitution and needed to be authorised specially. Although clumsy, this solution protects national sovereignty and the constitution efficiently. The new transfers granted by future treaty revisions will need to be similarly authorised and the list can only lengthen. Furthermore, the success of this constitutional 'lock' requires the intervention of the Conseil constitutionnel. Until 1992, only four officials could refer a treaty to the Conseil; for the lock to be efficient, the reference system needed to be widened.

The Reform of Article 54

In 1992, Members of Parliament demanded the right to refer a treaty to the Conseil constitutionnel prior to its ratification. With this power, Members of Parliament hoped to keep a check on European integration. Consequently, article 54 was amended by the constitutional reform of 25 June 1992 to allow 60 *députés* or 60 *sénateurs* to refer a treaty to the Conseil constitutionnel. Although article 54 has been used 11 times since 1958, Members of Parliament have only referred a treaty to the Conseil in this way twice.[54]

Article 88-1[55]

Article 88-1 provision was not included in the original bill for the new title XV. It was the result of an amendment adopted by the Assemblée nationale. Although article 88-1 grants a constitutional basis to France's membership of the European Union, it refers to the treaty requiring a constitutional authorisation at the time. Indeed when this provision was first adopted, the authorisation was limited to the European Union as established by the Maastricht Treaty. At the moment, it refers to the Lisbon Treaty.

---

[54] See the decisions C cons no 92-312 DC, 2 September 1992, Maastricht II and C cons no 2006-541 DC, 28 September 2006, London agreements.

[55] See article 88-1: 'The Republic shall participate in the European Union constituted by States which have freely chosen to exercise some of their powers in common by virtue of the Treaty on European Union and of the Treaty on the Functioning of the European Union, as they result from the treaty signed in Lisbon on 13 December, 2007.'

While article 88-1 recognises the participation of France in the European Communities, it describes the European Union as 'constituted freely by States to exercise some of their competences in common'. This informs us of the nature of the European Union as captured by the French constitution: the European Union does not benefit from sovereignty, original or shared, and its existence is entirely dependent on Member States. This insistence on the intergovernmental character of the organisation ensures unequivocally the superiority of the French constitution.

An Increase of Parliament's Control

With the advent of the European Union, concerns were repeatedly voiced in the French Parliament with regard to European integration. Members of Parliament revised the constitution repeatedly to increase their control over European decisions and policies. Interestingly, these initiatives have been encouraged by recent treaty revisions.

From Parliamentary Delegation to Permanent Committee

The French Parliament tried to strengthen its control over the activities of the European Communities from the moment the European Parliament was directly elected in 1979. Members of Parliament feared the increased legitimacy of the European Parliament and predicted that an information gap would open between the two Parliaments. Consequently, a statute was passed on 6 July 1979 which authorised the creation of a permanent delegation for the European Communities in both houses of Parliament. Only a constitutional reform could establish an extra permanent committee, but there was no political momentum for this. Consequently, these permanent delegations could not benefit from much power.[56] Indeed, the status of the permanent delegations was in doubt until their introduction in article 88-4 of the constitution in 1992. It was not until the reform of July 2008 that the delegations were transformed into permanent committees for European affairs with the same powers as the other permanent committees.

The main role of these committees is to advise the house on draft legislation and provide information on any European Union issue of

---

[56] Permanent delegations could not resemble permanent committees, otherwise the Conseil constitutionnel would have interpreted the move as a blatant attempt to circumvent the constitutional prohibition and censored them.

interest and/or importance. To this effect, all documents produced by European institutions and all proposals transmitted to the Council are to be forwarded to the new committees.[57]

The Difficult Introduction of Resolutions

From the beginning, Parliament toyed with the possibility of adopting 'resolutions' on specific European issues in an attempt to influence the Government's European policy. As early as 1979, Members of Parliament contemplated granting such power to the new delegations. However, for historical reasons, resolutions were frowned upon; Parliament could not control or direct the activity of the Government outside the provisions of the constitution strictly construed.[58] The limitations were finally conquered when the permanent delegations for European Affairs were given the power to adopt resolutions by the constitutional reform of 1992.

Nowadays, the committee for European affairs examines all European Union proposals on transmission. The committee has three options. It can delay making a recommendation because of insufficient information and appoint a reporter to provide both information and analysis. If the committee has enough information, it can recommend the adoption or the rejection of the proposal; in both cases it can include a commentary or a draft resolution detailing the reasons for its position. When the committee for European affairs recommends a rejection, the draft resolution is necessarily forwarded to the relevant permanent committee. The permanent committee reports and decides on the draft resolution; it can adopt, reject or amend it. Once the permanent committee has decided, the resolution can be tabled for debate in the house. If the resolution is not tabled within eight days for the Assemblée nationale and 10 days for the Sénat, it becomes final and is forwarded to the Government. Resolutions are advisory and they have not always been successful in steering the Government's

---

[57] The delegations used to receive per year, on average, 300 proposals, 800 documents from the Commission and 1,500 documents from the Government. This figure is set to increase.

[58] Furthermore, by wishing to issue resolutions in relation to European Union matters, Members of Parliament may contravene yet another constitutional provision: according to the constitution, international relations are the quasi-exclusive domain of the President of the Republic. Indeed, Parliament may have wanted to use the resolutions to try and impose a mandate with regard to Council negotiations.

position in Council. An average of 10 resolutions are adopted every year in each house and of these, very few are adopted in plenary. This figure may seem low, especially when one considers the effort deployed to give this power to Parliament. Successive reviews have not identified this as a problem, however.

The Accession of New Member States to the EU

To ensure the approval of the Constitution for Europe by referendum, President Chirac promised in 2005 the addition of article 88-5 to the constitution: the treaty of accession to the European Union of a new Member State would need to be approved by referendum first. This was mainly to allay fears regarding the entry of Turkey. Article 88-5 may have been politically expedient but the rejection of the constitution for Europe by referendum left the French constitution lumbered with a rather infamous provision. Unsurprisingly, the revision of July 2008 tried to cure this by amending article 88-5: each house of Parliament can adopt a resolution with a 60 per cent majority to have the treaty ratified in the Congrès instead. The treaty is ratified by the Congrès with a 60 per cent majority.[59] This provision may increase the control of Parliament over the accession of new Member States but it may cause some serious problems in the future.

The Lisbon Treaty and the Role of National Parliaments

When examining the Lisbon Treaty,[60] the Conseil had declared that the new powers conferred on national Parliaments to control the European Union's decision-making process required an amendment of the constitution.[61] For this reason, two new articles were introduced in title XV.

Article 88-6 transcribes the powers protecting the principle of subsidiarity which can be found in article 12 of the Treaty on European Union (TEU) and in protocol no 2 of the Lisbon Treaty. To this effect, each house can forward to the European Parliament an opinion on the compatibility of a European act's proposal with the principle of

---

[59] This threshold is more demanding than the one required to amend the constitution.

[60] C cons no 2007-560 DC, 20 December 2007, Treaty of Lisbon.

[61] Already, the Constitution for Europe had adopted a protocol on the role of national parliaments in the European Union and granted them a number of prerogatives. The Lisbon Treaty contained a similar protocol and the role of national parliaments is also described in the new article 12 of the Treaty on European Union.

subsidiarity.[62] Furthermore, in the event that Members of Parliament believed that European legislation breached the principle of subsidiarity, an action in the European Court of Justice can be triggered by 60 *députés* and 60 *sénateurs*.

Article 88-7 creates a procedure for the French Parliament to oppose a decision to amend the decision-making process by reference to the simplified procedure or to the judicial cooperation in civil matters.

These new constitutional provisions are particularly interesting with regard to a reflection on multilevel constitutionalism. In this instance, a national constitution was amended to incorporate the provisions of an international treaty and give a national parliament powers of control over a supranational organisation.

CONCLUSION

With the rise of territorial government and the constitutional recognition of the European Union, the French constitutional order has evolved beyond recognition. Indeed, the core principles of indivisibility, unity and national sovereignty were adapted with comparative ease by successive constitutional reforms. The French constitution has thus embraced multilevel constitutionalism without much conceptual recognition of this fact or its implications. The present constitution may still proclaim the existence of a 'stand-alone' united and indivisible republic, but the contemporary picture of the French constitutional order is more complex and subtle. Pulled in opposite directions by demands for local autonomy (or even independence) on the one hand and for deeper European integration and international cooperation on the other, the original constitutional order has responded by dabbling in multilevel constitutionalism. However, with time, it may be necessary to capture and conceptualise these changes more fully and amend the constitution accordingly.

---

[62] For a recent use of this provision, see the resolution of the Assemblée nationale of 15 June 2011 (TA no 695) which states that the proposal amending Directive 2003/96/EC restructuring the Community framework for the taxation of energy products and electricity is in breach of the principle of subsidiarity.

FURTHER READING

S Boyron, 'The "New" French Constitution and the European Union' (2008–09) 11 *Cambridge Yearbook of European Legal Studies* 321

P Cassia, 'Le maire, agent de l'Etat' (2004) *Actualité juridique: droit administratif* 245

J-C Douence, 'Les métroples' (2011) *Revue française de droit administratif* 258

G Drago, 'La guerre des juges n'aura pas lieu' (2007) *Juris-Classeur périodique (administratif)* 29

J-Y Faberon, 'La Nouvelle-Calédonie, pays à souveraineté partagée' (1998) *Revue de droit public* 645

B Faure, 'La nouvelle compétence générale des départements et des régions' (2011) *Revue française de droit administratif* 240

A Levade, 'Première QPC sur une disposition législative transposant une directive: non-lieu à statuer ou la poursuite du dialogue avec la Cour de justice' (2011) *Constitutions* 54

X Philippe, 'France: The Amendment of the French Constitution "on the Decentralised Organisation of the Republic"' (2004) *International Journal of Constitutional Law* 691

O Pollicino, 'The Conseil d'Etat and the Relationship between French Internal Law and European Law after Arcelor: Has Something Really Changed?' (2009) *CML Rev* 1519

C Richards, 'Devolution in France: The Corsican Problem' (2004) *European Public Law* 481

J-P Thiellay, *Le droit des outre-mers*, 2nd edn (Paris, Dalloz, 2011)

8

The Dynamics of Constitutional Change

The Amendment Procedure: A Question of Choice? – The
Dynamics of Constitutional Change – The Trends for Constitutional
Reform – Conclusion

T HE INSISTENCE ON constitutional change in this last chapter should not surprise; it is an inevitable topic when surveying a
constitutional order. This study is also rooted in the belief that
constitutional change reveals the deep nature of a constitutional system
and that a careful study of this phenomenon provides a deeper level of
analysis of the constitutional settlement itself. The regulation of constitutional change is at the heart of the doctrine of constitutionalism.
Indeed, in most constitutional systems, the processes by which constitutional norms change will determine fundamental questions for the
regime such as its survival, efficiency and legitimacy.

Furthermore, the 1958 constitution introduced a new and remarkable
constitutional reality. For a long time, constitutional change was not
really framed by the formal procedures of constitutional amendment in
France. In previous regimes, constitutional change reflected a paradox:
while constitutional practices were often at variance with the provisions
of the constitution, it was quasi-impossible to amend the text formally.
Not only was constitutional change happening outside the formal
amendment procedure, but often it undermined the integrity of the
constitutional order. As a result, constitutions came and went and were
at the mercy of political actors and events. Constitutional documents
survived for as long as was politically expedient, but no longer. The
1958 constitution has evolved dramatically since its inception in 1958,
but it has done so 'quietly': the urge for revolutions and coups has finally
been controlled. For the first time in French history, a constitution has

been 'adjusted' successfully. Moreover, the number and extent of constitutional amendments demonstrate that there is no impediment to constitutional reform in the present regime. In fact, the constitution has been altered in so many ways and at so many levels that one would be well justified in considering the present French constitutional system to be a permanent and living experiment in constitutional change.

Amendment procedures are commonly used to classify constitutional systems and in this regard the 1958 constitution is a rigid constitution. The drafters of the 1958 constitution certainly aimed to protect the constitutional settlement by making the document comparatively difficult to amend. However, the distinction between flexible and rigid constitutions is at best misleading in the French context. It does not explain the reality of constitutional change, its depth, its effects, its import or even its success in altering the constitutional settlement legitimately. In many constitutions, constitutional reform does not tell half the story of change and this is particularly true in France. There, constitutional change is a dynamic, the complexity of which is not easily captured. Formal amendments have engendered deep political changes and finally triggered a virtuous synergy between law and politics. To concentrate on the formal and legal processes of constitutional reform would narrow considerably the analysis and would make it mostly vacuous.

Consequently, in this chapter, constitutional change will be explored in a number of ways: first, the amendment procedure will be presented; secondly, the dynamics of constitutional change will be identified and analysed; finally, the various trends of constitutional change will be identified in an attempt to assess their overall import.

THE AMENDMENT PROCEDURE: A QUESTION OF CHOICE?

Although the fifth Republic is undeniably a rigid constitution, the amendment procedure contained in article 89 achieves a good balance between flexibility and rigidity: it protects the constitution but is simpler than similar procedures in previous constitutions. Indeed, the 1958 constitution has been amended 24 times since its inception and the first stage of the 25th constitutional reform has just been completed.[1] This is

---

[1] See the constitutional bill on the equilibrium of public finance which was adopted by the Assemblée nationale on 12 July 2011.

a definite break from the past: constitutions were normally discarded rather than amended. Indeed, neither the third or fourth Republics managed to amend their constitutions to tackle dysfunctions. In fact, the amendment procedure of the 1946 constitution was such a drawn-out process that when the regime was abolished, two constitutional amendments were pending still (one had been initiated as early as 1955).

Still, in the early years, the amendment procedure was the subject of controversy: the second constitutional amendment was arguably a breach of the constitution. De Gaulle felt it politically expedient to resort to article 11 instead of article 89 to amend the constitution. Although this constitutional practice has been abandoned since, both provisions will be examined below.

Article 89

Article 89 has been used repeatedly and successfully to amend the constitution. Indeed, the number and ambit of the amendments have increased markedly since the 1990s. Article 89 sets out clearly the procedure to amend the constitution, but imposes strict limitations.

The Constitutional Limitations

First article 89 § 4 places some temporary limitations on the amendment procedure: it is not possible to amend the constitution when the French territory's integrity is compromised (eg in time of war). Constitutional change needs serenity and peace; otherwise the situation's urgency may result in the adoption of a rash, undesirable and possibly undemocratic amendment. This limitation sprang from the adverse experience of the constitutional revision of 10 July 1940: while the German army advanced rapidly through France, the French Parliament amended the constitution and handed all powers of the (third) Republic to General Pétain. This led to the Vichy regime and in effect ended the third Republic. Both the 1946 and 1958 constitutions learned from this and prohibited any constitutional amendment in such circumstances. In addition, other provisions of the constitution limit the timing of a constitutional amendment: according to article 7 § 6, it is not possible to amend the constitution when the President of the Republic has resigned, died or been impeached. The Conseil constitutionnel has also declared that no amendment can proceed as long as the President of the Republic is using the emergency powers of article 16.[2] These temporary limitations recognise that the revision process is intrinsically risky and needs to be shielded from adverse circumstances.

Finally, article 89 § 5 imposes a permanent prohibition on the amendment procedure: the republican nature of the Government cannot be altered. At first glance, this substantive limitation seems clear: France must continue as a republic, presumably as opposed to a monarchy or empire. However, it is possible to adopt a wider interpretation of this prohibition: the republican nature of the regime is dependent on a number of rights (eg equality) and principles (eg territorial unity); any change to these would consequently compromise the nature of the regime and the existence of the republic. The Conseil constitutionnel was called to rule on this question in 2003. Senators had referred the constitutional bill introducing the principle of decentralisation of territorial government in article 1 of the constitution: they claimed that this revision undermined the unitary and therefore republican nature of the regime. The Conseil, however, rejected this interpretation.[3]

If a proposed amendment does not fall within one (or more) of these limitations, the procedure of article 89 can be triggered.

The Amendment Procedure

The procedure reproduced in article 89 of the 1958 constitution contains three stages and specifies two possible routes.

The Right of Initiative

All constitutional amendments start in the same way: according to article 89, the right of initiative belongs equally to Members of Parliament and to the President of the Republic on a request from the Prime Minister. In reality, the right of initiative belongs largely to the President of the Republic. Although Members of Parliament have drafted and introduced constitutional bills to amend the constitution, none has ever succeeded. In fact, political reality makes it difficult for Members of Parliament to use their right of initiative fully: either they are members of the presidential majority and the Executive is better placed, both

---

[2] See C cons no 92-312 DC, 2 September 1992, Maastricht II.
[3] See C cons no 2003-469 DC, 26 March 2003, Decentralisation.

politically and constitutionally, to propose a constitutional amendment, or they are members of the opposition and their proposals can only fail. Although the three periods of 'cohabitation' provided an opportunity for Members of Parliament of the majority to propose constitutional amendments, none did so; they did not want to be responsible for the inevitable political tensions that would ensue between the parliamentary majority and the President of the Republic.

Similarly, the request of the Prime Minister for a constitutional amendment is mostly superfluous: for the majority of amendments, the initiative has come solely from the President. Only in cohabitation periods has the role of the Prime Minister been pivotal: President Chirac was not convinced that the presidential mandate should be shortened to five years in an attempt to avoid further cohabitation, but in 2000 he was forced to trigger a revision by Jospin, the Socialist Prime Minister.

The Pre-Legislative Stage

Once it has been decided that the constitution is to be amended, the Executive engages in a wide consultation exercise to determine the exact content of the reform. On five occasions, the President of the Republic first convened an expert committee of academics, experts and politicians to advise on this content.[4] Prior to making their proposals, the committees have all engaged in wide consultation. Although only a small number of constitutional reforms have resorted to expert committees, all five were potentially key reforms, either because of their subject matter or their ambit.

Once the Executive has negotiated the content of the reform with a wide cross section of the political community, a bill is drafted. At this stage, some of the proposals put forward by the committee of experts

---

[4] Expert committees chaired respectively by Professor Vedel and by Balladur were convened to make proposals prior to the two attempts at wide-ranging reform in August 1995 and July 2008. Furthermore, the reform of February 2007 clarified the criminal liability of the President of the Republic on the recommendations of another expert committee chaired by Professor Avril. Finally, the last two attempts at constitutional reform resorted to expert committees too: an expert committee chaired by Simone Veil was convened in April 2008 to investigate possible additions to the Declarations of Rights. An expert committee chaired by Michel Camdessus (honorary chairman of the Banque de France) framed the provisions contained in the recent constitutional bill aiming to introduce a 'golden rule' in the French constitution.

may be dropped.[5] Then, as with the ordinary legislative procedure, the Conseil d'Etat is consulted on the constitutional bill prior to its adoption by the Government in the Council of Ministers. Although the opinion of the Conseil d'Etat is only communicated to the Government, the annual reports of the Conseil d'Etat may contain some information. Generally, the Conseil d'Etat is less likely to proffer advice on the policy choices of any reform, constitutional or otherwise. Instead, the Conseil d'Etat concentrates on the means chosen to fulfil the policy objectives, their efficiency and coherence. Still, this advice may have the consequence of undermining the proposal itself, as exemplified by the opinion given on the constitutional bill on decentralisation in 2002.[6]

Adoption by Parliament

Once drafted, the bill is introduced in Parliament (in either chamber). Article 89 requires that both chambers approve the text in identical terms. The extent to which the ordinary legislative procedure can be used to vote on a constitutional amendment has been the subject of debates. As explained in chapter 4, the Government has any number of weapons to ensure that ordinary legislation is adopted by Parliament. However, commentators have argued against the use of these when debating and voting on a constitutional bill. This may be for political reasons – the Government needs to ensure the support of Members of Parliament – or because of legal arguments – there is uncertainty among commentators as to which weapon can be used legally. In reality, while threats have been made,[7] there seems to be a general reluctance to curtail the legislative process. In fact, the Government will often have tried to build strong support in favour of the proposal prior to its introduction.

The Final Approval: Two Routes

At this point, the procedure of article 89 allows two options: the constitutional bill needs to receive popular or parliamentary approval. The

---

[5] In 2008, the proposal to clarify the respective roles of President of the Republic and Prime Minister was abandoned at this stage.

[6] In its opinion, the Conseil d'Etat queried the need and merit of inscribing the principle of decentralisation in article 1 of the constitution. It also questioned the normative status of the principle of subsidiarity. See Conseil d'Etat, 'Rapport Annuel' (2003) 55.

[7] For instance, the Government threatened to use the 'blocked vote' during the vote of the constitutional reform necessary for the ratification of the Maastricht Treaty.

President has discretion over the route that the constitutional bill takes. The first option requires approval of the electorate by referendum. The second option requires that both chambers convene together in the Congrès. The constitutional amendment is carried if it receives at least 60 per cent of the votes. Although the drafting of article 89 implies that constitutional amendments should normally be approved by referendum, all constitutional amendments were adopted by the Congrès with the exception of the reduction of the presidential mandate to five years.

Article 11, Popular Sovereignty and the Revision of the Constitution

Article 89 may be straightforward, but the involvement of the French people in the successive constitutional reforms has been and is still controversial.

The Use of Article 11

In 1962 de Gaulle wanted to reform the electoral system for the President of the Republic, but feared that Parliament would oppose the introduction of direct universal suffrage. Unfortunately the legislative process contained in article 89 requires the approval of the constitutional bill by both houses before the referendum. For the reform to be successful, de Gaulle needed to bypass Parliament. For this reason, de Gaulle relied on article 11 instead. He reasoned that the legitimacy granted by direct democracy would be enough to quell any challenge. Indeed, the referendum was successful and made it difficult for anyone to contest the direct expression of the will of the Nation. Even the Conseil constitutionnel, when asked to review the constitutionality of the referendum, declined to do so. It would have been untenable for any constitutional court, however legitimate, to contest such a decisive declaration of popular sovereignty. Nevertheless, a continued use of article 11 to amend the constitution may have created problems in the long run: for instance, commentators began to wonder whether a new constitutional practice was fast emerging when article 11 was used a second time to amend the constitution in 1969. The failure of the 1969 referendum and the subsequent resignation of de Gaulle marked the end of this unorthodox interpretation of the constitution. Article 11 has been used sparingly since and never to amend the constitution: although the ambit of this provision was widened in the reform of August 1995, politicians have quickly learnt to be wary of the people's verdict.[8]

From Bypassing Parliament to Bypassing the People

In fact, since the departure of de Gaulle, there has been a tendency to exclude the sovereign people from decisions on constitutional reforms: since 1962, all constitutional reforms bar one have opted for the parliamentary route. This may be justifiable for small and technical amendments, but the parliamentary route was even preferred for the recent reform of the constitution. On 23 July 2008 the constitution was completely overhauled and one may wonder why the sovereign people was not asked to underwrite this major constitutional reform. It may be that its complexity did not lend itself to a referendum, but in view of the number and import of constitutional reforms in the last two decades, one may rightly question what role is left to the sovereign people in this regard. While de Gaulle strove to strengthen the foundations of the political system with universal direct suffrage and referendums, politicians nowadays tend to eschew the mechanisms of direct democracy: the sovereign is left without a voice. This is all the more surprising since the trend at present is to promote the use of mechanisms of direct democracy: increasingly, referendums – be they national or local – and popular initiatives are included in legislation and constitutions. The place of the French people in constitutional reform may have changed dramatically since the beginnings of the 1958 constitution, but it still triggers strong debate and controversy. Indeed, for some, the quasi-systematic use of the parliamentary route when revising the constitution has resulted in the emergence of a constitutional convention.

THE DYNAMICS OF CONSTITUTIONAL CHANGE

The regime of the fifth Republic established by the constitutional document is somewhat at variance with the one established in reality: present political practices seem to reveal the same disregard for the constitution

---

[8] See J-M Denquin, 'Le déclin du referendum sous la Vè République' in *Les quarante ans de la Vè République* (1998) *Revue de droit public (No Spécial)* 1582.

as in the past. However, unlike previous regimes, the constitution was formally amended to reflect and legitimise these evolutions. As a result, the present political system has achieved unparalleled stability. Although calls have been heard for the adoption of a new regime, the present constitution has stayed on top of the dysfunctions that have arisen so far. To understand this evolution and its implications, it is therefore necessary to analyse in some detail this dynamic of constitutional change. To do so, the various components of this dynamic will be identified and analysed.

The Emergence of Constitutional Conventions

The analysis of the various constitutional amendments that have taken place since 1958 reveals a surprising trend: the emergence of constitutional conventions. The procedure contained in article 89 may be clear and complete, but every stage of this process – the initiative, drafting and approval – seems to be witnessing the formation of constitutional conventions.[9] Concerning the initiative, although both President of the Republic and Members of Parliament have the right of initiative, all constitutional reforms so far have been triggered by the Executive (and with one exception by the President of the Republic). With regard to complex and/or controversial reforms, an expert committee of academics and politicians is convened by the President of the Republic to research and put forward proposals. Arguably, this helps to secure cross-party support later. Also, the route taken by the constitutional reform seems increasingly to give rise to stable political practices: once the approval of the constitutional reform by both houses is secured, the bill follows quasi-systematically the parliamentary route. The use of referendums is rare and restricted to reforms that can be encapsulated in a simple and clear question. Finally, a convention seems also to be dealing with constitutional reforms which have been abandoned after approval by both houses, but before their submission to the Congrès or the people. Generally, such reforms are regarded to have lapsed; they cannot be 'revived' years later. Although, the status of these practices is still

---

[9] See P Avril, 'Des conventions à la révision de la constitution' (2008) *Revue française de droit constitutionnel* (*hors serie* 49 and S Boyron, 'The French Constitution and the Treaty of Amsterdam: A Lesson in European Integration' (1999) 6 *Maastricht Journal* 169.

unclear, the formal procedure of amendment is informed and even framed by them. It demonstrates how well rooted in political life the process of constitutional reform is.

Beyond the establishment of these thriving practices, one can detect a momentous shift: there is a fervour for constitutional amendment in the fifth Republic that did not exist before. The emergence of this over-arching belief drives the whole evolution with regard to constitutional change in the fifth Republic. For the first time in France, formal provisions and constitutional practices and political beliefs are combining in a rational framework to facilitate constitutional reform.

The Mechanisms of the Dynamic

A healthy dynamic of constitutional change surfaced in the early days of the regime and engineered the necessary transformation to ensure an early and continued survival. To understand this dynamic, it is important to isolate its various components. The establishment of clear political practices is the first component. It is possible to cite the early presidential reading of the constitution or the transformation of the Conseil constitutionnel into a quasi-constitutional court as such examples. The creation of the responsibility of the Prime Minister before the President, the repeated use of referendums and the resort to article 16 may have been at the margin of constitutionality, but they all combined to give a presidential direction to the new regime. Similarly, by incorporating fundamental rights into the constitution in the 1971 decision, the Conseil constitutionnel transformed itself into a guardian of constitutional rights. However, for the dynamic to continue, it requires a second component: the intervention of formal constitutional amendment. With the 1962 referendum, the French people legitimised and institutionalised the presidential reading. Similarly, the early evolution of the Conseil constitutionnel was endorsed by the constitutional reform of 1974 by widening the access to this institution.

More interestingly, the dynamic rarely stops then; more often than not it triggers further political practices and constitutional amendments: in 1962 the emergence of the majority phenomenon in the Assemblée nationale secured the presidential interpretation of the constitution further. Also, in 2000, the reduction of the presidential mandate aimed to avoid further cohabitations and reassert the presidential reading. With regard to the Conseil constitutionnel, the reform of 1974 unlocked the potential of the institution: without this constitutional reform, the Conseil would have had a meagre legitimacy and very few cases to work with. Finally, it may have taken repeated efforts to grant ordinary citizens access to the Conseil constitutionnel, but this was finally done by the reform of July 2008. This completes the transformation of the Conseil constitutionnel into a formidable constitutional court.

The Virtuous Synergy of Constitutional Change

This dynamic created a virtuous circle of constitutional change: at last, constitutional practices and constitutional amendment combined together to transform the constitutional system. This created a virtuous circle or synergy between law and politics for the first time in France. The 1958 constitution has been able to capture and shape political practices – something that past constitutions struggled to do – but more importantly, it allowed political practices to emerge and to transform the constitution in turn. In a paradox of constitutional change, political practices were both constrained by the constitutional text and harnessed by the constitutional order to ensure its survival and establish a *sui generis* political regime. In the fifth Republic, politics may be constrained by law, but the law did not stifle the creative power of politics. Although the 1958 constitution is a rigid constitution, it evolves constantly. Interestingly, this has taken place without compromising the stability or integrity of the constitutional order. On the contrary, the permanent dynamic of constitutional change has ensured the stability of the regime and has helped shape the substantive content of the constitutional order.[10]

Surprisingly, the dynamic has managed to create a virtuous synergy of constitutional change in yet another way. Beneficial and destructive political practices are clearly distinguished and treated differently; in this context, not all political practices are recognised to hold the same intrinsic value. Constitutional reform has been used to eradicate those which disturbed or even endangered the regime. Indeed, the shortening

---

[10] For example, the attempt of the Conseil constitutionnel to draw the contemporary contours of the constitution was completed by constitutional reform: while the Conseil added the Declaration of 1789 and the Preamble of 1946 to the 1958 constitution, the constitutional amendment of 2005 annexed the Charter for the Environment.

of the mandate of the President of the Republic contributed to this virtuous synergy. The experiences of cohabitation came to be regarded as endangering the efficiency and stability of the regime and a term was put to them. Similarly, the constitutional reform of July 2008 has attempted to redress the flawed institutional balance and grant more power to Parliament; this move was necessary to retain and even regain the regime's legitimacy. So far, the dynamic of constitutional change has managed to distinguish between 'good' and 'bad' political practices. This would indicate that this constitutional dynamic is guided by overarching principles that assess and label the different practices. Although these principles may not be easily identifiable, many relate to the regime itself: stability, efficiency, legitimacy and continuity of the regime will be protected from political practices that seek to undermine them. Other guiding principles must consist of those reflecting long-held ideals of (French) constitutionalism (popular democracy, accountability of elected officers, constitutional guarantee of rights etc) and which until now had been implemented with difficulty. Still, this degree of constitutional 'discernment' demonstrates a constitutional maturity that France has not experienced much in modern history.

Constitutional Change, History and Taboos

As shown in chapter one, history has always been a determining factor with regard to constitutional change in France. As a result of a rich but complex history, the French carry a considerable amount of historical baggage, which has impacted constitutional change repeatedly. Experiences of previous regimes often constrain markedly constitutional reform in France: lessons are drawn from failures and successes and they inform the drafting of the next constitutional document.

Indeed, the hand of history has been felt on the process of constitutional change on numerous occasions during the fifth Republic. In some instances, this has had a stifling effect: the numerous restrictions imposed on the French Parliament are only lifted now after considerable time and debate. In fact, past history has a lot to answer for still, if one considers the debatable limitations on the number of permanent committees in each house. A close study of the constitutional reforms required before the ratification of the European treaties reveals that these concerns were so deep seated that they restricted unduly parliamentary controls over the

European Union; the right to issue resolutions in this context was fought long and hard and the committee for European affairs was only established in each house in July 2008. Even an external threat such as that of the European Union did not jostle the complacency of politicians quickly.

On the other hand, 'a lack of history' may well have facilitated the transformation of the Conseil constitutionnel into a constitutional court. Prior to the Conseil, there had never been much constitutional review in France; the Conseil benefited from a clean slate: it did not have a past to live up to or to break from. In fact, the Conseil did use constitutional history to its advantage: to legitimise its control, the Conseil relied upon two historical and symbolic texts – the Declaration of the Rights of Man of 1789 and the Preamble of the 1946 constitution. The Conseil has shaped its own history.

Interestingly, historical 'baggage', it seems, can be overcome with the passage of time: many important constitutional reforms were long in the planning and were attempted repeatedly before they were finally adopted. The reduction of the mandate of the President of the Republic, the extension of the powers of the Conseil constitutionnel, the creation of a status for the opposition had all been proposed before. Indeed, some were the subject of a failed or abandoned amendment procedure. For others, there had been successful constitutional amendments but these were deemed insufficient: the Conseil supérieur de la Magistrature was amended twice to strengthen its independence, the reform of August 1995 took small steps towards the rehabilitation of Parliament. This explains in part why the reform of July 2008 was drafted and adopted so speedily despite its ambit: a number of proposals had been debated before. This is an important point in view of the arguments discussed above: many of the more controversial reforms had acquired a history of their own before they came to be adopted. This may have been the key to their success: familiarity and the passage of time have given these reforms a certain maturity and provided them with a past detached from the experiences of previous regimes.

Finally, there remains some historical baggage in the form of constitutional taboos: some institutions or principles have left such an historical imprint that they are unlikely ever to be adopted or changed. For instance, it is unlikely that France will ever be able to resort to a single-chamber Parliament. Similarly, it is unlikely that the Declaration of Rights of Man of 1789 will ever be superseded by a new declaration of rights.

THE TRENDS FOR CONSTITUTIONAL REFORM

The 1958 constitution has been amended 24 times since coming into force and the pace of constitutional reform has quickened: while the constitution was revised 5 times in the first three decades, it has been amended 19 times in the last 20 years.[11] In fact, another constitutional reform is pending at the moment (although it is unlikely to be concluded in the near future). A study of the type and extent of these amendments will reveal much with regard to the evolution of the French constitution and the catalysts for constitutional change in France.

Confirming the More Creative Interpretations of the Constitution

As mentioned above, a number of constitutional amendments aimed at confirming existing interpretations, especially when those were quite remote from the original intention of the drafters.

First, the presidential reading of the regime was granted the constitutional seal of approval in 1962; this choice was reaffirmed in 2000. Secondly, the Conseil constitutionnel altered its role considerably in one judicial stroke. Far from resisting the change, the 1974 constitutional amendment confirmed this audacious alteration of the Conseil constitutionnel and amplified it. Similarly, the reform of July 2008, which came into effect in March 2010, strengthened this transformation further.

Holding the Executive to Account

Many politicians and commentators have lamented that the presidential interpretation of the constitution has created an imbalance to the detriment of the French Parliament. Also, many have argued that the new political configuration, while consolidating the role of the Executive as a whole, compromises the standard mechanisms for their political accountability, namely ministerial responsibility. This accountability gap was so strongly felt that it led to the passing of two constitutional

[11] Some commentators are concerned with the pace of these constitutional reforms: see P Pactet, 'La désacralisation progressive de la constitution de 1958' in *Mélanges Pierre Avril* (Paris, Montchrestien, 2001) 398.

amendments strengthening the judicial accountability of the Executive. Originally, a specialist court, the High Court of Justice, was given jurisdiction over the criminal liability of members of Government while in office and over the impeachment of the President of the Republic. However the failings of the High Court of Justice were highlighted by the contaminated blood affair.[12] The constitutional reform of July 1993 overhauled the criminal liability of government members and created a new court – the Court of Justice of the Republic – and a new head of criminal liability.

Furthermore, following the alleged involvement of President Chirac in illegal political party funding prior to his presidential mandate, the Conseil constitutionnel and the Cour de cassation gave conflicting interpretations of the provisions regulating his criminal liability. In July 2007 articles 67 and 68 were amended to clarify their ambit. Presidential irresponsibility is limited to actions and decisions arising from the presidential mandate. The irresponsibility for all other actions and decisions is only temporary: it is lifted one month after the end of the mandate. Article 68 was also modernised: the President of the Republic can be impeached if he/she fails to fulfil his/her duties in a way manifestly incompatible with the exercise of his/her mandate. Not only have these processes of accountability aimed to address the accountability gap, but they also reflect French society's deep change of attitude with regard to morality in public life.

Strengthening Parliamentary Democracy

The presidential reading of the constitution has had a negative effect on parliamentary democracy. Originally, the constitution curbed the powers of Parliament to avoid a return to the practices and instability of old. However, the emergence of the majority phenomenon has compounded the congenital weakness of the French Parliament: with so many constitutional limitations, Parliament has struggled to keep in check the formidable Executive. Arguably, the resulting accountability deficit ought to have been addressed in the 1970s or 1980s. The constitutional revisions, in 1995 and in 2008, have finally tried to redress the regime's original imbalance.

---

[12] See chapter 3.

Interestingly, the 1995 revision was originally triggered by Parliament's rebellion during the constitutional reform necessary to ratify the Maastricht Treaty. Parliament felt that it lacked the necessary power to protect French sovereignty. Arguably, years of 'parliamentary frustration' were also taking their toll. To meet the demands of Parliament and avoid a lengthy revision process, the President of the Republic, François Mitterrand, agreed to organise a constitutional reform soon after. In 1993 he convened an expert committee chaired by Professor Vedel to make a number of recommendations. However, parliamentary elections and a change of majority intervened before the process was completed. The revision was scaled down and many proposals abandoned. The resulting amendments were a far cry from what was really needed and soon demands for another reform were heard. This movement culminated in the reform of July 2008, which created a status for the opposition in Parliament, increased the number of parliamentary committees, bestowed on each chamber greater control over their agenda and limited the Government's legislative weaponry.

Increasing the Rights and Participation of Citizens

While reforming the executive and legislative branches has been an ongoing process, the interest in citizens and their rights is more recent. The initiatives in this domain tend to take two directions: a better rights protection and a more active political participation.

In March 2005, a new Charter for the Environment was annexed to the 1958 constitution. It aims to add environmental rights to the list of those already recognised by the Conseil constitutionnel. Consequently, the Charter reflects the present environmental concerns. It seeks to establish a constitutional framework of environmental rights and duties and ensure an effective protection for all in this domain. In addition, attempts have been made to promote women in public life: in July 1999 the constitution was amended to introduce a principle of gender parity in political life and in July 2008 the requirement of parity was extended to private companies, public corporations, charities, associations and so on. Also, the reform of July 2008 has made considerable efforts with regard to the protection of rights. Individuals can request the Conseil constitutionnel to give a preliminary ruling on an issue of constitutionality if it impacts litigation to which they are a party. Also, citizens can ask the new defender of rights to help them resolve a dispute with a public body.

Since the beginning of the twenty-first century, various reforms have improved the political participation of the sovereign people. The reform of March 2003 aimed to improve local democracy by introducing the principle of decentralisation into the 1958 constitution, establishing new constitutional foundations for territorial government and granting all territorial governments the power to organise local referendums. Also, the reform of July 2008 granted citizens a right of popular initiative. Although the trend to increase both participation and rights of citizens is comparatively recent, it has been translated into a notable number of constitutional reforms already.

Allowing the Ratification of International Treaties

No revision of the constitution was necessary prior to 1992 in order to ratify international treaties. However, the Treaty on European Union was found to contain provisions which contravened French national sovereignty. The 1958 constitution was duly amended and a new title was incorporated into the constitution. Not only were the necessary transfers of sovereignty authorised, but parliamentary control over European affairs was strengthened. Furthermore as Members of Parliament wished to keep European integration and future transfers of competences under review, the constitutional provisions do not contain a blanket approval for the European Union. In fact, Title XV has already being amended three times since then: for the ratification of the Amsterdam Treaty, the Constitutional Treaty and the Lisbon Treaty.

Other international treaties have triggered constitutional reforms. The treaty creating the International Criminal Court was found to interfere with the constitutional regime determining the liability of members of the Executive.[13] Also, the *Conseil constitutionnel* decided that the constitution needed to be amended prior to the ratification of the second optional protocol to the International Covenant on Civil and Political Rights.[14] Once ratified, the death penalty is irrevocably abolished even in

---

[13]   See C cons no 98-408 DC, 22 January 1999, International Criminal Court.

[14]   See C cons no 2005-524/525 DC, 13 October 2005, International agreements relating to the death penalty.

the event of exceptional circumstances endangering the existence of the Nation. The constitutional reform of 23 February 2007 added to the constitution a new article 66-1 stating that 'no one can be condemned to death'.

CONCLUSION

With the reform of July 2008, not only did the French Parliament adopt the most comprehensive revision of the 1958 constitution yet, but it engineered the regime's final break from the past. This 'modernisation' of the constitution will allow the fifth Republic to survive well into the twenty-first century and should silence the voices previously calling for the adoption of a new regime and sixth Republic. Some may well have believed that both regime and constitution were irremediably flawed or that the institutional imbalance was a fatal 'congenital' defect, but it shows that old habits die hard: the choice of drafting a constitution anew instead of amending it was casting a long shadow. Hopefully, the success of the 2008 constitutional reform has marked the end of this tradition. Indeed, this reform has allowed new constitutional values to come to the fore: constitutional continuity and regime longevity. However flawed the fifth Republic may be, neither politicians nor electors were ready to see it go. There is a first time for everything . . .

However, the moment of euphoria that followed the reform of July 2008 was very short lived. Opposition and majority fought each other with renewed passion over the organic laws necessary to implement the new provisions of the constitution. Furthermore, the latest attempt at constitutional reform – the introduction of the golden rule[15] into the constitution – has met with little success; although adopted by both houses, a vote in the Congrès has been postponed indefinitely.

FURTHER READING

S Boyron, 'France' in C Fusaro and D Oliver (eds), *How Constitutions Change: A Comparative Study* (Hart, 2011) 115

---

[15] The golden rule would create a duty of the French State to respect a strict budgetary equilibrium in public finance.

G Conac, 'Article 11' in F Luchaire, G Conac and X Prétot, *La constitution de la République française*, 3rd edn (Paris, Economica, 2008) 403

O Duhamel, 'Du comité Vedel à la commission Balladur' (2008) *Revue française de droit constitutionnel* (*hors-série*) 9

J Gicquel, 'Le Congrès du Parlement' in *Mélanges Pierre Avril* (Paris, Montchrestien, 2001) 449

P Jan, 'Article 89' in F Luchaire, G Conac and X Prétot (eds), *La constitution de la République française*, 3rd edn (Paris, Economica, 2008) 1991

Index

www.ingramcontent.com/pod-product-compliance
Lightning Source LLC
Chambersburg PA
CBHW071844270326
41929CB00013B/2100